HEART,
SELF, & SOUL

HEART, SELF, & SOUL

The Sufi Psychology of Growth, Balance, and Harmony

∾∘∾

ROBERT FRAGER, PH.D.

A publication supported by
THE KERN FOUNDATION

Quest Books
Theosophical Publishing House

Wheaton, Illinois ◆ Chennai (Madras), India

Praise For *Heart, Self, & Soul*

"Dr. Frager offers illuminating insights into the mystical path of Sufism, grounded in love and truth. He presents a fascinating blend of Islamic philosophy, teaching stories, and personal anecdotes. His psychological perspective makes it easy for a Westerner to understand."

—Frances Vaughan, author of *Shadows of the Sacred*

"In the same person, Dr. Robert Frager, pioneer in transpersonal psychology, is at the service of Shaikh Ragip of the Halvati-Jerrahi order. He takes us into the Sufic space of the miraculous dimension to share with us the classic treasures of the spirit bequeathed to him by his lineage master. This book is a luminous, clear, and generous invitation to join him in the sacred feast."

—Rabbi Zalman M. Schachter-Shalomi, coauthor of *From Age-ing to Sage-ing*

"Robert Frager speaks with authority yet is able to make a warm and remarkably intimate connection with his audience. I have to say that there are few authors whom I would recommend so unequivocally."

—Hal Zina Bennett, Ph.D., author of *Follow Your Bliss*

Quest Books
Theosophical Publishing House
P. O. Box 270
Wheaton, IL 60187-0270

www.questbooks.net

Library of Congress Cataloging-in-Publication Data

Frager, Robert.
Heart, self, & soul: the Sufi psychology of growth, balance, and harmony /
Robert Frager.
        p.   cm.
Includes index.
ISBN 978-0-8356-0778-0
1. Sufism—Psychology. I. Title. II. Title: Heart, self and soul.
BP189.65.P78F73   1999
297.4'01'9—dc21   99-31635
                                                            CIP

Second printing

Printed in the United States of America

Dedication

To my late Sufi master, Sheikh Safer Dal, who embodied the highest ideals of Sufism, and who told me to write this book because he knew I could.

And to my beloved wife, Ayhan Frager, whose faith and love of God are constant inspirations.

ACKNOWLEDGMENTS

I wish to thank many people who have helped with the development of this book. First is my late sheikh, Safer Dal Effendi, whose teachings and living example formed the foundation of my understanding and practice of Sufism. Sheikh Tosun Bayrak's talks and guidance are an unceasing source of inspiration and growth. Imam Bilal Hyde was an invaluable help with Arabic terms and Koranic references. Yannis Toussulis and Sam Goldberger have clarified for me many aspects of Sufi thought and Sufi psychology. Selim Ozich Baba has been very generous with his time and deep understanding of Sufism. Robert Clark and Hal Bennett read the manuscript and made encouraging comments. Jim Fadiman made profoundly insightful comments on the manuscript as did Rabbi Zalman Schachter-Shalomi. John Firman and Ann Russell were extremely helpful in commenting on my use of Assagioli's concepts and diagrams. Susan Newton and Steven Sulmeyer read the manuscript closely and made many useful suggestions. I also want to thank my dervishes and the Institute of Transpersonal Psychology faculty and students, who have heard and discussed most of the material presented here. If, in spite of all this help, there remain errors of fact or interpretation, I am sure that they are mine alone.

Contents

PREFACE

H istorians usually describe Sufism as the mystical core of Islam and date its appearance at about the ninth century A.D., approximately two hundred years after the birth of Islam. In its universal sense, however, Sufism includes the mystical dimensions of all religions. Religion is a tree whose roots are outward religious practices. The branches of that tree are mysticism. The fruit of the tree is truth.

Sufism is no different from the mysticism at the heart of all religions. Just as a river passes through many countries and is claimed by each as its own, there is only one river. All mysticism has the same goal, the direct experience of the divine.

One who practices Sufism is called a *Sufi, dervish,* or *fakir. Sufi* has several meanings in Arabic, including "pure" and "wool." (Early sufis wore simple wool cloaks and they sought inner purity.) *Dervish* is a Persian term derived from *dar,* or door. It refers to one who goes from door to door (begging) or one who is at the threshold (between awareness of this world and awareness of the divine). *Fakir* is Arabic for "poor person." In Sufism, this does not refer to those poor in worldly goods, but to those who are spiritually poor, who recognize their need for God. Their hearts are empty of attachment to anything other than God.

The adoption of the moral and ethical teachings of Islam created a climate in which Sufism could develop and flourish. Although Sufism is more prominent in the Middle East, North Africa, Europe, Central Asia, India, Pakistan, China, and Indonesia, its ideas, practices, and teachers are found throughout the world. Like any genuine mystical tradition, Sufism has changed its form to fit the cultures and societies in which it is practiced.

Sufism and Religion

Most Sufis believe that there is a fundamental truth in all religions and that the great religions are the same in essence. The various prophets and spiritual teachers are like light bulbs that illuminate a room. The bulbs are different, but the current comes from one source, which is God. In a room with many light bulbs, you cannot distinguish the light of one bulb from the light of another. It is all the same light, and the individual bulbs all receive electricity from a single source, even if some bulbs provide more light than others. The quality of the light is the same and so is the source.

Ibn Arabi, the most celebrated Sufi sage, wrote that there are four levels of practice and understanding in Sufism: *shariah* (exoteric religious law), *tariqah* (the mystical path), *haqiqa* (truth), and *marifa* (gnosis). Each is built upon the stages that go before.

First is the *shariah*, which is the foundation for the next three levels. In Arabic, *shariah* means "road." It is a clear track, a well-traveled route that anyone can follow. The *shariah* consists of teachings of morality and ethics found in most religions. The vast majority of Sufis have been Muslims, and so the *shariah* that Sufism is traditionally based on is that of Islam. The *shariah* provides guidance for us to live properly in this world. Trying to follow Sufism without following the *shariah* is like trying to build a house on a foundation of sand. Without an ordered life built on solid moral and ethical principles, no mysticism can flourish.

Second is the *tariqah*, which refers to the practice of Sufism. *Tariqah* literally means the trackless path in the desert that the Bedouin follow from oasis to oasis. This path is not clearly marked like a highway with exit signs. It is not even a visible road. To find your way in the trackless desert, you need to know the area intimately, or you need a guide who knows the destination and who is familiar with local landmarks. As the *shariah* refers to the outer practice of religion, the *tariqah* refers to the spiritual practices of Sufism. The guide you need in order to find your way is the sheikh. The *shariah* makes our outsides clean and attractive. The *tariqah* is designed to make our insides clean and pure. Each of these supports the other.

Third is *haqiqa*, or truth. It refers to the inner meanings of the practices and guidance found in the *shariah* and *tariqah*. It is the direct experience of mystical truth. Without this experiential understanding, we are fated to follow blindly and imitate mechanically those who have attained the station of *haqiqa*. The attainment of *haqiqa* confirms and solidifies the practice of the first two stages. Before *haqiqa* all practice is imitation.

Fourth is *marifa*, or gnosis. Gnosis is deep wisdom or knowledge of spiritual truth. It is the knowledge of reality, attained by a very few. This is the station of the messengers, the prophets and the great sages and saints.

Ibn Arabi explained these four levels. At the level of law (*shariah*), there is "yours and mine." That is, religious law guarantees individual rights and ethical relations between people. At the level of the Sufi path (*tariqah*), "mine is yours and yours is mine." The dervishes are expected to treat each other as brothers and sisters—to open their homes, their hearts, and their purses to each other. At the level of truth (*haqiqa*), there is "no mine and no yours." Advanced Sufis realize that all things come from God, that they are really only caretakers, and that they possess nothing. Those who realize truth have gone beyond attachment to possessions and externals in general, including fame and position. At the level of gnosis (*marifa*), there is "no me and no you." The individual realizes that all is God, that nothing and no one is separate from God. This is the ultimate goal of Sufism.

Becoming a Dervish

In my own Sufi order, the Halveti-Jerrahi Order, there are three ways to become a dervish and enter fully into the practice of Sufism. The first way is to dream of becoming a dervish. The second is to fall in love with a sheikh, and the third way is simply to ask.

Through dreams. If someone dreams of becoming a dervish, he might take that dream to a sheikh for interpretation. The sheikh may also consult his or her dreams to confirm the prospective dervish's dream. In my order, we believe that certain dreams can provide spiritual guidance.

My first Sufi master, Sheikh Muzaffer, had been a famous religious teacher and preacher in Istanbul. One of the larger and more famous Sufi orders invited him to join and offered to initiate him immediately as a sheikh. Muzaffer replied that he would have to wait for guidance from a dream. Soon after, he dreamed that he was worshiping in the Halveti-Jerrahi lodge as its current sheikh sat by the window. The next day he presented himself to that sheikh and related his dream. The sheikh told Muzaffer Efendi[1] to wait for a week while he consulted his own dreams; then he initiated him. Thus Muzaffer Efendi became a novice dervish of the Halveti-Jerrahi Order instead of a sheikh in a much larger and better-known order.

Some years later, the Halveti-Jerrahi sheikh passed away. He had designated Muzaffer Efendi as his successor, but some of the older dervishes disagreed. When they met in order to decide who would be sheikh, the man who had been most opposed to Muzaffer Efendi said to him, "I am now convinced that you are to be our head sheikh, and I want to be the first to kiss your hand and accept you as my new spiritual guide." The other dervishes were completely surprised by this man's abrupt change of heart. The man went on, "I have changed my opinion because of a dream I had last night," he explained. "I dreamed that I was leading the dervishes in the ceremony of Remembrance of God, but nothing went right. There was no unity in the chanting or in the movements of the dervishes. Then Muzaffer Efendi led the ceremony and everything went perfectly smoothly. I am convinced that this is a sign that he should be our head sheikh." The rest of the dervishes unanimously agreed, and so Sheikh Muzaffer, who had become a dervish because of a dream, now became head sheikh as the result of another dream.

Falling in love with the sheikh. The second way to become a dervish is to fall in love with the sheikh. That is how I became a dervish. I first met Sheikh Muzaffer in spring 1980. He had been invited to visit the graduate school I had founded, the Institute of Transpersonal Psychology. He came with a group of about twenty-five dervishes, including singers and musicians, in order to be able to perform the Sufi ceremony of Remembrance of God.

Sheikh Muzaffer was the head of a Sufi order and a well-known religious teacher in Turkey, and we were delighted to have him visit and teach our graduate students. (The Institute is devoted to exploring the interface between psychology and religion, and we have invited representatives of many of the world's religious and spiritual traditions as guest presenters.)

The day the dervishes were to arrive, I was in my office talking on the telephone. The door was cracked open and I could see into the hall-

Preface

way. A heavyset man wearing a white hat passed by and glanced at me. He never broke stride, so the glance could have taken only a microsecond. For me, however, time stood still. I felt that all the data of my life had been absorbed and integrated as if by a giant computer and that this man not only knew my past, but also my future, including the results of the telephone call!

I don't usually talk to myself, but an inner voice said, "I hope that was the sheikh, because if he wasn't, I don't think I'm ready to meet this man's teacher." I finished my telephone call and located our guests. I introduced myself as the president of ITP and welcomed them. To my relief, the man who had walked past my office was Sheikh Muzaffer.

That afternoon I was invited to take tea with the dervishes, and the sheikh told several Sufi stories. I immediately realized that the living reality of this tradition was far richer than the books I had read about Sufism. The stories retold in books don't have a fraction of the impact they do when told by a teacher, who also provides a context and emphasis on central issues embedded in the story.

I had been deeply interested in mysticism for a long time. For over ten years, I had pursued an active and disciplined meditation practice. I eventually began psychotherapy with a spiritually oriented therapist. As I started to work on a whole host of emotionally charged personality issues, my meditation practice left me. It was as if Freud's idea of libido was correct; that is, I had only had so much psychic energy, and now that it was focused on working out personal material, it was no longer available for spiritual work. I couldn't even feel guilty for not meditating, because this change was so clearly a shift of internal energies rather than the result of laziness or a failure of will.

When I met Sheikh Muzaffer, I was still in therapy and still in a kind of spiritual limbo. I wasn't sure I was ready for a new spiritual practice, but I certainly missed my old one. Sheikh Muzaffer was a man of great heart and charisma and wisdom. Coming into his presence was like entering the presence of a sultan or an emperor. It felt to me as though his personal power was balanced only by his great love and compassion. In addition, Sheikh Muzaffer was a marvelous storyteller with a wonderful sense of humor.

I will never forget hearing Sheikh Muzaffer pray for the first time. Two of our students, a religious Jewish couple, asked him to pray for them and for their marriage. Sheikh Muzaffer raised his hands, palms up, and began to pray. I suddenly realized that I had never heard real prayer before. It seemed as if he went up to a heavenly place and brought the words of prayer down to earth. Before this, all I had ever heard were either rote prayers using the words of others, or prayers made up intellectually in an everyday state of consciousness. Sheikh Muzaffer's prayer was totally different. I was also struck by the fact that he never asked about the couple's religion or beliefs. It was clearly irrelevant to him, and he could not possibly have prayed more sincerely and deeply even for his own dervishes. (In fact, this couple did become his dervishes the next year.)

I was also struck deeply by the wisdom and practical relevance of Sheikh Muzaffer's teachings. Many of my earlier spiritual teachers had been unworldly monastics. In fact, I was a little tired of hearing lectures on work or relationships by people who had never had jobs or families. Sheikh Muzaffer was extremely grounded and knowledgeable about the world. He had a business (a religious bookstore), a wife, and he was raising two children.

I also came to appreciate deeply the men and women who traveled with the sheikh. They included lawyers, doctors, business people, professors, and laborers. I was particularly impressed by the sense of brotherhood among these men. They had all served in the Turkish army; I could tell that they had been disciplined, tough soldiers, but there was no sense of machismo among them. These men rushed to pour each other a glass of water or a cup of tea. They often laughed together and even tickled each other. This was the kind of male group I had always longed for.

At the end of this first visit, I was struck with how the teacher, his teachings, and the community of dervishes paralleled the three jewels of Buddhism—the Buddha, the *dharma* (Buddhist teachings), and the *sangha* (the community of practicing Buddhists). Any one of the three would have been enough for me to consider seriously following this path, and I realized these three aspects combined to make a single, powerful whole.

Sheikh Muzaffer and the dervishes returned the following year, and I cleared my calendar to be with them as much as possible. Even though I had been deeply touched by the first trip, I had never dreamed of becoming a dervish. On the first day of this second trip, however, a young woman approached Sheikh Muzaffer and asked hesitantly, "Can an American become one of your dervishes?" Clearly her question was more personal than theoretical, but Sheikh Muzaffer smiled sweetly and simply mirrored her question, "Yes, an American can become one of my dervishes."

"Is it possible to live here in America and still be your dervish?"

The sheikh mirrored her again. "Yes, it is possible to live here in America and be my dervish."

Finally, the young woman broke down and sobbed, "Can *I* become your dervish?" Sheikh Muzaffer put her head in his lap and stroked her hair and told her kindly, "My daughter, you are my spiritual child already!"

As the thought that I might become his spiritual son came into my mind, I felt my eyes watering. I rarely cried in those days, and I quickly realized that these were not tears of sadness or even of joy; they were a sign that I had been deeply moved. (I've become much better at crying since; a dervish is supposed to have a soft heart.) For the next day or so, every time I thought of becoming a dervish, I would jump up and go to my office and cry. Finally, I asked one of the American dervishes if I might become a dervish. He replied that he would ask one of the senior dervishes to ask the sheikh.

As soon as I made the request, a series of strange thoughts came into my mind. First, I thought that I might become quickly initiated as a dervish and then get to go on stage the following evening for the Remembrance of God ceremony. Then I began to think of all the reasons I shouldn't or couldn't become a dervish. Would I have to become a Muslim? Would I have to renounce my love of other religions? Would I have to give up wine? Obviously something in me was extremely resistant to becoming a dervish. (It was my first introduction to the *nafs*, the lower self.) The very idea that I would pursue a path that might lead to inner transformation terrified this part of me.

The next evening, following the remembrance ceremony, which I got to watch from the front row, we all had dinner together. Afterward, the sheikh began to recite a blessing in Turkish. This one felt very different from the others I had heard. I didn't understand a word he said, but I felt as though I were bathed in light throughout his blessing. Then his translator, who was sitting next to me, leaned toward me and said, "That was in honor of you and in honor of what is to come next."

Once the dinner tables were cleared and put away, the sheikh went to the front of the room. I was seated in front of him, my knees touching his, my right hand holding his. The ceremony was conducted in Turkish and Arabic, and I had no idea exactly what was going on. I was given a dervish hat, prayer beads, a silver medallion, and a dervish vest. The vest had belonged to the sheikh, and it was much too big for me. When one of the dervishes pointed that out, Sheikh Muzaffer laughed and said, "He will need it to be big so he can shelter his dervishes under it." Even at the very beginning, I was given a hint that there was a lot more in store for me on this path.

After my initiation, I suddenly noticed that a number of my students looked the same way I felt—dazed and lovestruck. One by one, they asked to become dervishes. When we compared notes, we all noticed that our chests ached, as though they were being stretched by our newly expanded hearts. We were in love! Our love for Sheikh Muzaffer was a kind of romantic, but asexual love.

This process is also called the sheikh's heart opening to the dervish. The underlying principle is that individuals fall in love with a sheikh only if the sheikh already feels love for them. Love is said to move from the higher concentration (the sheikh's heart) to the lower (the heart of the prospective dervish). Similarly, when the love for God grows in our hearts, it is a sign of God's love for us. As Bayazid writes, "At the beginning, I was mistaken in four respects. I sought to remember God, to know Him, to love Him, and to seek Him. When I had come to the end, I saw that He had remembered me before I remembered Him, that His knowledge of me had preceded my knowledge of Him, His love toward me had existed before my love to Him, and He had sought me before I sought Him."[2]

Eventually, twelve of us became dervishes. This core group founded our California center.

Asking to become a dervish. The third and least auspicious way to become a dervish is simply to ask. In this case, the desire to enter the Sufi path comes from the head rather than the heart. The following story was first told to me the day after I became a dervish. In our Order it is traditionally told at the time of initiation.

Mehmet, a young dervish, had a close friend named Hasan. Hasan said to Mehmet, "Would you please ask your sheikh if I might become a dervish too?" Mehmet went to his sheikh and said, "I have a good friend named Hasan. He is honest and hardworking, and he asked me to ask you if he could become a dervish." The sheikh made no reply. (A sheikh will often remain silent rather than speak negatively or give answers or solutions that a dervish should figure out for himself.)

Eventually, after Mehmet had approached his sheikh for the third time, the sheikh said, "Let your friend come and serve in our lodge, and we will see if he is ready to become a dervish."

Hasan was kept busy sweeping and cleaning up the kitchen. He could hear the dervishes chanting and praying and listen to them chatting and joking at meals. After some time, Mehmet asked the sheikh again about his friend. The sheikh said, "Let him serve me a glass of water next week, during our next festival. If he can serve me successfully in front of the distinguished crowd, that will be a sign that he is ready."

On the day of the festival, Hasan kept busy in the kitchen as he waited anxiously to be called. After the meal, the sheikh began his talk. Finally, he signaled that he wanted a glass of water. Hasan rushed in with the glass of water on a tray and knelt before the sheikh. The sheikh was telling an involved story, and as he gestured to make a point, he knocked over the glass. Hasan was so mortified that he shut his eyes in horror.

When he opened them, Hasan found himself at the edge of a cliff in a forest. He made his way through the woods and came to a town. There were wonderful smells coming from a restaurant, and Hasan realized that he was very hungry. Although he knew he wasn't carrying his wallet, Hasan decided to order a nice hot meal. After dessert and coffee, a well-dressed man came up to his table. "I hope you enjoyed your meal," he said. "Oh yes, everything was delicious. Are you the owner?"

asked Hasan, pretending to search for his wallet. "Yes," replied the man, "and I am delighted that you enjoyed our humble cooking."

"I can't find my wallet," Hasan exclaimed. "I must have dropped it. How can I pay you?"

"You must be new around here. I don't need any payment. But I would very much appreciate it if you would say a prayer for the souls of my parents, who passed away recently."

Hasan made an eloquent prayer for the souls of his host's parents. The restaurant owner thanked Hasan profusely and insisted that he come back tomorrow for another meal.

Bemused, Hasan left, feeling full and content. The evening was cool and as he passed a tailor's shop, he stopped to admire a beautiful coat. Just then a young man came out of the shop. "Do you like that coat?" he asked.

"It is beautiful," replied Hasan, "and I love the workmanship on the embroidery."

"Thank you," said the young man. "It is yours."

Hasan tried to refuse but the tailor insisted. "You are not from around here, are you?" asked the tailor. "Do you have a place to stay?" Hasan admitted that he did not. "Then you can do me a favor. I need someone to stay in the apartment above my store and mind the shop in case of fire or some other emergency."

Hasan sat in his new apartment with his new coat, his stomach filled with delicious food. He thought that he must be in heaven, as all his wants and needs were so miraculously taken care of.

Just then, he heard dozens of soft voices outside. He looked out and saw that the street was filled with women chatting and calling out to friends. As Hasan looked out, his eyes fell on the most beautiful woman he had ever seen. Hasan could not sleep all night. The next morning when the tailor came to open the shop, Hasan explained his experience of the night before.

"Thursday night," the tailor explained, "is our ladies' night. The women of the town spend the evening together and *the men all stay at home. Many men have first seen their wives-to-be on such evenings. When this happens, our custom is that the young man goes outside on a Thursday evening carrying a lighted candle. He presents it to the young woman of his choice, and if she accepts the candle it means that she accepts his proposal."*

On the following Thursday evening, Hasan offered a candle to the beautiful woman who had captured his heart. She took it from his shaking hands and smiled at him. Not knowing what more to do, Hasan rushed back to his apartment

The following morning, Hasan was summoned to the magistrate's office. He was in a panic. Was it the free meals at the restaurant, the coat, the apartment, or the candle? The magistrate was a stern-looking distinguished gentleman, whose gaze pierced Hasan to his core. To Hasan's shock, the magistrate smiled and said, "It appears that my daughter has accepted your proposal." The magistrate went on. "Her dowry includes a house and enough money for servants and for you to make investments to support yourself. However, before you marry my daughter, you must promise to meet three conditions."

Hasan was willing to promise anything to gain the hand of his beloved. He said, "Yes, of course. What are the conditions?"

"You must promise to guard your tongue, your hands, and your genitals. Do you promise?"

"Yes, I promise."

And so Hasan was married. He felt he must be the happiest man alive to be married to the woman he loved and living the life of a wealthy man.

One morning as Hasan and his wife slept late, there was a knock at the door. Instantly Hasan remembered that he had promised to see some people about an investment. He said to his wife, "Dear, I made a business appointment but I don't want to bother with it just now. Would you please tell the men at the door that I have gone out already and that I'll see them this afternoon?"

His wife, amazed, said, "What? What do you want me to tell these men?"

Somewhat impatiently Hasan repeated, "Tell them I've gone out and that I'll see them this afternoon!"

His wife, obviously upset, quickly dressed and rushed out of the room. After some time had gone by and she did not come back, Hasan went out to look for her. He thought that she might be visiting her father, so he went to his father-in-law's house. The magistrate said angrily, "You did not keep your first promise! Worse, you not only had no concern for your own tongue, but you even asked my daughter to lie for you. This is unforgivable!"

Hasan begged and pleaded and promised that it would never happen again. His father-in-law relented and Hasan's wife agreed to return. Soon everything was back to normal.

Some weeks later, Hasan and his wife took a basket of food and went out for a picnic. While his wife rested, Hasan took a walk and passed by a fruit orchard. A peach had just dropped down onto a bush growing outside the orchard wall. It was ripe and looked absolutely delicious. Hasan thought that it would make a perfect dessert.

He brought the peach back to his wife and asked her to cut it up. "Did someone give it to you, or did you buy it?" she asked.

Hasan replied, "No, I found it on the road. It had fallen down and I picked it up."

"You mean that no one gave the peach or sold the peach to you. You just took it."

"Yes, it was lying out in the open, right on the path."

The wife began to cry and ran off through the woods. When Hasan returned home, no one had seen her come back. Some hours later, he reluctantly went to see his father-in-law. The magistrate was even more stern than before. "You broke your second promise! You failed to guard your hands."

"But the peach was lying along a public pathway," argued Hasan.

"It doesn't matter. You did not grow that peach, you did not buy it, and you did not receive it as a gift. It was not yours to take."

Again, Hasan begged forgiveness. He promised that he would never again make such a mistake, and eventually his wife agreed to return home.

After some months, Hasan noticed that the younger women of the town gathered at the river every Tuesday to do their washing. Although his wife was very beautiful, he had grown accustomed to her looks. These young women were each lovely and charming in their own ways. Hasan began to make a habit of walking by this section of the river every Tuesday, and each week he paused longer and longer to admire their young, beautiful bodies. One Tuesday, as Hasan crouched behind a bush to peer at the young women, he was grabbed from behind and lifted off his feet. A huge soldier marched him to his father-in-law's office.

The magistrate looked coldly at Hasan. "You have failed your third promise! Even if you did not act on your thoughts and feelings, in your mind you were unfaithful to my daughter." Then the magistrate turned to the soldier. "Throw him back to where he came from!"

The soldier marched Hasan through the woods to the edge of the cliff and threw him over. In terror, Hasan squeezed his eyes shut.

When he opened his eyes, he was back in front of the sheikh, still holding the tray with the glass of water. The sheikh leaned over and whispered to Hasan, "You see, you are not yet ready!"

The world that Hasan entered is very much like the world of the dervish. If a dervish sincerely pursues the Sufi path, outer benefits frequently come and worldly difficulties are often eased. While traveling in the United States and the Middle East, I have frequently been entertained royally by brother and sister dervishes simply because of the spiritual path we share.

Sometimes, however, when one becomes a dervish the opposite

may occur, and things may seem to fall apart. Both success and difficulty are tests on this path. Some people forget God when they enjoy peace and material abundance. Others may forget God when they suffer hardship. Real success is to develop a level of inner peace and communion with God that cannot be shaken by the ups and downs of temporal events.

To be a dervish is to guard your tongue, your hands, and your genitals. It is that simple—and also that difficult. Most of us struggle every day with issues of honesty and integrity, and the more you advance on the path, the more demanding the discipline. A novice is expected to make mistakes and learn from them. Far greater awareness and self-control are expected of a senior dervish.

Sheikh Muzaffer used to explain this with the following analogy. When the grand wazir became a father, he brought his infant daughter to the sultan. The sultan took the infant on his lap. Suddenly the sultan's lap became very wet. He handed the girl back to her father, saying in a teasing tone, "Look what your daughter has done! Now I'll have to change my clothing."

The sultan forgave the baby for wetting his lap, but if the grand wazir had done so, the sultan would have had the man's head cut off. We are like babies sitting in God's lap. Whenever we make a mistake it is like wetting God's lap. God forgives us over and over again, but as we mature, we should strive to do all we can to prevent such lapses.

Chapter One

The Psychology of Heart, Self, and Soul

"Know, O beloved, that man was not created in jest or at random, but marvelously made and for some great end."

—Al-Ghazzali[1]

If someone sits with me
And we talk about the Beloved,

If I cannot give his heart comfort,
If I cannot make him feel better
About himself and this world,

Then, Hafiz,
Quickly run to the mosque and pray—
For you have just committed
The only sin I know.

—Hafiz[2]

Basic Concepts in Sufi Psychology

In this book, we will focus on three central concepts in Sufi psychology—the *heart*, the *self*, and the *soul*. Each is a technical term and has a set of connotations different than its everyday English usage. Each term includes overtones of meaning from

Koranic usage and from centuries of Sufi discussion and commentary. These concepts come from a rich, thousand-year-old tradition, and hundreds of books have been written about each.

Heart. This means the spiritual heart. For instance, we say that someone who is sincere and well motivated is someone "with heart." Spiritual seekers write about the importance of finding "a path with heart." We also talk about the opposite; someone who has no compassion is "heartless."

According to Sufi psychology, the heart contains our deeper intelligence and wisdom. It is the place of gnosis, or spiritual knowledge. The Sufi ideal is to develop a soft, feeling, compassionate heart, and to develop the heart's intelligence. This is a deeper and more grounded intelligence than the abstract intelligence of the head. It is said that when the eyes of the heart open, we can see beyond the superficial exterior of things, and when the ears of the heart open, we can hear the truth hidden behind the words.

The heart holds the divine spark or spirit within each of us. In effect, the heart is a divine temple. Sufis try and remember to treat all other people with kindness and respect, as the owners of this infinitely precious temple. As we will see, Sufism stresses conscious human relationships and service as fundamental spiritual disciplines.

Love is another basic Sufi spiritual discipline, and the home of love is the heart. The more we learn to love others, the more we become capable of loving God. One of the great lovers mentioned in the Torah was Zuleika, the wife of Potiphar. There are many stories of Zuleika and Joseph in the Sufi tradition. Zuleika fell in love with Joseph, who was her husband's slave. It is said that Joseph was one of the most handsome men who ever lived. When Zuleika's friends began to tease her about her outrageous love of Joseph, she invited them all to tea. While her friends were peeling the fruit she served them, Zuleika summoned Joseph. When the other women saw him, they were so distracted by his beauty that they all cut themselves. Zuleika said, "Now that you have seen my Joseph, can you blame me?"

Eventually, Potiphar divorced Zuleika because of her scandalous love for Joseph, and she had to live among the poorest workers and beggars. Years later, when Joseph had become the second most powerful man in Egypt, he saw Zuleika one day in the street. She was dressed in rags and looked old and worn from her difficult life. He said to her tenderly, "I could not love you when your were married and I was your husband's slave. But now I am free to marry you and will do so gladly because of your love for me." With shining eyes, Zuleika relied, "No, Joseph, my love for you was a veil. I have long since come to love the Beloved directly. I need nothing and no one in this world any longer." Her love for Joseph had opened her heart.

Self. In Sufi psychology the self, or *nafs*, is an aspect of the psyche that begins as our worst adversary but can develop into an invaluable tool. The lowest level is the tyrannical *nafs*. It is a collection of all those forces within us that lead us off the spiritual path. These forces cause tremendous pain and suffering and lead us to hurt those we love.

In a passage from the Koran, Zuleika admits that she sought to seduce Joseph, and then says:

> Nor do I absolve my own self
> Of blame: the self
> Commands [us] to do evil,
> Except for those my Lord
> Has had mercy on. (12:53)

NAFS - NEG. TENDENCIES
EGO - UNCONSCIOUS

I have translated "the self that commands us to do evil" as the tyrannical *nafs*, because these negative tendencies can dominate our lives like an absolute tyrant. At their root are egotistic impulses that are often deeply unconscious. Many Western psychologists, philosophers, and other authorities on human nature who are still very much under the influence of the tyrannical *nafs* tend to treat this state as normal. According to Sufi psychology, however, the tyrannical *nafs* is at the root of the worst distortions of thinking and perception and the source of the greatest danger to ourselves and others. Sufism provides powerful and effective tools for understanding and transforming the tyrannical *nafs*. These tools include self-observation, self-discipline, and seeing oneself in others.

At the other extreme, the highest level of the *nafs* is known as the pure *nafs*. At this stage, the personality is like a pure and perfect crystal that reflects God's light with almost no loss or distortion. This final

PURE NAFS

transformation of the *nafs* is an extremely rare achievement, found only in the greatest saints and prophets. The poet Hafiz illustrates this state:

> I am happy even before I have a reason.
> I am full of Light even before the sky
> Can greet the sun or the Moon.[3]

Soul. Sufi psychology includes a model of the human soul based on the principles of evolution. The soul has seven aspects or dimensions: the mineral, vegetable, animal, personal, human and secret souls, and the secret of secrets. Each of us possesses these seven levels of consciousness. The goal in Sufism is for all of them to work in balance and harmony.

Many psychological and spiritual systems stress only one or two levels of functioning. In Sufism, emotional well being and healthy, nourishing relationships are as essential as spiritual and physical health. The ideal is to live fully in the world without becoming attached to it or forgetful of our spiritual nature and spiritual aims.

Sufism provides a truly holistic approach to spiritual psychology in which the soul avoids the dangers of the linear and hierarchical models found in many spiritual systems, models that have been used to justify the oppression of women and minorities. In Sufism, there are absolutely no spiritual distinctions between men and women or between different races or nationalities.

This model integrates the physical, psychological, and spiritual. The physical aspect of our lives is sustained by the age-old wisdom of the mineral, vegetable, and animal souls. Our psychological functioning is rooted in the personal soul, which is located in the brain and is the seat of ego and intelligence. Our spiritual nature is a qualitative jump beyond the physical and psychological (which are both rooted in our physical bodies and material existence). The human soul, secret soul, and secret of secrets are located in the nonmaterial spiritual heart. The human soul is the seat of our compassion and creativity. The secret soul is the location of Remembrance of God, and the secret of secrets is the infinite, divine spark within us.

Some Comparisons Between Western and Sufi Psychology

1. Traditional psychology assumes that the universe is completely

material and without meaning or purpose. According to Sufi psychology, the universe was created in accordance with God's will and is permeated with God's presence. The Koran states, "To God belong the East and the West; Wherever you turn, there is the Face of God." (2:115)

To me, this is a particularly powerful and moving phrase. God's face is everywhere, always in front of me, even though I usually remain unaware of it. Rumi beautifully illustrates how the world is filled with God's presence. "For sixty years I have been forgetful,/every minute, but not for a second/has this flowing toward me stopped or slowed."[4]

The universe is meant to be the place of the search for God. In a famous *hadith* (saying of the Prophet), God says, "I was a hidden treasure. I longed to be known, and so I created Creation." At one level this means that the universe is a mirror of the divine. God is fully present in everyone and everything. But to find God, we have to look beneath the surface, to see the inside as well as the outside of things. At another level, it means that humanity was created in order to seek the hidden treasure which is God. The universe is a cosmic hide-and-seek game. Our purpose, the reason we were created, is to seek God, and the greatest human beings are those who have found Him. The Turkish Sufi poet, Yunus Emre, writes, "Men of God's truth are an ocean,/Lovers must plunge into that sea;/The sages, too, should take a dive/To bring out the best jewelry."[5]

2. Traditional psychology assumes that the human being is nothing more than a physical body and a mind developed from the physical nervous system. An important element in Sufi psychology is the spiritual heart, which is the location of inner intuition, understanding, and wisdom. We are more than mind and body; we are the embodiment of divine spirit. Whenever we explore human psychology in depth, we encounter this infinite divine spark. It is important to know where we came from and where we are going. Our souls existed before we were born and continue to exist after we die. Our goal is to uncover this divine spark within ourselves and to learn to live by the inner guidance of our divine nature. Inner guidance from the spiritual heart is more available as we progress along the Sufi path. Eventually we can be guided by our own hearts rather than by external rules or principles. However, this is a relatively advanced stage of practice.

3. In Western psychology, descriptions of human nature focus primarily on human limitations and neurotic tendencies, or on innate human goodness and our essentially positive nature. The first approach is typical of clinical psychology and the second of humanistic psychology. According to Sufi psychology, all human beings are located between the angels and the animals. We share both natures and have the potential to rise higher than the angels or to sink lower than the animals. Therefore, we need to struggle in order to counter our negative habits and tendencies. This is known as the inner *jihad*, the inner struggle or inner holy war. We also need to develop our intellect and will power in order to actualize positive, spiritual tendencies. The inner struggle becomes more demanding and more subtle as we progress on the Sufi path.

4. According to traditional Western psychology, our highest state of consciousness is the rational, waking state. Sufi psychologists point out that, for most people, this is actually a state of "waking sleep." Most people are habitually heedless and relatively unaware of themselves or the world around them. Other states are possible, including those of remembrance, humility, awe and finally of unity with God. They can be accessed only through spiritual disciplines that lead to remembrance of God, transformation of the self, and the opening of the heart.

In addition to an extensive classification of spiritual states of consciousness, Sufi psychology distinguishes between these temporary states (known as *hal*) and stable states of development (known as *makam*). One may remain at a given level of development for months or years. These states of development include:

- INITIAL AWAKENING—The recognition that the spiritual search is more important and meaningful than our previously valued worldly goals and ambitions.

- PATIENCE AND GRATITUDE—The development of patience and perseverance is essential for spiritual development. So is a sense of gratitude. A dervish feels gratitude for receiving the teachings of the Sufi path and for having the capacity to follow them.

- FEAR AND HOPE—Fear of losing our love of God and sense of connection with Him motivates the developing dervish. Also essential is a sense of optimism—a hope that in spite of our shortcomings we will make progress.

- SELF-DENIAL AND POVERTY—This means denial of the negative ego's incessant demands for pleasure and power, and dedication to the service of others instead of self-promotion. A dervish is also known as a *fakir*, literally a poor person. The Prophet said, "I am proud of my poverty." Poverty means lack of attachment to possessions and a heart that is empty of all desire except the desire for God.

- TRUST IN GOD—At this stage, we realize that everything we have comes from God. We rely on God instead of on this world.

- LOVE, YEARNING, INTIMACY, AND SATISFACTION—We have one major desire, to love God, to yearn for and feel God's presence, to be satisfied only by God's love and to desire nothing else.

- INTENT, SINCERITY, AND TRUTHFULNESS—A concern for intention rather than the outer form of action. The more advanced we become, the more our intentions become clear and pure. Sincere, truthful intent gives meaning to all actions.

- CONTEMPLATION AND SELF-EXAMINATION—This capacity develops only over time. According to a famous Prophetic saying, an hour of contemplation is worth seventy years of conventional prayer.

- RECOLLECTION OF DEATH—We realize that our time is limited and therefore priceless. The world has no attraction any longer, and as advanced dervishes, we are totally devoted to the pursuit of God. Abraham Maslow, the founder of transpersonal psychology, pointed out that recollection of death can bring about the "plateau experience," a state in which our experience is transformed.[6]

5. Western psychologists hold that self-esteem and a strong sense of ego identity are important; that loss of identity is pathological. In Sufism, the sense of a separate identity is one of the veils between us and God that distorts reality and prevents us from knowing our true divine nature. Our goal is to transform our egos and to lose our sense of separate identity. When we finally realize our nothingness, we can perfect our unity with the infinite.

Sufi psychology distinguishes between the healthy, positive ego and the self-centered, negative ego. Swiss psychologist Carl Jung writes that the ego needs to be strong in order to handle the radical changes and intense demands of the spiritual path. This means self-respect, self-esteem, and a realistic sense of our own positive traits and capacities.

A positive ego serves us and helps us to achieve our goals. The negative ego displays an inflated sense of self-worth, a self-centered, egotistical approach to life. It continually tries to get us to serve it; it is like a donkey that we carry on our backs instead of being carried by the donkey.

6. Western psychologists assume that personality is a relatively unified structure. In Sufi psychology, the human being is seen as a diverse collection of traits and tendencies, many of which are related to different stages of evolutionary development. One of our tasks is to balance these various traits and to strengthen our spiritual development. Unity of personality is an advanced state.

For most people, inner unity is an illusion. We often make intentions and begin projects with great optimism and then never follow through. Let me give you a common example. On Friday evening, we set the alarm for six A.M. in order to finish up all kinds of tasks before breakfast. When the alarm rings next morning, we immediately turn it off, roll over in bed, and curse the *idiot* who decided to wake us at such an ungodly hour.

As William James, the father of American psychology and a pioneering spiritual psychologist, pointed out, most of us want to be known as generous philanthropists and sophisticated socialites, philosophers and athletes, sex idols and spiritual role models. We know that these various roles are basically mutually incompatible, but we want it all. True inner unity is a rare achievement.

7. Western psychology considers logical reasoning the highest human skill and the way to knowledge and wisdom. In Sufi psychology, the abstract, logical intellect is called the lower intellect. It is useful at school and also for learning skills related to worldly success. But knowledge must be put into practice, and there is also a higher intellect that enables us to understand spiritual truths and the meaning of life. If

the intellect serves as a tool of the ego, it can become the enemy of growth and development. The abstract intellect *needs* the light and wisdom of the heart.

Hafiz reminds us how limited the intellect is in the face of the infinite:

> If you think that the Truth can be known
> From words,
>
> If you think that the Sun and the Ocean
> Can pass through that tiny opening
> Called the mouth,
>
> O someone should start laughing!
> Someone should start wildly laughing—
>
> Now![7]

8. Western psychology believes that almost all significant knowledge can be transmitted using logically organized rational prose. Sufis know that the written word is limited. The highest states of spiritual development are beyond rational description, and to achieve them, the rational, separate ego must be dropped. Poetry may be a more appropriate medium to express the most profound human experiences, and for centuries, great Sufi poets have captured spiritual truths. The following riddle poem is from Yunus Emre.

> I climbed up the plum tree
> And plucked the grapes there;
> The master of the garden asked angrily:
> "Why are you eating my walnuts?"
>
> I grabbed a sparrow's wing
> And loaded it on forty ox-carts.
> All forty were unable to pull it,
> So it remained stuck there.
>
> The words that Yunus speaks
> Are like no other words.
> Thus he veils their inner meaning
> From the closed minds of the hypocrites.[8]

In addition, many Sufi teachers use stories and parables to transmit subtle truths. These stories are not rigid and unchanging; a skilled teacher will adapt the story to fit the needs of the audience.

9. For Western psychologists, faith means believing in things that are not real or ideas that have no solid evidence. For Sufi psychologists, faith means belief in the truth behind the varied appearances of material creation. Faith puts the individual into the right relationship with the universe and with the divine.

To Sufis, one of the most important sayings of Muhammad is, "Those who know themselves know their Lord." Sufism is a process of deep self-searching. An essential aspect of this search is the fundamental belief that the divine is fully present within us, even if we cannot experience it at present. Without faith, any understanding of ourselves or the universe is distorted, because we cut ourselves off from the only perspective that leads to real understanding.[9]

Our Origins: The Story of the Descent of the Soul

The following account of the descent of the soul is taken from the writings of Hazreti Ibrahim Hakki Eruzumi, a well-known Turkish Sufi saint. He begins with the creation of the universe and the descent of the individual soul into material creation.[10]

The universe began with God's command, *Kun*, "Be." With this word, the universe began to unfold. In Arabic, *Kun* is composed of two letters, *K* and *N*. The *K* stands for *kemal*, or "perfection," and *N* stands for *nur* or "light." Thus came the creation of perfect light. This first creation has been called the light of prophethood, or the pure light that precedes the material universe. It is the building block out of which all souls and all material things were built. It is like the *Logos* of the Greeks, the Thought that precedes energy and matter. Everything has been created from this, except for God.

God created souls before material creation, and souls existed in a more subtle realm, a world that is closer to God than this one. Here there are virtually no veils between souls and God. We all existed for millennia in a heavenly realm, sitting at God's feet, bathed in God's divine light and love.

God asked the souls, "Am I your Lord?" The sound of that divine voice became the root of all music that touches the heart, inspires, and uplifts us. The souls knew that God had created them; they were in harmony with God's will, and they were profoundly inspired by being in the divine presence.

Then God sent the individual soul down to the material world, and it became immersed in each of the four elements of creation. First it passed through water and became wet; then it passed through earth and became muddy. It passed through air and became clay, and finally, it passed through fire and became baked clay. Thus the nonmaterial soul passed through all the basic material elements that generate the material world, and the soul of light became embedded in a pot of clay—the physical body.

This includes not only the material body, but also emotions, thoughts, and energies. These various levels of embodiment are summarized by the four elements. The soul is still perfect and divine and close to its Lord, but it is now covered, hidden. However, God sent with the soul the Divine Attributes so that each individual is a link between heaven and earth.

Unfortunately, once we were embodied in materiality, we became blind to that secret within us. We cannot, as material beings, manifest those divine qualities when we are deeply attracted to the things of this world.

But God also gave us the tools to return to this original level of awareness, to break out of the clay pot. The tools are mind and will. The mind gives us the ability to know right from wrong, and the will provides the capacity to choose right action. We all have this will but few of us exert it enough. The basic principle is simple. As the Prophet Muhammad said, "Do what is lawful and healthful; do not do what is unlawful and unhealthful, and if you are not sure, . . . do not act until you become sure." This is basically very simple, but it becomes complicated because the will is not strong enough. All too often, we know what to do, but we don't do it; then the ego takes over and we make excuses for ourselves.

Practical Mysticism for the Modern World

Sufism is of particular relevance today, because it is a sophisticated mystical path that includes in its practice work, family, and the other experiences of daily life. While some Sufis have been wandering mendicants, most have held regular jobs and raised families.

The great Sufi teachers have had a wide variety of professions. Some were artisans, such as Attar the perfumer/pharmacist and Omar Khayyam the tentmaker. Some were wealthy merchants and landowners or powerful advisors to sultans and emperors. But all of the great Sufi teachers managed to fulfill their duties in the world while seeking God.

Living in the world but not of it. The Sufi tradition teaches us to use our duties and experiences as part and parcel of our spiritual journey rather than treating worldly work as a distraction from our spiritual work. Sheikh Muzaffer, my own spiritual teacher, was fond of saying, "Keep your hands busy with your duties in the world and your heart busy with God."

Very few of us are able to take years from our lives in order to join an ashram or monastery. We all can learn a great deal from the Sufis about how to continue our daily lives without sacrificing our spiritual journey. One of the goals of Sufism is that daily life itself becomes a profound spiritual practice.

The Sufis believe that our minds and bodies are gifts from God, and that as a sign of our gratitude we should do our best to develop these gifts and use them well. My sheikh used to point out that if someone bought you a beautiful and very expensive hat, one that suited you perfectly, wouldn't you feel very grateful? How much more grateful should you be to the one who gave you the head to put it on!

Rather than avoiding worldly responsibilities, the Sufis teach us to fulfill our responsibilities even more so than the average person, because we are dedicated to using our God-given capacities to the best extent possible. A real dervish is a harder and more honest worker than anyone else; a dervish tries to be a better husband or wife, a better parent, and a better son or daughter. If we cannot love our families and serve our employers to the very best of our ability, how can we even begin to think of loving and serving God?

A multicultural tradition for all people. Sufism is of great value today because it is a spiritual discipline for all peoples and cultures. Sufism has never been an elitist spirituality. Many of the greatest sheikhs have been poor and illiterate. It is the quality of the heart that matters, not the externals of clothing and pocketbook. Sufism is a thousand-year-old unbroken mystical tradition, and Sufi psychology contains the wisdom of centuries of practice and guidance. Various modes of chanting, meditating, body movement, and other spiritual disciplines have developed among many different races and cultures.

In Turkey, different Sufi orders have developed among various classes and types of people. For example, the Bektashi Order appealed primarily to soldiers and farmers. The Naqshbandi Order attracted theologians and scholars. The Mevlevi Order, with its beautiful music and poetry, was of special interest to the artistically inclined. The Halveti Order has included sultans, generals, influential governors, and administrators.

Many of those who were wealthy gave up their wealth when they became dervishes. When the founder of my order became a dervish, he told his family to distribute all his wealth and possessions as if he had died. Others have used their wealth to support charities or the work of their order.

The Paths of Sufism

Sufism is a spiritual path that can take us from wherever we are now to union with the infinite. It is said that there are actually as many paths to God as there are created beings. Within the Sufi tradition, we can distinguish at least five roads; each road appeals to large numbers of people. These are the paths of heart, head, community, remembrance, and service. Each has developed sophisticated practices and a rich literature.

The path of the heart. Devotion to God is one of the most basic Sufi practices. This devotion is reflected in the heart-warming poetry of Rumi and other Sufi poets. Rumi reminds us of the power of love:

> Since hearing of the world of Love,
> I have given my life, my heart,
> And my eyes this way.

13

At first, I believed that love
And beloved are different.
Now, I know they are the same.
I had been seeing two in one.[11]

It is said that love is what elevates us above the animals—even above the angels. At the opening of one of the great mosques in Istanbul, the sultan invited a Sufi sheikh to give the first sermon. Everyone in the neighborhood crowded into the mosque and, just as the sheikh got up to deliver his sermon, a water carrier grabbed his sleeve. "I lost my donkey," he said desperately, "and I really need him so I can deliver water. Since everyone is here today, would you please help me find it?"

When the sheikh began his sermon, he asked if there were anyone present who had never loved another, not even a pet? One man slowly stood up. Encouraged by his example, two others stood up as well. The sheikh turned to the water carrier and said, "You lost one donkey, but I have found you three!"

Sufis learn to love their sheikh and to love and serve their brother and sister dervishes. They learn to love the Prophet and all other great spiritual teachers. When I first became a dervish, my master said that to be a dervish is to love Moses and his teachings as much as, if not more than the Jews, and to love Jesus and his teachings as much as, if not more than the Christians.

Years ago, when Sheikh Muzaffer and a group of dervishes visited Paris, they were invited to perform Islamic prayers at one of the cathedrals. Afterwards, the senior priest said, "I have let you make your prayers in my cathedral. Will you let me perform mass in one of your mosques?" Sheikh Muzaffer immediately replied, "Absolutely not!" The priest was shocked at this apparent inequity, but Sheikh Muzaffer continued, "I have the right to pray in your cathedral because I love Jesus. But you cannot pray in our mosques because you do not love Muhammad."

The path of the head. In addition to the inspiration of poets and lovers, the Sufi tradition has been enriched by the wisdom of scholars and sages. However, the sages of Sufism access a deeper wisdom and more complete intelligence than that of the average bookish scholar. Sufis are fond of the saying, "A scholar who does not practice what he has learned is like a donkey with a load of books." The books carried in the donkey's saddlebags cannot transform the donkey, and neither can the books that are only carried in the scholar's head. Real wisdom means to learn something well and then to apply it.

> A poor dervish once approached a teacher of Arabic who had no classroom. The teacher wrote his lessons in chalk on the city wall. The dervish asked the teacher if he might learn to read and write. Taken with the dervish's sincerity, the teacher offered free lessons. He drew a single straight vertical line on the wall and explained, "This is the letter alif; it is the first letter of the alphabet." The dervish bowed, thanked the teacher and walked away. The teacher, who was accustomed to teaching at least the first half of the alphabet in the initial lesson, was astonished. This was going to be a long process!
>
> The dervish did not come back the next day or the next week, and eventually the teacher forgot all about him. Months later, the dervish appeared, his eyes shining with an inner light. He bowed deeply and announced that he was ready for his next lesson. The teacher thought, "We will never get through the alphabet at this rate," but all he said to the dervish was, "All right. First, let's review your first lesson. Write the letter alif on the wall."
>
> The dervish wrote the letter alif, and the wall crumbled.

This story reminds us that there is far more in simple beginnings than we generally realize, and that the secret of spiritual progress is not how much we learn, but rather our mastery of it.

The path of community. In our isolated modern society everyone hungers for community. Sufism is very much a communal path. One of the central practices is the weekly *dhikr*, or remembrance ceremony. The dervishes chant, sing and encourage one another. They also teach each other, often as much as the sheikh teaches them. The Koran says that the believer is the mirror of the believer. Newer dervishes can see in senior dervishes more developed faith, greater capacity for service, and deeper remembrance of God. We learn from role models, and the more good ones, the better.

According to the Prophet, "Your faith is not complete until you wish for your neighbor what you wish for yourself." Ask yourself, do you really care for your neighbor? Are you committed to helping your neighbors if they are in need?

The Prophet also said that you are not a believer if you eat when your neighbor is hungry. Even in modern Turkey it is a custom is to keep the windows closed when cooking, because the smell of your cooking might make the sparse diet of the poor even more difficult to bear. In fact, when Turks barbecue outside, they often send a plate of food to their neighbors.

Today the world has shrunk, and our neighbors include the hungry on all parts of the globe. To be a dervish is to be committed to social justice, to do what we can to alleviate hunger and suffering. The heart that does not feel the pain of others cannot love God.

Dervishes learn to love and serve each other. Ideally, friendship among dervishes is based on their mutual love of God; there is no temporal ambition or hidden agenda attached. Most worldly friendships end whenever the bond that they are based on is over. For example, friends who enjoy expensive entertainments are not likely to remain friends if one of them can't keep up the same lifestyle. Genuine spiritual love is not superficial, and the joy of that kind of friendship is its own reward. It is a reflection of God's endless love. There is a story, found in various cultures and traditions, that clearly illustrates the power of community.

> One of the old Sufi orders had shrunk over the years, until only one sheikh and three dervishes were left. They lived together in the order's lodge, spending their days in prayer, contemplation and tending their fields and orchards. As the four men grew older, they became concerned that their rich tradition might die out altogether.
>
> One of the dervishes suggested that the sheikh visit the local rabbi, known as a very wise man. "He is also a spiritual teacher," said the dervish, "and I'm sure he has had to deal with this same question of attracting the younger generation." The sheikh went to the rabbi, and over tea, told the rabbi his dilem-

ma. The rabbi laughed and said, "I have the same problem. I really don't know how to interest the younger generation of my own community. However, I can tell you one thing: in my meditations it has been revealed to me that one of you is the qutub of the age."

In Sufism the qutub, literally "the pillar," is the hidden spiritual leader of humanity. There is always a qutub, whose identity is known to only a handful of saints. The qutub channels the light and wisdom of the heavens onto the earth plane. Without a qutub, the world would slowly become dark and spiritually void.

The sheikh returned to his dervishes and told them what the rabbi had said. Immediately the three dervishes concluded that the sheikh must be the qutub. But then they reflected and wondered if the qutub might be Mehmet, who led them in prayers every day and who had memorized the entire Koran. Or perhaps the qutub was Ahmed, who gave the call to prayer and whose beautiful voice always inspired whoever heard him. Or the qutub might even be Daud, who was quiet and humble and was there whenever anyone needed help.

The little community of sheikh and dervishes began to treat one another as if each was the qutub. Their love and respect for each other deepened and their sense of joy as a community was greatly intensified. The Sufi lodge was located on beautiful grounds and people often came to picnic. Soon the new atmosphere of the community began to attract more and more visitors. Some stayed to participate in prayers or in the remembrance ceremony, and eventually, a few young people began to ask about the possibility of becoming dervishes.

The path of service. Closely related to the path of community is the path of service. If we truly care for one another, we will want to serve one another, and in doing so, we also serve the divine within them; our service is a privilege and a gift.

Furthermore, it is not the amount of service but our intention that counts. As Mother Theresa said, "It isn't what you do, but the amount of love that you do it with that counts." Mother Theresa is a marvelous example of the transformative power of service. As a young nun, she showed no signs of becoming a mystic or spiritual leader. By all accounts, she was an average nun and an average teacher in a Catholic school in Calcutta. She was transformed into a saint only after she dedicated herself to serving lepers and the poorest of the poor.

Years ago, the mother of the sultan was known as a great philanthropist. She planted trees to give the people of Istanbul shade in the summer and paid for a system of wells so that people could get water more easily. She built mosques and also schools and a hospital, which she endowed with income-producing lands so that they could function in perpetuity.

While the hospital was under construction, she visited the site. There she noticed an ant fall into wet concrete. Deciding that no creature should suffer from her acts of charity, she stuck her expensive French parasol into the concrete and lifted the ant out.

Years later, on the night of her death, several of her close friends dreamed of her. She looked young and radiant, and when they asked if she were in Paradise because of all her generous charities, she replied, "No, the state I enjoy now is all because of one little ant!"

We do not need to possess great wealth in order to perform acts of compassion. As Jesus once said, God takes note of even the sparrow's fall.

The path of remembrance. Sufism is a discipline of remembering the divine within us. Sufis believe that God places a divine spark in each of us, hidden in our heart of hearts but veiled by our love of everything that is not God, our attachment to the trivialities of this world, and our heedlessness and forgetfulness. Yet the veils themselves are unreal. Through the Prophet, God said, "There are seventy thousand veils between you and Me, but there are no veils between Me and you."

Most dervishes observe daily practices of remembrance, generally consisting of so many repetitions of the divine names or attributes and recitation of prayers and passages from the Koran. In most orders, there is also a weekly community ritual of remembrance. The dervishes recite prayers and chant selected divine names. The most famous of these rituals is the Mevlevi practice that includes music, chanting, and the "whirling" or turning of the dervishes. Other orders place more emphasis on chanting or certain prayers. Some orders practice remembrance sitting, others practice standing, and some combine both.

There is great power in the belief that God is fully present within us already, and that remembrance serves only to make us conscious of what we already know. One saint expressed this idea as follows: "O seeker, know that the path to Truth is within you. . . . There is no arriving or leaving; . . . What is there other than God?"[12]

A well-known Sufi teacher said to his dervishes, "You must keep knocking on the gate with the faith that the gate will eventually open to you." Rabia, a saint, was passing by and heard his words. She commented, "When has the gate ever been closed?" The teacher bowed to her.

Exercise

The Sufi journal. Many Sufis keep a daily journal in order to practice self-observation and self-awareness. Ibn Arabi wrote that his teachers would sit alone every evening to reflect upon their daily actions and experiences. If their actions required forgiveness, they asked for forgiveness; if their actions merited repentance, they would repent. Ibn Arabi emulated their example.

Begin the practice of journaling every evening, and reflect on the implications of what you said and did during the day. The more deeply we reflect on our experiences and actions each day, the better we will come to know ourselves. Self-understanding is at least half the battle in self-transformation.

Chapter Two

OPENING YOUR HEART

*Dear friend, Your heart is a polished mirror. You must
wipe it clean of the veil of dust that has gathered upon it,
because it is destined to reflect the light of divine secrets.*

—AL-GHAZZALI[1]

A sheikh had just recovered from an illness. It was winter, so his dervish always got up early to heat water for the sheikh's predawn ablutions. One morning the dervish got up and saw that his master was already awake. The dervish jumped out of bed, grabbed a pitcher of water, and held it tight against his breast. When he began to pour the water, it scalded the sheikh's hands. Amazed, the sheikh asked his beloved dervish, "Where did you boil this?" The dervish replied, "On the fire of my heart."

The Heart as Our Spiritual Center

Western education tends to overemphasize the head and ignore the heart. The education basics—reading, writing and arithmetic—all involve learning of the head. Subjects that develop the heart, such as music, art and social skills, are generally treated as second-rate, frill subjects. This has led to the stereotype of the highly educated college graduate who is very intelligent but not very smart. In contrast, Sufi psychology stresses the need to nourish and develop the heart. One whose heart is open is wiser, more compassionate and more understanding than one whose heart is closed.

By heart I mean our inner spiritual nature, not the physical heart. Our hearts are the source of inner light, of our inspiration, creativity, and compassion. A real Sufi is someone whose heart is alive, awake, and filled with light. In the words of one Sufi master, "If words come from the heart, they will enter the heart, but if they come from the tongue, they will not pass beyond the ears."

Love is at the core of Sufism, and the locus of love is the heart. The Sufi poets are probably the clearest in describing the power of love and the importance of an awakened heart.

Once a young woman asked me,

"How does it feel to be a man?" And I replied,

"My dear,
I am not so sure."

Then she said,
"Well, aren't you a man?"

And this time I replied,

"I view gender
As a beautiful animal
That people often take for a walk on a leash
And might enter in some odd contest
To try to win strange prizes.

My dear,
A better question for Hafiz
Would have been,

'How does it feel to be a heart?'

for all I know is Love,
And I find my heart Infinite
And Everywhere!"[2]

Comparing the Spiritual and Physical Hearts

The spiritual heart functions very much like the physical heart. The physical heart is located in a central place in the torso; the spiritual heart is located in between the lower self and the soul. The physical heart regulates the body; the spiritual heart regulates the psyche. The physical heart nourishes the body by sending fresh, oxygenated blood to every cell and organ in the body. It also receives impurity-filled blood through the veins. Similarly, the spiritual heart nourishes the soul by radiating wisdom and light, and it also purifies the gross traits of the personality. The heart has one face turned toward the realm of spirituality and one face turned toward the realm of the lower self and our negative traits.

If the physical heart is injured, we become ill, and if it is severely damaged we die. If our spiritual heart is infected with the negative characteristics of the *nafs* (or lower self), we become spiritually ill. If the outer heart becomes completely dominated by the *nafs*, our spiritual life dies.

The heart is not to be confused with emotionality. Emotions like anger, fear, and greed come from the *nafs*. When people talk about their "heart's desire," they are usually referring to the desires of the *nafs*. The *nafs* is attracted to pleasure and does not care about God; the heart is attracted to God, and seeks pleasure only in God.

The heart is directly responsive to our every thought and action. My sheikh used to say that every kind word or act softens the heart, and every unkind word or harmful act hardens it. The Prophet referred to the central importance of the heart when he said, "Indeed, in the human body there is a piece of flesh which, when at peace, brings peace to the rest of the body and when corrupt, corrupts the rest of the body; and that is the heart."[3] The poet Rumi teaches us:

> Become a person of the heart
> or at least the devotee of one;
> Or else, you will remain
> like a donkey stuck in the mud.
> If one has no heart,
> one can gain no benefit;
> In wretchedness, one
> will be famous in the world.[4]

NAFS - PLEASURE
HEART - GOD

23

Opening the Heart

We can open the eyes and ears of the heart to perceive more deeply the inner realities hidden beneath our complex material world. In the words of one Sufi master:

> The heart has an eye with which it enjoys visions of the Unseen, an ear with which it listens to the speech of the inhabitants of the Unseen and the Speech of God, nostrils with which it smells the perfumes of the Unseen, and a palate whereon it perceives the taste of love, the sweetness of faith, and the savor of gnosis.[5]

The heart is a temple that has been placed by God in everyone, a temple that is meant to house the divine spark within us. In a famous *hadith*, God says, "I, who cannot be fitted into all the heavens and earths, fit in the heart of the sincere believer." This temple within each of us is more precious than the holiest shrines and temples on this earth. It is a greater sin to injure the heart of another human being than to harm one of the earth's holy places.

To be a dervish is to remember that the heart of each person we meet is God's temple. Many hearts have been wounded, and we can serve God's creation by working to heal those wounded hearts. This kind of service also heals and opens our own hearts as well. In the words of the Sufi teacher Ansari, "The more we love, the more we open our hearts. Action without love and without the sincere intention of the heart has little or no meaning."[6]

Many of us have allowed the worship of idols into our hearts (by idols, I mean the ephemeral things of this world, such as fame, money, and power) and devoted ourselves to their pursuit. One of the fundamental practices of Sufism is to repeat the phrase, *la ilaha illallah*, "There are no gods but God." The discipline of Sufism includes the cleansing of our hearts, making them suitable temples for God's presence.

The Arabic term for heart, *qalb*, comes from the root "to turn" or "to revolve." In a sense, the spiritually healthy heart is like radar, which constantly rotates and scans, never becomes fixed on or attached to anything in the world; it always seeks the divine. With the litmus test of *la ilaha illallah*, the heart tells us that nothing in the world is worthy of our worship, yet God is everywhere.

> On one religious holiday, the Caliph Harun al-Rashid
> put on his best robes and rode among the people. Everyone
> cheered and admired his beautiful clothing. Then Bahlul the
> Wise Fool stepped in front of the caliph and said:
>
> > The festival is not a matter of dressing up
> > in fine new clothes,
> >
> > The festival is celebrated by serving God
> > and being aware of your Lord.
> >
> > To celebrate the festival is to be sultan of
> > the heart, not sultan of the realm.
> >
> > Sultans of the realm pass into oblivion, but
> > the sultan of the heart is never forgotten.
>
> Hearing this, Harun al-Rashid was moved to tears.[7]

The Four Stations of the Heart

According to the sage al-Tirmidhi, the heart has four stations: the breast, the heart, the inner heart, and the innermost heart.[8] These four stations fit within each other like nested concentric spheres. The breast is the outermost sphere, the heart and the inner heart are in the two middle spheres, and the kernel of the heart is at the center.

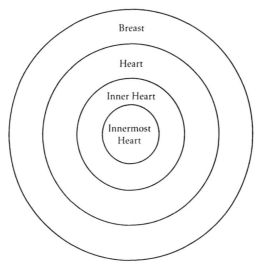

Each station houses a light. The breast is the home of the Light of Practice of the outer forms of any religion. The heart houses the Light of Faith. The inner heart holds the Light of Gnosis, or knowledge of spiritual truth. The innermost heart holds two lights, the Light of Unification and the Light of Uniqueness, which are two aspects of the divine.

The four stations are like the different areas in a homestead. The breast is the outermost area, like the edge of the property that borders on the outside, most open to wild animals or strangers. It is the interface between the heart and the world.

The heart corresponds to the house itself. It is surrounded by walls and kept secure with a locked gate or locked doors. Only family members and invited guests can enter. The inner heart is the locked treasure room for the most valued heirlooms of the family. Very few have the key.

Each station is also associated with different spiritual stages in Sufism, different levels of knowledge and understanding and different levels of the *nafs*:

Breast	Heart	Inner Heart	Innermost Heart
Light of Practice	Light of Faith	Light of Gnosis	Lights of Unification and Uniqueness
seeker[9]	believer	gnostic	unified
knowledge of right action	inner knowledge	inner vision	divine grace
tyrannical	regretful[10]	inspired	serene

The Breast

The Arabic word for breast, *sadr*, also stands for "heart and mind." As a verb, it means to go out, to lead, and also to resist or oppose. Located between the heart and the lower self, the breast might also be termed the outermost heart. It is a meeting point between them and prevents either from infringing on the other. The breast leads our interactions with the world, and in it we resist the negative impulses of the lower self.

The breast is the main battleground between the positive and negative forces within us where we are tested by our negative tendencies. If the positive forces are strong, the breast is filled with light and comes under the influence of the divine soul, located in the kernel of the heart. On the other hand, if negative traits such as envy, desire, passion, and arrogance enter the breast, or if the breast contracts due to sorrow, suffering, or tragedy and persists over an extended time, darkness will come to dominate the breast. The heart contracts and becomes hardened, and the inner lights of the other stations of the heart are obscured.

The Light of Practice. The breast is directly affected by our words and actions and is nourished by devotion, prayer, charity, service, and the practice of fundamental principles found in all religions.

With positive actions, the breast expands and the Light of Practice grows. This is why service is an essential aspect of the Sufi path. In one sense, the path is easy. All we need to do is to avoid harming or taking advantage of others and dedicate ourselves instead to serving and helping. Then our hearts open more and more, and we move swiftly and surely along the spiritual path. Sincerity of effort is also important. For example, we serve others for their sake, not for praise or personal gain. As we will see later in this chapter, sincerity comes from the inner stations of the heart.

The work of Sufism includes the inner work of the cleansing of the breast and the opening of the heart. One remedy for hard-heartedness is remembrance of God. Two of the greatest forms of remembrance are formal prayer and the recitation of the Names or Attributes of God.

Sheikh Muzaffer used to say that it is relatively easy to learn the outer forms of prayer, but it is much harder to teach our hearts to pray. It is not difficult to bathe and put on clean clothing, but it can be very difficult to cleanse our insides. The goal of Sufism is to develop hearts that can pray. It is through sincere, patient, steadfast practice of prayer and other spiritual exercises that the breast becomes cleansed and expanded. As these practices dissipate our negative tendencies, the inner lights of the heart become stronger and continue the cleansing process. The cleansing of the heart is fully accomplished only through divine help. The Koran points out that "God might test what is in your breasts and purge [purify] what is in your hearts." (2: 154)

The *nafs* is an essential component in all our outer actions, because our capacity for action resides in the *nafs*. In a sense, the heart feels and the *nafs* acts. We might say that the outer practice of religion is the use of the *nafs* in accordance with God's will. It is the surrender of our individual will to God's will, dedication to serving the divine, and following the path that brings us closer to God.

Paradoxically, we also need to use our individual will to do what is right instead of what is easy or most attractive. We need to exert our individual will to follow the path of truth found in all religions. One student was struggling without much success to break some old habits. She asked her teacher for his blessing. The teacher replied, "You have my blessing to succeed, and you also have God's blessing. Now all we need is *your* blessing!"

In a sense, the *nafs* enters into the breast in order to test us. To succeed we must hold to our religious and spiritual practices and continue to act sincerely and compassionately. These actions disperse our negative tendencies; then the heart's Light of Faith illuminates the breast and prevents the *nafs* from dominating the breast. Even then, we must continue to struggle against negative, unbalanced traits.

The knowledge of the breast. As mentioned earlier, the Arabic word for the breast is also related to the same root as "mind," which is the place of all the knowledge that can be learned through study, memorization, and individual effort and can be discussed, written down, or taught to others. Knowledge kept in the breast has been called outward or worldly knowledge, because it can be useful in earning a living and effectively handling worldly affairs. However, this kind of knowledge also tends to increase our pride and arrogance. We begin to think, "*I* know," and "*I* accomplished," and also "I know *more* and have accomplished *more* than others." The knowledge that comes into the breast from the outside becomes firmly established only through effort, through repetition, and through concentration.

Another kind of knowledge enters the breast from the inside, from the heart. This inner knowledge is more easily established in the breast; it includes the subtleties of inner wisdom and indications of divine grace. However, we have to *act* on this knowledge to maintain it. Inner wisdom that is not reflected in action soon fades.

Rumi refers to these two processes of knowing as the "complete intellect" and the "acquired intellect." The acquired intellect has many different levels, but each acquires knowledge from the outside. The complete intellect knows from within.

> The intellect is of two kinds: The first is acquired. You learn it . . . from books, teachers, reflection and rote, from concepts and from excellent and new sciences.
>
> Your intellect becomes greater than that of others, but you are heavily burdened because of your acquisition. . . . Seek the fountain from within yourself![11]

The Heart

When we have cleansed our breasts and our hearts are open, we begin to perceive beyond the superficial externals to what is hidden within. As mentioned earlier, action that harms others or violates universal spiritual principles (like honesty, integrity, compassion) tends to close or harden the heart. To be a dervish is to have a soft, vulnerable, sensitive, and knowing heart.

The knowledge of the heart. The Prophet Muhammad said, "Knowledge is of two kinds: knowledge of the tongue . . . and knowledge of the heart, which is the truly valuable knowledge." In the West we overemphasize the "knowledge of the tongue," or book learning, which is one of the levels of the acquired intellect. This is the limit of traditional Western psychology, which does not yet recognize the deeper knowledge of the heart, the complete intellect.

The brain is like a computer that can store data and rearrange stored information, but creativity comes from the heart. Unfortunately, the heart's creativity can be misused by the *nafs*, as we can see in many creative individuals who are still arrogant, worldly, and egotistical.

As mentioned earlier, one essential element in the knowledge of the heart is the *practice* of what we know. Heart knowledge is deepened by experience. My teacher, the late head of the Halveti-Jerrahi Order, Sheikh Safer, said with great humility, "I don't know a great deal about Sufism, but I have loved whatever I have learned, and I have lived it for over forty years." These are the words of a real dervish and a real sheikh. Sufism is a lived teaching. A little applied knowledge brings wisdom, but too much book learning results in mental and spiritual indigestion.

Nasruddin, a Sufi master, was serving as the local judge. A woman came to him with her son and complained that her son had an uncontrollable sweet tooth. She asked Nasruddin to tell the boy to stop eating sweets all the time. Nasruddin nodded sagely and told her to come back in two weeks. When they returned, he simply said to the son, "Boy, I order you to stop eating sweets!"

The mother asked, "Why did you make us wait for two weeks? Couldn't you have said this to my son when we first came to you?"

Nasruddin answered, "No, I couldn't possibly have told that to your son two weeks ago."

"Why not?" asked the mother.

"First," Nasruddin replied, "I had to stop eating sweets!"

In the West, we are so used to learning and talking without doing that this story seems funny. Actually, we are the funny ones. Another story illustrates the difference between knowledge of the head and knowledge of the heart.

One day, a scholar was out rowing on a large lake. He heard a voice coming from a small island. Curious, he rowed to the island and found a hermit practicing dhikr, *Remembrance of God, by sitting and reciting a holy phrase over and over.*

The scholar called out to the hermit and explained that he was pronouncing the formula, which was in classical Arabic, incorrectly. The scholar felt gratified to have been able to correct the unlettered hermit. After all, it was said that those who mastered this holy phrase could even walk on water.

The scholar rowed away, pleased with his good deed. Then he heard a noise behind him and turned to look. The hermit was running after him over the water. "O scholar, I've said the formula the old way for too long! Please repeat it correctly for me once again."

The heart contains the fundamental principles of knowledge. It is like a spring that feeds the pool of knowledge in the breast. The heart is the root and the breast is the branch that is fed by it. Both the inward knowledge of the heart and the outward knowledge of the mind (or breast) are necessary.

Outward knowledge includes information we need to survive, including our professional skills and the intelligence needed to make a home and raise a family. It is also necessary in order to live a moral and ethical life; we have to know right from wrong.

Inward knowledge is the understanding of reality that must accompany the outward form to give it meaning and life. Inner knowledge needs outer practice to support and sustain it, and to deepen it through experience.

The Prophet Muhammad said, "Actions are only according to intentions," and "No action is attributed to one who has no intention." The value of any outer action is given meaning and value only through the sincere intention of the heart. The heart houses the Light of Faith, and also the traits of love, piety, calmness, fear of wrongdoing, humility, softness, tranquillity, submission, patience, refinement, and purity. God had mercy on us by placing the heart beyond the authority of the *nafs*. The breast is the farthest limit of the influence of the *nafs* and our negative tendencies.

While the breast may expand or contract depending on our actions, the light of the heart, like the light of the sun, remains whole and unchanging. The sun does not change, even if it is obscured by clouds, fog, or the darkness of night. Neglect, forgetfulness, or disobedience may veil the light of the heart, thus lessening its power over the lower self. However, if we sincerely repent, the coverings may be removed, the veils pierced, and the Light of Faith will shine through once again. For this, we need divine help and grace.

The Light of Faith. The Light of Faith is like a wonderful lamp that has been covered with many layers of veils. Even though the light itself is full and perfect, we need to remove the veils that obscure it. There is no original sin in Sufi psychology. We are not fundamentally evil; in fact, we were born with innate wisdom and goodness. We all have HEART the same inner Light of Faith. Even if the light is completely covered, it is still fundamentally full and flawless. It is our job to uncover the light that God placed within our hearts and to pray to God to help us and to make our efforts bear fruit.

To some who touch the depths of the heart, God reveals inner knowledge of spiritual virtues, such as noble character, generosity, patience, and striving against negative tendencies. Others are given the ability to speak eloquently about God and God's attributes of mercy, beauty, grandeur, and forgiveness. Some are granted the ability to write inspiring poetry or prose about God and about the spiritual path. Still others experience profound contemplation of God's uniqueness and oneness, so they see nothing but God within themselves. The truly wise are like pearl divers who keep seeking deep within.

Fear of God. The heart is the home of *taqwa*, which is often translated "fear of God." At the lowest level, this means fear of God's punishment. For Sufis, *taqwa* means fear of losing our love for God, our sense of closeness to God, and our sense of God's love. Those who fear God in this way act joyfully in accord with God's commandments, not out of fear of punishment. A better translation for this might be "awareness of God." Those who know say that fear of God guards us against doubt, worship of false gods, infidelity, insincerity, and hypocrisy.

Another translation of *taqwa* is "consciousness of God." This ongoing awareness makes us think and act more carefully and consciously.

> One of the early caliphs, Hazreti Osman, once asked a wise rabbi to explain the meaning of taqwa. The rabbi asked, "Did you ever run barefoot in the desert when you were a small boy?"
>
> Osman replied, "Yes, of course. We all ran around barefoot as boys."
>
> "How did you walk when you were in an area filled with nettles and sharp rocks?"
>
> "Very carefully. I paid attention before I took each step."
>
> "That is it! That is taqwa."

If we remember that every word and action can either bring us closer to God or take us further away, we would have the beginnings of *taqwa*. We would become far more aware and more heedful of all our actions.

The Inner Heart

The inner heart is the place of inner vision and the locus of the Light of Gnosis. Gnosis means "inner wisdom" or "knowledge of spiritual truth."

The heart and inner heart are very closely linked and, at times, almost indistinguishable. The heart knows, and the inner heart sees. They complement each other, just as knowledge and vision complement each other. If knowledge and vision are combined, the unseen becomes seen, and we become certain in our faith.

Those who have knowledge without vision are like scholars who have studied a foreign country for many years but have never visited it. No matter how much they may study from afar, there will always be something lacking in their understanding.

Similarly, vision without knowledge is not enough. This is like the tourist who visits a foreign country but who knows nothing of the country's language, history, or customs. The tourist may have firsthand experience of the country but lacks the knowledge to appreciate or understand it. Only those who both know and experience for themselves have certain knowledge.

> Beyond wanting, beyond place, inside form,
>   That One. A flute says, *I have no hope*
>   *for finding that.*
> But Love plays
>   and is the music played.
> Let that musician finish this poem.
>   —Rumi[12]

Awareness of God's presence. The angel Gabriel asked the Prophet Muhammad, "O Muhammad? What is *ihsan* (beautiful action)?" The Prophet replied, "That you worship God as if you saw Him, for if you do not see Him, truly God sees you."

The believers see their Lord with the eyes of their hearts, or else they know with their hearts that God sees them. If we knew that we were always in God's presence, if we truly *felt* that divine presence, wouldn't our lives be quite different?

The vision of the inner heart is illustrated in the following story:

Sheikh Junaid had a young dervish he loved very much. Junaid's older dervishes became jealous. One day, Junaid told his dervishes that each of them was to buy a chicken, then sacrifice it in a place where no one could see them. No one at all. Whatever they did, the dervishes were to return by sundown at the latest.

One by one the dervishes returned to Junaid, each with a slaughtered chicken under his arm. Finally, the young dervish returned with a live chicken still squawking and struggling under his arm. The older dervishes laughed and whispered among themselves that the young man had finally revealed how foolish he was. He couldn't even carry out his sheikh's orders!

Junaid asked each dervish to describe how he had carried out his instructions. The first man to return said that he had purchased his chicken, gone home, locked the door, closed the curtains and slaughtered the chicken. The second dervish said that he returned home with his chicken, locked the door, pulled the curtains, entered a dark closet and slaughtered it there. The third dervish also took his chicken into a closet, but in addition, he blindfolded himself so that even he could not see the slaughtering. Another dervish went into a dark, deserted area of the forest to sacrifice his chicken. Another went into a pitch black cave.

Finally, it was the young man's turn. He hung his head, embarrassed. His chicken was still squirming under his arm. In a low voice he said, "I brought the chicken into my house, but everywhere in the house there was a Presence. I went into the most deserted parts of the forest but the Presence was still with me. Even in the darkest caves the Presence was there. There was no place I could go where I was not seen." The young man had ihsan. Then the other dervishes realized why Junaid loved him.

The inner heart's perception is true perception. "The heart in no way falsified that which it saw." (53:11) True wisdom comes from inner knowing combined with inner vision.

The Innermost Heart

The innermost heart, or the heart of the heart, is infinite in its scope and radiance. It is like a great axis that remains stable as everything else revolves around it. In Arabic, *lubb*, the term for the innermost heart, means "kernel" and "inner understanding," which is the true foundation of religion. All the heart's other lights are based on the innermost heart's Lights of Unification and the Uniqueness of God.

The innermost heart is irrigated with the water of God's kindness, and its roots are filled with the lights of certainty. God cultivates the innermost heart directly, without any intermediary. The *nafs* with its passions and ignorance cannot even approach it, and its trees have brought forth the Light of Faith. "But God has endeared the faith to you, and has made it beautiful in your hearts." (49: 7)

Those who have turned from their negative traits and have developed access to their innermost hearts attain inner understanding. "He grants wisdom to whom He pleases: and he to whom wisdom is granted receives indeed a benefit overflowing; but none will grasp the Message but men of understanding." (2: 269) The deepest truths are understood only through the innermost heart.

Stages of reason and understanding. Inner understanding is often thought of as something similar to intelligence or reason, but one is like the light of the sun and the other like the light of a lamp. Both are lights, but the lights of the innermost heart are constant and come directly from the divine. Reason varies from person to person, and it changes over time with study and experience. The mature reason of a wise person is an ally of the deep inner understanding of the heart of hearts.

The first stage of reason is innate reason. It develops when we are small children as our capacity for language grows. At this stage we can understand commands and prohibitions given by others and can distinguish right and wrong, strangers and relatives.

The second stage is reason of evidence, which occurs at puberty. At this stage the light of reason becomes firm. The adolescent is expected to act responsibly, to think logically, and to have the capacity to follow the teachings of morality and religion. Along with this greater capacity for reason comes greater responsibility to behave correctly.

The third stage is reason of experience. The wise attain knowledge of what is not known by means of what *is* known. This is the most useful and the highest form of the three stages of reason. First comes understanding through evidence. This is secondhand knowledge, based on others' experience. It is like learning about the United States from others, never having visited it. Some of the stories may be exaggerated or untrue, but it is difficult to judge without firsthand experience.

Next is the understanding of the eye, of direct vision. First-time foreign visitors to New York City can see for themselves from the window of the airplane the Statue of Liberty and the skyscrapers of Manhattan.

The next stage is that of understanding through direct experience. This comes only after the visitors get off the plane. They meet many different Americans and see, hear, taste, smell, and feel what life is like in the United States.

Finally, the ultimate level of understanding would be to transform oneself, to go from being a visitor to becoming an American. Similarly, the inner knowledge of the heart of hearts is perceived only by those who have undergone a profound inner transformation and removed the veils that cover this light.

All those who know God have developed their reason, but reason and knowledge alone are not enough. There are many persons who know a tremendous amount, but their intellects are used mainly in the service of the ego. True wisdom and spiritual understanding are a light that God has placed in our heart of hearts, and it functions like a lamp that enables us to see clearly. In those without faith, this light is veiled.

Among those of faith there are different levels of understanding. Those with only outer knowledge will understand the outer forms of religion. For example, we may understand the literal meaning of scripture and then take this level of meaning as law. Those with inner knowledge understand in terms of the heart. Thus, they comprehend the inner, symbolic meanings behind the outer forms of practice and the deeper, symbolic meanings of the words of scripture.

As mentioned earlier, the breast is the seat of outer knowledge, and its light increases with study and use. Inner knowledge is the comprehension of the inner levels of the heart; it affects the person's whole life. Scholars who merely accumulate outer knowledge without putting into practice what they have learned are like donkeys carrying a load of books. Just as the words carried in the minds of such scholars have no real effect on their lives or their hearts, the books have no real impact on the donkey.

The Lights of the Heart

Spiritual understanding is the light that God projects into the heart. It is like a lamp that allows us to see. Each of the lights described earlier, the Lights of Practice, Faith, Gnosis, Unification, and Uniqueness are similar to each other. They originate in the same divine source.

Each of the lights of the heart is like a mountain. The Light of Practice in the breast of the believer is so solid and stable that nothing in this world can destroy it as long as God preserves it. The farthest limits of this mountain are striving against one's negative traits and the performance of good actions. On it lives a bird, the tyrannical *nafs*, the lowest level of the *nafs*. This bird flies in the valleys of worship of false gods, disbelief, doubt, hypocrisy, and the like. The Prophet says, "Many are the valleys and ravines in the heart of man, and in each of these lies gorges."[13] We must not let ourselves fall down into the gorges of doubt or hypocrisy.

The mountain of the Light of Faith is located in the heart, and on it is the bird of the inspired *nafs*.[14] It flies in the valleys of both piety and wickedness. This mountain is even greater and more stable than the mountain of the Light of Practice. Muhammad said of the believers, "The faith in their hearts is like firm mountains." Although the *nafs* is an integral part of all our outward actions, including our prayers and other religious practices, it has no part in the inner knowing of the heart. The farthest limits of this mountain are trust in God and vision, perceiving by means of the Light of Faith that which is not visible to the eye.

On the mountain of the Light of Gnosis in the inner heart is the bird of the regretful *nafs*. It sometimes flies in the valleys of exultation, might, pride, and joy in God's favors. At other times it flies in the valleys of need, humility, scorn of itself, and the vision of humbleness, destitu-

37

tion, and poverty. It includes the quality of self-blame and repentance for mistakes.

The mountain of the Light of Gnosis is larger and more splendid than the first two, as it is the source of vision, and vision is more sure than knowing. By this light we perceive what passes away and perishes, and we also know God, who abides eternally.

The mountain of the Lights of Unification and Uniqueness in the innermost heart is infinite in size and splendor. On it sits the bird of the serene self, which flies in the valleys of serenity, contentment, modesty, firmness in unification, and the sweetness of remembrance of God.[15]

These images are extremely striking. The positive Lights of Practice, Faith, Gnosis, and Unification are like great mountains of light within our hearts, while our negative tendencies are tiny and weak like small birds that perch on the tops of these great mountains. If we identify with these small birds of the limited self, they can lead our minds into valleys of darkness.

In Western psychology, this image is generally reversed. According to most Western psychological theories, we are dominated by the limitations and defects of our personalities. Our spiritual tendencies are minor and minimal, like tiny birds of light perched atop the dark mountains of the limited personality.

The Sufi psychology of the heart is a profound spiritual psychology. It does not ignore our negative tendencies, but it does put them in perspective. Compared to the inner lights of the heart, these tendencies are relatively small and insignificant. Only when we allow ourselves to identify with them and follow them do they have any real power over us. We would be much wiser to identify with the far greater light and truth within us, to follow its guidance, and to actualize it in our own lives.

The light verses. The lights of the heart are described in one of the most famous and most beautiful passages in the Koran:

God is the Light of the heavens and the earth.
The parable of His Light is as if there were a Niche
And within it a Lamp;
The Lamp enclosed in Glass,
The Glass as it were a brilliant star

Lit from a blessed Tree,
An Olive, neither of the East nor of the West,
Whose Oil is well-nigh luminous, though fire scarce
    touched it;
Light upon Light! (24:35)

The "niche" is the foundation upon which the lamp rests, as the breast is the foundation upon which the heart rests.[16] Before electric lighting, lamps were set in wall niches designed to reflect the light throughout the room.

The "glass" protects the flame from being put out by a sudden breeze. It is like the personality, which obscures the light less and less as it is purified and refined. Glass is made from sand and other opaque materials that are refined and transformed until they become transparent to the light and can transmit it unchanged. The glass does not possess its own light, but when light comes into it, it shines like a brilliant star.

The "lamp" itself and the pure flame represent the divine spark within our hearts. Those who have unveiled this flame within themselves are able to ignite other hearts. The light of truth has existed in all the prophets and in all great spiritual teachers. In a real sense, all of God's prophets are the same. Their pure hearts appear to be self-luminous, although in reality all light is but a reflection of a single source—divine light.

The olive tree is not very impressive to look at. It is relatively small and its leaves are a dull greenish-brown. But the olive fruit makes wholesome food and wonderful oil. The olive, the source of the oil, is universal, just as God's light is not localized and divine truth does not belong to any single locality or people. The oil is like spiritual truth, which illuminates the mind and heart almost before we have been consciously touched by it.

The path of the heart. Some travelers on this path were just beginning their journey when they were overtaken by night inside a dark house. They acquired a lamp and with its light, they were able to open the windows and the door. Then the moon shone into the house and provided still more light. Next, the travelers went out into the desert, and under the full moon they no longer needed the lamp. Then dawn came and overwhelmed the light of the moon. Finally, the sun reached its zenith, and the light of dawn was but a pale memory.

The dark house represents the tyrannical *nafs*, which cuts off all light. The lamp is the Light of Reason. As reason increases and is applied to knowledge of outer action, it is like the rising of the moon (the station of the breast). The Light of Faith is like the break of dawn (the station of the heart). Through vision obtained through divine grace, the light grows (the station of the inner heart). It increases still more through the Light of Unification and attains its greatest power (the station of the innermost heart).

The state of unity. One of the crowning achievements of Sufi psychology is the description of the highest state of human experience, the state of unity with the divine. Of necessity, any portrayal of this state must go beyond logic and our usual categories of description.

> The Sufis see without knowledge, without sight, without information received, and without observation, without description, without veiling and without veil. They are not themselves, but insofar as they exist at all, they exist in God. Their movements are caused by God, and their words are the words of God uttered by their tongues, and their sight is the sight of God, which has entered into their eyes. So God Most High has said, "When I love a servant, I, the Lord, am his ear so that he hears by Me, I am his eye so that he sees by Me, and I am his tongue so that he speaks by Me, and I am his hand so that he takes by Me.[17]

The reality of Unity transcends our language just as it transcends our everyday experience.[18]

Believers who have attained the level of unification have drowned in the divine ocean. It is as if the divine sun, veiled until now, is at its zenith with no clouds between it and the believers. The sun burns the believers and changes them within and without.

Those who have attained unification think only of God. They are like someone facing a hungry lion, certain of their destruction. They know beyond any doubt that there is no help except from God. They are beyond convention because they are no longer concerned with worldly matters. They fear their own hidden faults and lack of faith in their secret souls. They will not turn toward anything other than God.

The unified are at once watered and thirsty, hungry and fed, naked and clothed, seeing and blind, learned and ignorant, wise and foolish, rich and poor, living and dead. The state of the unified cannot be understood by reason or logic alone, because God has become their friend, help, and support. They have humbled and controlled their selves. Their state is beyond the comprehension of reason.

Conclusions

In our Western view of human nature, someone with "heart" is one who feels deeply. The Sufi concept of heart is far richer and more complex. The heart is a divine temple found within the breast of everyone, made by God to house the spark of God within us. One of the foundations of Sufism is to cleanse and open the heart, to make the heart a fit temple for God's presence.

If we remember that our hearts are divine temples, our sense of self and our whole psychology is transformed. From this perspective, we are not worldly creatures seeking the spiritual; we are spiritual beings seeking to discover our own true nature. What we truly are is to be found in our heart of hearts.

If we remember that everyone's heart is a divine temple, then we will see everyone differently and behave with greater love and caring. After all, the holy temples of this world have been built by prophets and saints, but the temple of the heart was created by God. This image of others is the foundation of the Sufi practice of service. To remember to honor the heart in each person is a great discipline. We so often forget. But if we could remember, our lives and all our relationships would be transformed. A working Sufi community is, in part, designed to foster this remembering.

The model of the heart presented in this chapter also stresses that our knowledge is not complete unless we act on what we know. Every action affects the heart. A kind word or helpful act softens and opens the heart, while harsh words or harmful acts harden and close it.

The model presented here is a classic model of four layers of the heart. It dates back to the eighth century. The first layer, the breast, is the locus of action. It is the place of interaction between our personality and our spiritual nature. We need our personality to act, but we also need to be guided in our actions by the deeper wisdom of the heart. In the breast we can transform our negative tendencies into positive ones, a major work of psychospiritual alchemy.

The second layer, the heart proper, is the place of deeper knowing and faith in the truth of genuine spiritual and religious teaching. It is also the place of our awareness of God's presence, an awareness that leads to transformation of our thoughts and actions.

The third layer, the inner heart, is deeper but closely related to the heart proper. It is the place of direct knowing. The heart proper knows intellectually that we are in God's presence, but at the level of the inner-most heart, we *feel* God's presence so clearly and concretely that it is as if we actually see God in front of us.

At the fourth level, the innermost heart, we enter the realm of the infinite. It is beyond words, theories, and thoughts. At this level, the sages break into poetry instead of prose, and their linear arguments are transformed into paradoxes.

The deeper we enter into our own hearts, the closer we get to God. What then prevents most of us from exploring the depths of our hearts? One obstacle is negative habits. As mentioned above, every negative action hardens the heart and makes it less accessible. Also, we have each suffered in our worldly relationships, and we have learned to armor our hearts against more pain. Another obstacle is our tendency to seek happiness and satisfaction without instead of within. To the extent we look for satisfaction in the world, we forget to search within our own hearts, which contain the goal we all seek, consciously or unconsciously.

An old Indian parable is an excellent metaphor for this tendency. The musk deer smells the intoxicating scent of musk, which comes from its own scent glands. Not realizing the source, a young deer races madly through the jungle seeking the source of the wonderful scent and leaps over a cliff to its death in search of what was, all along, within it. Or perhaps we don't see the world correctly. If our hearts are opened, everything in the world can remind us of God.

I rarely let the word "No" escape
From my mouth
Because it is so plain to my soul

42

That God has shouted, "Yes! Yes! Yes!"
To every luminous movement in Existence.[19]

Exercises for Opening the Heart

When the eyes of the heart open, we see the inner realities hidden behind the outer forms of this world. When the ears of the heart open, we hear the truth that is hidden behind words. Through an open heart, our nervous systems can become so closely attuned to the nervous systems of others that we know what they think and how they will act.

The following exercises work. They have the capacity to open your heart and transform your life. If that is what you truly want, I encourage you to practice these exercises sincerely and patiently and with focused intention.

Remembering God: A prayer at bedtime. Before going to bed, say silently in your heart three times, "God is with me. God beholds me. God watches over me." You may increase this to seven times a night, then eleven.

A Sufi sheikh, when he was three years old, was taught this prayer by his uncle. After he repeated the prayer three times a night for several nights, the uncle told him to say it seven times, then eleven. The child reported that he felt a sweetness growing in his heart. His uncle said, "Keep doing this all your life, for it will help you in this world and in the next." Later on the boy said, "After several years I found an ever-deepening sweetness within myself."

A heart prayer. The Prophet taught this prayer to his companions: "O God, grant me love of You and to love those who love You and to love whatever brings me nearer to You. O God, make Your love more precious to me than cool water to the thirsty."

The blessing of an open heart. This technique is adapted from the Divine Light Exercise of Swami Radha, who learned it in India during an unexpected encounter with an ageless yogi on the day of her initiation as a swami. This yogi, called Babaji, is similar to the hidden, undying Sufi teacher, Khidr.

Once you have felt the heart opening in this exercise, keep that sense of your heart overflowing with divine light and sending it to everyone you meet. As a spiritual guide, Swami Radha was able to reveal the most difficult insights to her students, without them closing down or resisting, because she could hold them in the light.

Stand with feet comfortably apart, knees relaxed. Raise your hands and gradually tense your whole body, then relax. Feel your body fill with energy and light. Then lower your arms and again tense and relax, feeling your body filled with divine energy.

Next, let your arms relax and turn your hands with palms facing in front of you. Visualize a divine sun directly overhead. The golden rays of this divine source shine down upon you and permeate your body until you are filled with divine light.

First, the light fills your feet and rises to your ankles. It gradually moves up to your calves, fills your legs, then the buttocks and pelvis. The light continues to rise through your torso to your arms and hands, your neck and your head.

Now imagine that there are double doors in front of your heart. Once your body is completely filled with light, open these doors and let the overflowing light stream out from your heart and the palms of your hands.

Visualize a friend or loved one in front of you. Send the light to them. Allow it to swirl in a clockwise direction around their body, rising from feet to head. As the light fully enfolds them, visualize it permeating their being to effect physical, emotional, and spiritual healing. Allow the light to purify and melt away any illness, pain, or impurity. When the light has fully permeated them, visualize it returning to its divine source.

Allow the doors of your heart to close and turn your palms to your sides. Take a moment to savor the wonderful feeling of divine energy within you. You may recall Jesus' words about inner light: "The light of the body is the eye: If therefore thine eye be single [your mind concentrated], thy whole body shall be full of light." (Matthew 6:22)

Your heart as a sunflower. This is an excellent followup to the previous exercise. As you go about your daily business, think of your heart as a sunflower that radiates light to everyone and everything you meet. Feel that you have a miniature sun in your chest. While your head and your mouth are busy with conversation, let the light from your heart touch and warm the heart of the other.

Let your sunflower touch the sunflowers of everyone you meet. No matter who they are or what their personality is like, their heart is a sunflower just like yours, yearning for divine light.[20]

Your heart as a divine temple. Sit alone in a quiet place and become still and quiet inside. Free yourself of any preoccupations and concerns. Let nothing but thoughts of God enter your mind. Once you are still say, "God, God." Keep your mind in your heart, focused on this word alone.

Polishing the lamp of the heart. Aladdin was able to summon a *jinn*, or genie, by rubbing a magic lamp. Perhaps the lamp represents the heart (which contains the divine spark). When your heart awakens, it becomes a guide and an ally far more useful than any genie.

Begin by watching your breath, gradually refining it and making it rhythmical. As you breathe, mentally recite "God" with each inhalation and each exhalation. Focus on your heart center in the middle of your breast. Feel your breath gradually massaging and soothing your heart center. Continue this until it becomes natural and without mental strain.

Next, look into your heart and feel the impressions lodged there. There may be mundane worries of daily life. Notice and release all of these impressions by the gentle massaging action of the breath on the heart.

As you continue, deeper memories or feelings may make themselves known. You might come face to face with rejection, self-pity, fear, or anger. Whatever comes up, observe it directly and shine the light of awareness on it. Continue the massaging action of the breath.

You may come upon thoughts or feelings that resist your efforts; they have lain in your heart for so long that they are rusted in. Know that by patient effort and trust in God, even the most persistent patterns can be released—if not in one session, then perhaps in one hundred and one.

Essential to this practice is the suspension of judgment. Don't condemn your heart impressions; simply remain aware of them. Also, don't try to change your behavior or correct other people. Just gently and patiently massage and release the old mental and emotional blockages inside yourself.

Chapter Three

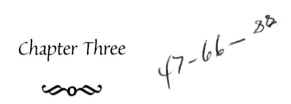

~∞~

Transforming Your Self

The nafs is like a flame
both in its display of beauty
and its hidden potential for destruction.
Though its color is attractive, it burns.

—Bakharzi[1]

A dervish was taking a long journey. After walking for weeks, he finally came to the foot of a steep hill that loomed like a mountain in front of him. He raised his hands and prayed, "Oh Lord, you know that I have been traveling for your sake. You are in charge of everything and everyone. Please send me a donkey to help me up this hill." (Those who know say that when we act sincerely, for God's sake, God will send us the help we need.)

Immediately he heard the sound of braying and, sure enough, there was a small donkey caught in the bushes. He thanked God for the gift and was just about to mount the donkey when a bandit rode up on an Arabian stallion. The bandit was a big, fierce-looking man with huge mustachios, bulging muscles, and a pistol and scimitar in his belt.

The bandit snarled, "Aha! A dervish. I hate dervishes! You are always talking about honesty, humility, and helping others. Who are you to dare criticize my way of life? And here you are, a big man about to ride that little donkey. Better that the donkey should ride you. Yes, that's it! Pick up the donkey

47

and put it on your back."

The dervish looked at the bandit in dismay. "Pick up the donkey?"

The bandit put his hand on his scimitar. "I said pick it up and put it on your back!"

Reluctantly, the dervish complied. Then the bandit growled, "Now, carry the donkey up the hill."

"Up the hill?"

Again the bandit reached for his scimitar. "Carry the donkey up the hill," he ordered.

The dervish began to walk up the hill with the donkey on his back. Each time he glanced back, he saw the bandit waiting, hand on scimitar. Finally, the exhausted dervish reached the top of the hill. He set the donkey down and raised his hands to God once again. "Lord, I know that you see everything and that you know everything. But sometimes you get it backwards!"

Like the poor dervish, most of us have been carrying our donkeys on our backs. We have been working for our *nafs*, for our personality, instead of having it work for us. God meant the self to be a tool for us, and of course it is we who have gotten things backwards, not God.

What Is the Nafs?

One of the most common terms in Sufi psychology is the *nafs*, or the self. This term is sometimes translated as "ego" or "soul." Other meanings of *nafs* include "essence" and "breath." However, in Arabic, *nafs* is most commonly used as "self"; for example, in everyday words like *myself* and *yourself*. When most Sufi authors use the term *nafs*, they refer to our negative traits and tendencies. At its lowest level, the *nafs* is that which leads us astray. We all struggle to do those things we clearly know we should do. We often struggle even harder to avoid those actions we know are wrong or harmful.

Why the struggle? If we were of a single mind, there would be no struggle. But our minds are split. Even when we are convinced of what is

48

right, there is some part of us that tries to get us to do the opposite. That part is the lower self, in particular, the lowest stage of the *nafs*, the tyrannical *nafs*.

The *nafs* is not so much a static psychological structure as a process created by the interaction of spirit and body. There is nothing essentially wrong with either the spirit or the body. However, the process that results from the combination of the two can become distorted. When the spirit enters the body, it is exiled from its nonmaterial origins and the *nafs* begins to form. The spirit is thus imprisoned in material creation and begins to take on its aspects.

Because the *nafs* has its roots in body and spirit, it includes both material and spiritual tendencies. At first, the material dominates; the *nafs* is attracted to worldly pleasures and rewards. What is material is naturally attracted to the material world. As the *nafs* transforms, it becomes more attracted to God and less attached to the world.

Many Sufi authors have written about seven different levels of development of the *nafs* founded on references in the Koran. This chapter is based primarily on the explanations of Sheikh Safer Dal, the late head of the Halveti-Jerrahi Order, supplemented with material from various other sources and with my own interpretations.

Divine names. Each level of the self is associated with one of the names or divine attributes of God. There are ninety-nine names mentioned in the Koran. Repetition of these names and contemplation of their meaning can be an effective medicine for curing the diseases of the self at each station. In the Halveti-Jerrahi Order, the individual practice of remembrance includes the names listed below. In addition to weekly group practice, dervishes are assigned various names for individual daily practice.

Levels of Nafs	Divine Name	Color
1. tyrannical[2]	*La ilaha illallah* (No god but God)	light blue
2. regretful	*Allah* (God)	red
3. inspired	*Hu* (Thou)	green
4. serene	*Haqq* (Truth)	white

49

Levels of Nafs	Divine Name	Color
5. pleased	*Hayy* (Ever living)	yellow
6. pleasing	*Qayyum* (Eternal)	black/dark blue
7. pure	*Qahhar* (Omnipotent)	no color/black

The divine name connected with the first stage is *La ilaha illallah*, which means "there is no god but God." The first half of this phrase is a negation and the second part is an affirmation; it means, "No god, there is God." In one sense this phrase is like the koans of Zen Buddhism; that is, it cannot be comprehended fully through logic alone. "No god"—with our limited capacities, there is nothing we can see or experience or imagine that is God. Also, "There is God"—God exists and is everywhere and everything; there is nothing that is not God.

The deepest meanings of *la ilaha illallah* contain the most subtle truths of Sufism. This phrase, *la ilaha illallah*, is also known as the phrase of unity. It affirms that there is nothing divine outside of God, that all power and creativity rest with God. At another level, it asserts that there is nothing that is separate from God.

Many people follow their own moods and inclinations as if their personality were God. They are pulled this way and that way from moment to moment. The Koran refers to this as *hawa*, or "caprice." "Who is more misguided than he who follows his own caprice without guidance from God?" (28:50)

Western society places great value on personal freedom. But for many this is merely freedom to follow their own misguided inclinations. Paradoxically, submission to spiritual discipline is the beginning of real freedom, because it is the beginning of freedom from the tyranny of the *nafs*.

For centuries the basic practice of Sufism consisted of repetition and contemplation of *la ilaha illallah*. A central part of the affliction of the tyrannical *nafs* is addiction to worldly pleasures and lack of faith. One cure for this condition is the realization that God exists and that this world and its pleasures are not all there is to life.

Allah is known as the greatest name, and it contains all the divine attributes indicated by the other names. One meaning of Allah is "the One worthy of worship." Nothing else is worthy of our worship. A cure for hypocrisy, the main disease of the regretful *nafs*, is to worship God and to serve creation for God's sake instead of acting to feed our egos or fill our pockets.

Hu refers to God without attributes, an intimate way of addressing God, which can be translated simply as "Thou." According to some Sufis, it is the pronunciation of the "h" at the end of "Allah." This intimate, wordless connection with God is found in the heart. It is small and faint at the level of the inspired *nafs* and grows with each successive level. The connection with God is the source of the inspiration of the inspired *nafs*.

Haqq means "Truth," and God is the unchanging truth. All other truths change and become invalid in time, as everything that is not God changes. The contentment of the serene *nafs* comes from seeking God instead of the finite and ever-changing things of the world. The stage of the serene *nafs* is the stage at which we begin to know truth.

Hayy means "Ever living." Everything that exists partakes of this divine attribute, as God is the source of life and existence in all things. The atoms of everything in creation vibrate with this name. People differ in their degree of aliveness, according to their knowledge and actions. Those who sense God as *Hayy* in everyone and everything have attained the stage of the pleased *nafs*.

Qayyum means "Eternal." God's existence depends on none other than God. Everything else in the universe relies on something or someone outside itself to survive. Only God is eternal and has no need of anything. When the universe is experienced as nothing other than God, the individual has reached the stage of the *nafs* pleasing to God.

Qahhar means "Omnipotent" or "Overwhelming" and refers to God's attribute of irresistible, unstoppable power that totally obliterates any obstacle. Nothing can escape God, and all the millions of universes bow their heads before God. To reach the stage of the pure *nafs*, all sense of our separate "I" must be eradicated. This final attainment is possible only through God's unlimited power.

Colors. The colors associated with each level of the *nafs* are often used by the sheikhs in dream interpretation to assess the level of their dervishes. When dervishes dream of wearing yellow clothing, for example, it may be a sign that they have begun to work on the stage of the pleased *nafs*. The sheikh will add recitation of *Hayy* to their spiritual practice along with other changes in their spiritual duties.

The Tyrannical Nafs

This stage, the *nafs ammara*, has also been translated as the "commanding *nafs*," the "domineering *nafs*," or the "*nafs* that incites to evil." The term *ammara* literally means "to habitually or repeatedly command," so this stage might even be called the "nagging *nafs*." The tyrannical self attempts to dominate us and to control our thoughts and actions. Unfortunately, it is often successful. When speaking of the *nafs* in general, many Sufi authors refer only to this lowest station of the *nafs*. The Koran describes it thus: "The tyrannical self certainly impels to evil, unless my Lord bestows Mercy upon me." (12:53)

In the Koran, the verb *amara*, "to command," is frequently used. It generally refers to God's commands; for example, "God commands the believers to be generous in charity." The intensive form of the verb, *ammara*, is used only once, in the above Koranic passage. Just as God commands us to do good, there is something in us that pushes us to do the opposite. Under the influence of the tyrannical self, the commands of the lower self *are* stronger than the commands of God.

Some who are dominated by the tyrannical *nafs* may engage in all the outward forms of religion, but it is all an empty show designed to impress others. In the words of one sheikh, "The *nafs* is an attribute that becomes tranquil only in deceit; being calmed only by what is other than God, the *nafs* will never submit to the way of God."[3]

At this first stage, we are ruled by our cleverness. This is intelligence without faith in anything outside ourselves. It is devoted to the accumulation of riches, power, and ego satisfaction no matter what the cost. There is no love of God, no sense of inner restraint or even sin, because there is no inner morality. We can see this clearly in psychopaths who cheat, steal, and even murder without remorse.

Addiction to the demands of the tyrannical nafs. Many at this stage are slaves to pleasure; for example, they will do virtually anything for sexual gratification, choosing as sexual partners whoever is available without regard to health or safety. Often they choose people who abuse them. At this level we are addicts in denial, dominated by uncontrollable addiction, yet we refuse to recognize that we even have a problem. There is no hope of change until we can acknowledge that we are actually controlled by our tyrannical *nafs* and that our lives are not really under our own control.

Perhaps the worst characteristic of this level is the addiction to praise and adulation, which in many ways is a more difficult and more dangerous addiction than drugs and alcohol and is often far more deeply rooted in the psyche.

The *nafs* wants everyone to notice us, to think well of us. It never stops wanting more and more; nothing is good enough for it. If others like us, we want them to love us. If they love us, we want unconditional obedience. If they obey us, we want them to worship us. This part of us will destroy others to raise itself up. Sufi teachers have described this lowest level of the *nafs* as follows:

> One of the latent vices and secret maladies of the *nafs* is its love of praise. Whoever imbibes a draught of it will move the seven heavens and seven sublunar realms for the very flutter of an eyelash. The symptom of this affliction is that when the *nafs* is deprived of praise, it falls into indolence and laxity.[4]

This kind of addiction is not well described in the literature of psychology because most of us, including psychological theorists, suffer from it. We are in the middle of it and so we cannot see this addiction in others or in ourselves. We are like fish who do not know what water is because they have never known anything else.

There is at least a spark of the tyrannical *nafs* in virtually all of us. We may have to look closely to see it because the tyrannical *nafs* is an expert at hiding from consciousness. An old sheikh noted that if someone says, "What a fine person you are!" and this pleases you more than hearing, "What a bad person you are!", know that you are still a bad person.

There are, in each of us, tyrannical forces or impulses that sometimes propel us toward wrongdoing. For example, we lash out at others, hurt those we love, and act as our own worst enemies. Then, almost immediately afterwards, we rationalize what we have done and claim that we are in charge of our lives. "The *nafs* is like fire. When at the point of being extinguished, it always flares up somewhere else; if the *nafs* is calmed in one area, it ignites in another."[5]

The tyrannical *nafs* generally operates outside conscious awareness. It seems to speak with our own voice and to express our own innermost desires, so we rarely resist it. It is a skilled ruler who rarely has to rely on naked force. If the authority of the ruler is taken for granted, there is little possibility of revolt. The tyrannical *nafs* dominates us without our knowing it, and to the extent this is true, we don't even try to counter its influence; the thought of revolt never arises. This is why so many people operate for much of their lives under the domination of the tyrannical self.

Descriptions of the tyrannical nafs. Various Sufi teachers have described the dynamics of this stage of the self as follows:

> In the early stages of the Path, as long as one is under the control and domination of the *nafs*, it is known as the commanding *nafs*. In these circumstances, where the *nafs* is still rooted firmly in material nature, it constantly seeks to drag the spirit and the heart down from a higher to lower level, namely, to its own established level. It constantly presents itself as an adorned object of adoration to others . . . thereby bringing the lofty spirit low, and defiling the pure heart with trickery.[6]

> In most situations, the outward aspect of the *nafs* differs from the inward, and it acts differently in the presence of others than it does in their absence. It praises people in their presence, feigning honesty to their face, while in their absence it does the opposite. This attribute can be removed from the *nafs* only through sincerity.[7]

> The *nafs* is persistently obsessed with . . . the good opinion of people, regardless of whether God may disapprove. The result . . . is the increase of possessions and pride therein,

as well as arrogance, self-importance and contempt. It avoids or ignores whatever people disapprove of, even though God may be pleased with these things; for instance, spiritual poverty, neediness and helplessness.[8]

The *nafs* is constantly preoccupied with the virtues of its attributes, contemplating its states with contentment and reverence. It considers important the least thing it has done for anyone, remembering it for years afterwards, being overwhelmed by its own kindness. Yet however great the favors others do for it, it places no importance on them, forgetting them quickly.[9]

Whatever possessions and objects of its desires the *nafs* may obtain, it hangs on to them. . . . When this attribute gains strength, it spawns envy, and covets the property of others. The *nafs* does not want anyone to receive anything from anybody. . . . When such envy becomes strong it turns to spite, whereby the *nafs* persistently seeks the destruction of anyone who comes to share in whatever bounty is meted out.[10]

The *nafs* is never constant. Continually subject to notions and whims, . . . only wanting to finish everything quickly. Its movements are arbitrary and unreliable; it is in a hurry to fulfill its desires, acting precipitously. Certain sages have likened it . . . to a ball rolling giddily down a slope, constantly in motion. This attribute can only be removed from the *nafs* through patience.[11]

It is important to remember that the above quotes all refer to the lowest level of the *nafs*. Some people are stuck at this level. Many others manage to live relatively ethical and moral lives and only occasionally become caught by the influence of the tyrannical *nafs*.

Working with the negative ego. It is not easy to control the insatiable negative ego found at the stage of the tyrannical *nafs*. Ascetic practices alone will not work. In fact, they often bring about inflated pride or arrogance. The Sufi saint Bayazid says, "The thickest veils between man and God are the wise man's wisdom, the worshipper's worship, and the devotion of the devout."[12] The Malami School of Sufism is particularly devoted to the control of the negative ego. Part of its practice is to avoid fame and also actions or appearances that might lead to praise or special recognition.

One evening Sheikh Muzaffer went out to dinner with a group of people at a fancy Istanbul restaurant. The waiter came to the table with bottles of wine and other alcoholic beverages. One of the group angrily scolded the waiter, "Don't you know this is a famous religious teacher? How dare you bring alcohol to our table?"

Sheikh Muzaffer quickly said, "Don't be upset. The waiter is only doing his job. The restaurant makes most of its money on these drinks. We shouldn't take away our waiter's livelihood. Waiter, put all these bottles on the table." They ate dinner with the bottles remaining on their table, untouched.

The Malami approach is a sophisticated psychological asceticism, the discipline of sacrificing the desire for praise, even for acceptance by others. In order to eliminate insincerity, the Malamis erase all outward signs of piety and even pretend to be less than respectable. They seek to deprive the negative ego of all that feeds it—especially the desires for outer recognition and reward.

We may never fully eliminate in ourselves the influences of the tyrannical *nafs*. At best we can control them and cause them to lie dormant. There remain traces even at the most refined levels of the self. For example, Moses had a strong temper; he even struck and killed a man. Although even prophets still have vestiges of the tyrannical self, they don't *follow* these tendencies. They are like puppets in God's hands and they can do nothing by themselves.

Rumi tells the story of a dragon hunter who went to the mountains to trap a dragon. He finally discovered the frozen body of a great dragon in a cave high up on a tall peak. He brought the body to Baghdad and exhibited it on the bank of the river. Hundreds of people came to see it. As the sun gradually warmed the dragon's body, it slowly began to stir out of its winter sleep. The people screamed and stampeded and many were killed. The dragon hunter was frozen in terror, and the dragon swallowed him in a single gulp.

Such savagery is easy for that which is a bloody tyrant.
Your *nafs* is such a dragon: how can it be dead?
It is merely frozen due to lack of means.

. . . .

Let that dragon of yours remain dormant.
Should it be released it will devour you.[13]

In a dramatic way, Rumi cautions us not to take our tyrannical self for granted. We may feel we have dealt with our anger, pride, addictions and so on, but a sudden situation may reawaken them. The only real solution is to transform the *nafs*.

> A dervish had been traveling and regretted that he had been unable to attend his sheikh's talks. When he returned, his sheikh told him there was no need for regret. Even if he missed the sheikh's lectures for ten years it would not matter, because he always said only one thing: "Sacrifice your ego; nothing more!"

The inner pharaoh and the inner Moses. This first level of the *nafs* is like a proud, tyrannical pharaoh. It was not enough that the pharaohs of Egypt were the absolute rulers of the most powerful and most advanced civilization on earth. They also had to be worshiped as gods. That desire for power, praise, adulation, and even worship is typical of this stage of the *nafs*.

Rumi cautions us to treat Moses and pharaoh as living, inner realities, and not merely as irrelevant historical figures:

> The light of Moses is *here* and *now*, inside you.
> Pharaoh as well. The ceramic lamp and wick change,
> but the light's the same. If you keep focusing
> on the translucent chimney that surrounds the flame,
> you will see only the Many, the colors
> and their variations. Focus on a light within
> the flame. You are that.[14]

The story of Moses leading Israel out of slavery is, on one level, an allegory for the process of freeing ourselves from the tyrannical self.

Each of us has a pharaoh within us, and each of us also has a Moses, a divine messenger who can lead us from slavery to freedom. Remember that God working *through* Moses brought the children of Israel to freedom. So too, we have to realize that we need divine grace to overcome the power of our tyrannical self. Each of us has an inner Moses, and we have to nourish and honor that liberator and divine servant within us.

There are many lessons for us in the story of Moses and Pharaoh. For example, Moses had to go to Pharaoh over and over again to ask for freedom for the children of Israel. Pharaoh would recognize the divine power in Moses and agree, then change his mind, almost as soon as Moses left. We too have been convinced of the truth of spiritual principles and ideals and vowed to live our lives differently, and then changed back to our old habits almost as soon as our resolution was made. It is as if the tyrannical *nafs* has the power to hypnotize us and make us unconscious once again.

Once beyond the pharaoh's immediate control, the children of Israel had to enter the Red Sea in spite of the fear that it would roll back and drown them. That took tremendous faith and courage. Imagine living as a slave, with no sense of power or control over your life. Then, suddenly you are told to cross a great sea, to walk over the wet sea bottom with the waters piled up on either side. You are told to have faith that a God you have just heard of will hold back the waters for you. According to one tradition, the Red Sea did not part until the first Israelite actually set foot in it, believing it *would* part.

It is not easy to escape the domination of the tyrannical *nafs*. The process often brings fear of the new and unknown. True transformational change is a process of literally turning our backs and moving away from our old way of life.

Often our old habits and way of life seem overwhelming, just as Pharaoh's army completely outclassed the children of Israel. The army of Egypt was the greatest in the world, while the Israelites had been slaves for generations and most had never even held a weapon in their hands. This represents a crisis that often occurs after an initial spiritual change. Parts of the psyche try to pull us back to our old, comfortable ways and warn us that if we do not go back, we risk disaster. However, our old habits lose their grip on us once we put our feet sincerely into the Red

Sea of change. Through God's grace, what was so irresistibly attractive in the past loses its charm.

At first the children of Israel could not understand Moses or his teachings. They even had to create a golden calf in order to worship. They were still an undisciplined rabble. It took time—two generations, or forty years in the desert—to overcome their slave mentality and conditioning. For us too, real change takes time. We begin with an undisciplined, unfocused collection of thoughts, feelings, and actions. Our negative ego and pleasure-loving instincts are still powerful forces within us. All too often nothing seems to be happening as we integrate inner change. It may even feel like forty years in the desert!

These forty years, however, were also a time of retreat with their prophet. Traditionally, a dervish spent years with his or her sheikh, living together and learning through all the different activities of the day, from prayer to work to shopping to laundry and other mundane tasks. Every activity can be an opportunity for the most profound lessons. Sheikh Safer once commented that he spent fourteen years, day and night, with his own sheikh. He would often go to see him immediately after work and stay until it was time to go back to work again.

The forty years spent with Moses provided the opportunity for a profound transformation of the children of Israel, from oppressed slaves to free believers. In one sense they enjoyed a forty-year retreat, not with just a spiritual guide, but with one of God's beloved prophets. A common Sufi tradition is the forty-day retreat, a time to be away from the world and close to God, just as Moses himself spent forty days on Mount Sinai.

When the children of Israel complained they would starve in the desert, God told Moses that manna would fall from heaven to feed them. The Israelites were to gather only one day's supply at a time. This was a test of discipline and of their faith in God as a provider. When some gathered extra manna and kept it overnight, it became rotten and full of maggots, a graphic reminder of the dangers of greed and excess regarding gifts of the spirit.

It is also psychologically significant that forty years represents two generations. By the end of their desert retreat, the vast majority of those who entered the land of Canaan had never known slavery. The only life they knew was the one with their prophet. So too with us old habits of thinking and acting can be gradually replaced by new, healthier habits.

There are three kinds of prophets: those who came to bring the law, the outer forms of religious observance and moral practice. Moses is the best example of this. The second type brings us the inner spirit behind the law. Jesus is a wonderful example of this type. Finally there are those who come to teach the unity of the inner and the outer. Both Abraham and Muhammad are examples.[15]

Moses is also associated with liberation from the tyrannical *nafs*, which needs the clear boundaries of law in order to restrain it. Without any belief in religious law, people are constrained only by fear of punishment.

The city of the tyrannical nafs. There is a wonderful unpublished manuscript on the self that was written by a Naqshbandi sheikh who lived more than 150 years ago. The sheikh asked that it not be published until after his passing.[16] He describes each station of the self as a city, nested one within the other. Sheikh Safer has commented that this manuscript is one of the most useful and important works in Sufism, and that all Jerrahi dervishes should read it often.

> As if in a dream, I reached a city that was all in the dark. It was so vast, I could neither see nor conceive of its limits. This city contained people from all nations and races. All the ugly actions of all the creatures, all the sins known and unknown to me, were all around me.
>
> What I observed led me to think that never, since the beginning of time, had a ray of light from the sun of truth fallen upon this city. Not only were the sky and the roads and houses of this city in total darkness, but its citizens, who were like bats, had minds and hearts as dark as night. Their nature and their behavior were like those of wild dogs. Growling and fighting with each other for a mouthful of food, obsessed by lust and anger, they killed and tore each other apart. Their only pleasure was in drinking and in shameless sex, without discrimination of male and female, wives and husbands or others. Lying, cheating, gossiping, slander, stealing was their custom, with total

absence of concern for others, conscience, or fear of God. Many among them called themselves Muslims. In fact, some were considered by them to be wise men—shaykhs, teachers, men of knowledge and preachers.

[A native of the city] told me that it was Ammara, . . . the city of freedom, where everyone did what he pleased. . . . I asked him the name of their ruler. He informed me that he was called His Highness Cleverness, and that he was an astrologer, a sorcerer, an engineer, . . . a doctor who gave life to the ones who otherwise would die, an intelligent, learned king who had no equal in this world. His advisers and ministers were called Logic, his judges depended on the ancient Law of Common Sense, his stewards were called Imagination and Daydreaming. . . . [A]ll the citizens were totally loyal to their ruler, not only respecting and appreciating him and his government, but loving him, for they all felt an affinity in their nature, in their customs, in their behavior. . . .

I went to His Highness Cleverness and daringly asked, "How is it that the men of knowledge of your realm never act on their knowledge and fear God? How is it that none in this city fear the punishment of God, while they fear your punishment? How is it that there is no light here, nor outside, nor in your people's hearts? How is it that your subjects appear as human beings, yet their nature is like that of wild animals, and worse still?"

He answered, "I—the one who can figure out how to derive personal benefit from this world, even if my benefit is their loss—am their ideal. I have an agent in each of them. They are my servants and the servants of my agents in them, but I also have a master who guides me, and that is the Devil.

Controlling the tyrannical nafs. Sheikh Nurbakhsh, who is also a psychiatrist, makes the important point that the tyrannical *nafs* should never be destroyed; it is to be transformed into good qualities and actions. To destroy the tyrannical self is to destroy ourselves.

When Sufis speak of the destruction of the *nafs*, . . . they use the expression "annihilation of the *nafs*." This signifies the annihilation of those characteristics associated with the *nafs* and their transformation into qualities associated with a true human being. The *nafs* itself, however, is indestructible. . . . When Sufis say that "so-and-so" has no *nafs*, they mean that the characteristics of that person's *nafs* have been transmuted into positive human qualities, such that no trace of the *nafs* remains visible in them.[17]

How can we learn to control ourselves and escape from this stage of the tyrannical *nafs*? How can we transmute our negative characteristics into positive qualities? It is possible to change one trait at a time; for example, to transform miserliness into generosity, anger into tolerance, and greed into nonattachment. In addition, we must also purify and open our hearts.

One way to purify the heart is through the practice of detachment from the world and remembrance of God, which bring out the lights of the heart and makes us aware of the operation of the *nafs*. Sheikh Nurbakhsh writes:

Continuous attention to God causes remembrance of God, which drives awareness of other things out of one's consciousness, causing the desires of the *nafs* to become gradually forgotten.

Continuous attention to God engenders the gradual transmutation of the attributes of the disciples' *nafs* into the Attributes of God.[18]

Also, the heart is opened by kindness and service. Sheikh Muzaffer used to say that every smile and every kind word softens the heart, but every hurtful word or action hardens it. In fact, our actions have repercussions beyond ourselves. He explains that acting well is a struggle:

There is a battle between the self, the lower self, and the soul. This battle will continue through life. The question is,

Who will educate whom? Who will become the master of whom? If the soul becomes the master, then you will be a believer, one who embraces Truth. If the lower self becomes master of the soul, you will be one who denies Truth.[19]

Sheikh Nurbakhsh also points out that another tool for controlling the tyrannical self is devotion to one's sheikh.

Devotion to the master engenders the Sufi's preference for the master's contentment over that of the *nafs*, thus reducing attention to the *nafs* and its desires. It also causes the energy of the *nafs* to be expended in service to the master and the desire to fulfill the master's wishes, such that the force of the *nafs* becomes weakened thereby.

Sheikh Tosun Bayrak has explained that the tyrannical *nafs* is like a thief who sneaks into your house at night to steal whatever is valuable and worthwhile. You cannot fight this thief directly, because it will mirror whatever power you bring against it. If you have a gun, the thief will also have a gun. If you have a knife, the thief will have a knife as well. To struggle with the thief is to invite disaster. The only practical solution is to turn on the lights. The thief, who is a coward at heart, will then run out of the house.

How do we turn on the light in our own lives? It is through the practice of remembrance, awareness, and heedfulness. As mentioned earlier, this level of the *nafs* is ignored in most Western psychological theories. We generally think of spiritual systems as focused only on the higher realms of human nature. Paradoxically, spiritually oriented theories such as this one may also describe more accurately the real problems and limitations of "normal" states, because such theories have been developed by those who are no longer in the grip of their negative egos. The sheikhs have attained a perspective from which they can see and understand the limitations of our so-called normal states because they themselves have transcended them.

A diagram of the tyrannical nafs. There is a diagram of the psyche that fits closely the Sufi model of the transformation of the self. The diagram was originally developed by Roberto Assagioli, an Italian psy-

63

chiatrist who studied with both Freud and Jung. I have adapted his diagram to fit the model of the seven stages of the self. In this basic diagram, the upper third of the oval, the higher unconscious, represents the spiritual, transcendent, or transpersonal parts of the psyche.

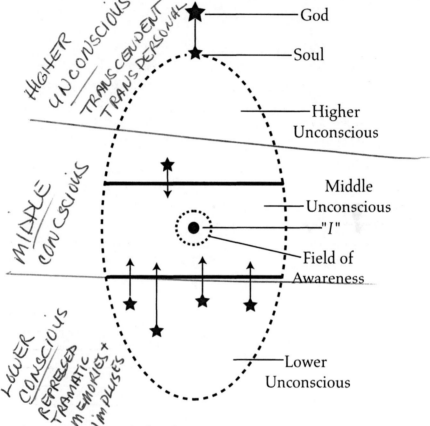

Figure 1. The Tyrannical Nafs

The middle unconscious includes the field of awareness, or the currently conscious part of the psyche. The area outside this circle contains memories that are not currently conscious, but easily retrievable; for example, your mother's maiden name. The "I" is placed in the center of the middle unconscious. It is the center of our awareness, our limited sense of who we are. The "I" has the ability to affect our experience by focusing our awareness, expanding or contracting it.

The lower third corresponds closely to Freud's concept of the unconscious. The lower unconscious is filled with repressed traumatic memories and powerful, often unacceptable impulses. There is a powerful repression barrier that maintains a separation between daily awareness and past traumatic experiences or deeply painful memories. If material from the lower unconscious breaks through this barrier, we may be surprised by pain or anger. Also, unconscious impulses of greed or sex may suddenly color or distort our behavior.

The higher unconscious is that realm of human experience encountered most dramatically in mystical or deeply spiritual experience. At such times, we may feel that the veils between us and God have suddenly lifted. We sense God's presence far more deeply than usual, often in the form of profoundly experiencing God's attributes, such as love, compassion, beauty, or unity.

At the stage of the tyrannical *nafs*, a powerful barrier separates the higher unconscious from awareness. Life is uninspired, cut off from any sense of love, meaning, or joy. If material from the higher unconscious does manage to break through into awareness, we experience a sudden, startling peak experience. We become surprised by joy.

The Soul is placed at the top of the oval, although it is actually the center of the entire psyche. The soul can be said to pervade all of the oval, to be distinct but not separate from the rest of the psyche. (It is extremely difficult to diagram something as complex as the psyche in only two dimensions, and some compromises are inevitable.) The soul is directly connected with the divine, even if the individual is unconscious of that connection. It is a source of deeper wisdom and guidance and can operate beyond the control of awareness of the conscious personality. One fundamental principal of Sufi psychology is that this connection with God is present in all people at all times, and therefore every individual deserves to be treated with respect and compassion.

At this first stage, the spiritual parts of the psyche are mostly cut off. The border between the middle and higher unconscious is thick and virtually impermeable. The "I" mistakenly sees itself as the center of the psyche, because the rightful center, the soul, is completely out of contact.

The border between middle and lower unconscious is also thick, but not completely impermeable. This represents the individual's lack of awareness of the id impulses, which, as a result, tend to erupt suddenly into consciousness. The less aware we are of these impulses, the greater their power. Therefore, the individual is most strongly dominated by the impulses of the id. The ego ("I") is also powerful, because at this stage we have no sense of either the spiritual or unconscious dimensions of the psyche.

The Regretful Nafs

Under the reign of the tyrannical *nafs*, we are basically unaware and unconscious. We cannot see the state we are in, and we do not realize the harm we do to ourselves and others. Even though it is weak and faint at first, as the light of faith and inner understanding grows, we begin to see ourselves clearly, perhaps for the first time.

In the Koran, the original reference to the regretful self, the *nafs lawwama*, is, "I call to witness the regretful self." (75: 2) The sense of the Arabic word *lawwama* is that of resisting wrongdoing and asking God's forgiveness after we become conscious of wrongdoing. At this stage, we begin to understand the negative effects of our habitual self-centered approach to the world, even though we do not yet have the ability to change. Our misdeeds now begin to become repellent to us. We enter a cycle of erring, regretting our mistakes, and then erring again.

> The blaming [regretful] *nafs* is that which has become illuminated by the light of the heart. When remembrance of God becomes established in the *nafs* that commands one to evil, it becomes like a lamp in a dark house, at which point it turns to 'blaming' [regret], for it notices that the house is full of filth and dogs, pigs, tigers, panthers, donkeys, cows, elephants, in short everything that is blameworthy. Having observed these things, it strives to expel the filth and the animals' savage presence from the house, whereupon it is accompanied by remembrance of God and contrition, until the remembrance overwhelms these things and drives them out.[20]

Those at this stage are like addicts who now finally realize the extent and implications of their addiction. They have harmed their families, damaged their careers, driven away their friends, and injured their own bodies. Unfortunately, no matter how clear or painful, these realizations are not enough to break the hold of the addiction. That requires far stronger medicine.

The ruler of this stage is still worldly cleverness, and the prime minister is still egotism or self-love. However, its attributes are softer than those of the tyrannical self. They are spiritual pride, hypocrisy, rigidity of belief, reliance on alcohol or drugs, seductiveness, and emphasis on seeking worldly and sensual pleasure.

The city of the regretful nafs. The traveler through the stages of the *nafs* asks the king to permit him to go to the great castle in the middle of the city:

> The king answered me, saying, "I rule over that castle also. That district is called Regret. . . . In the City of Regret, imagination does not have total power. They also do what is called sin—they commit adultery, they satisfy their lust with men and women alike, they drink and gamble, steal and murder, gossip and slander as we do, but often they see what they have done, and regret and repent." . . .
>
> [I met a man of knowledge in this city.] He confirmed that they were under the jurisdiction of His Highness Cleverness, but that they had their own administrators, whose names were Arrogance, Hypocrisy, Bigotry, and Fanaticism.
>
> Among the population were many . . . men who appeared to be virtuous, devout, pious, and righteous. I . . . found them to be afflicted with arrogance, egotism, envy, ambition, bigotry, and, in their friendship, insincerity. . . . What I can say for the best of them is that they prayed and tried to follow God's commandments because they feared God's punishment and Hell. . . .
>
> When I had first come to the City of Regret, I had seen that in its center there was yet another castle . . . . I asked the learned inhabitant about it. He said that it was called the City of Love and Inspiration. I asked about

its ruler and was told that he was called His Highness Wisdom, Knower of God. This king, said my informant, had a prime minister whose name was Love.

"If ever any one of us enters the City of Love and Inspiration, " [my informant] went on, "we don't accept him back to our city. For anyone who goes there becomes like all the rest of that city's population—totally attached to that prime minister . . . and is ready to give up anything—all that he has, his possessions, his family and children, even his life—for the sake of that prime minister called Love. Our sultan, His Highness Cleverness, finds this attribute absolutely unacceptable. He fears the influence of those who have this quality, for both their loyalty and their actions seem to be illogical and are not understandable by common sense."

"We hear that the people of that city call upon God chanting and singing, even with the accompaniment of the reed flute and tambourines and drums, and that doing so they lose their senses and go into ecstasy. [These are the Sufis, chanting and calling out to God.] Our religious leaders and theologians find this unacceptable. . . . Therefore, none of them even dreams of setting foot in the City of Love and Inspiration."

Hypocrisy. One of the strongest negative tendencies of this stage is hypocrisy. Because we have some knowledge of a correct way of life, we tend to think we have achieved these ideals already. As opposed to the shameless state of the tyrannical self, people at this stage are drawn to what is good, even if they cannot achieve it. It is not easy to admit that we are struggling and that we fail more often than not. So we pretend that we have achieved something, that we are the wise, fine person we would like to be.

At this stage we are like a false lover who claims to love the spiritual with all his heart but is still eyeing other possibilities. Sheikh Muzaffer used to tell the following story.

A man fell madly in love with a beautiful woman. Finally

he declared his undying love in the most flowery of terms. He went on and on, until the woman interrupted. "Your words are lovely, but my sister is coming along behind me. She is far more beautiful than I am, and I'm sure that you will prefer her to me."

As the man spun around to look at the beautiful sister, the woman slapped him sharply on the back of his neck. "I thought you said that your love for me was all consuming and undying," she exclaimed. "The instant I mentioned a more beautiful woman, you turned away from me to look at her. You don't even know the meaning of love!"

True sincerity is a rare achievement. One of the greatest Sufi masters once said, "If I knew that I had taken only one single step in sincerity, I would give no value to anything else."

A diagram of the regretful nafs. The oval model of the psyche, the barrier separating the spiritual aspects of the psyche has become thinned at this stage. As the light of the higher unconscious enters our awareness, we begin to see more clearly who we are and what our mistakes are. We can no longer remain in blissful ignorance and total denial. Because of this, we are also more aware of the impulses of the lower unconscious, and this very awareness reduces their power. However, these unconscious impulses are still relatively strong, and the arrogance of the ego is very much intact despite our growing inner awareness.

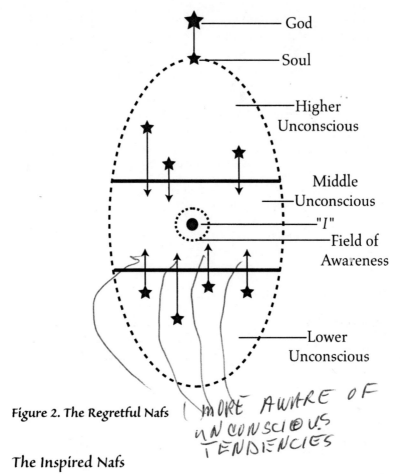

God

Soul

Higher
Unconscious

Middle
Unconscious

"I"

Field of
Awareness

Lower
Unconscious

Figure 2. The Regretful Nafs

MORE AWARE OF UNCONSCIOUS TENDENCIES

The Inspired Nafs

At this third stage, we begin to take genuine pleasure in prayer, meditation, and other spiritual activities. We begin to experience for ourselves the religious and spiritual truths we have only heard or read about up until now. We begin to feel genuine love for God and for others. This is also the beginning of the real practice of Sufism. Prior to this, the best we can accomplish is superficial understanding and mechanical worship. The ruler of this stage is wisdom and the prime minister is love. The traits of this stage include generosity, satisfaction with small things, surrender to God, humility, and repentance.

Repentance. Repentance is far different from the self-blame and regret of the prior stage. In repentance, we become aware of doing wrong and vow never to do it again. There are three aspects to sincere repentance. Repentance of the past is to see clearly our errors without rationalizing or making excuses. Repentance of the present is to make amends to anyone or anything injured by our past errors. Repentance of the future is to vow sincerely never to repeat that mistake again. The sign of God's acceptance of our repentance is that those things that were so attractive to us in the past have become unattractive—God has taken that temptation from our hearts.

We have all had the experience of failing time after time in changing old habits. Then suddenly these habits lose their hold on us. What was so attractive suddenly becomes unattractive. This is a sign that God has accepted our repentance. At this point, my sheikh used to say that we are no longer responsible for those old sins. We have truly changed and we are now someone who is not even tempted to commit them.

A classic example of the power of repentance can be seen in the story of Moses. When Moses and the children of Israel finally left Egypt and the pharaoh, this symbolized real repentance. Once they put their resolution into action, God removed the last barrier by parting the Red Sea. This symbolizes the removal of old temptations we truly repent. The Koranic reference for this stage is:

> By the *nafs*
> And the proportion and order
> Given to it;
> And its inspiration
> As to its wrong
> And its right;
> Surely the one succeeds
> Who purifies it,
> And the one fails
> Who corrupts it. (91: 7–10)

Inspiration. The individual begins to hear the inner voice of guidance. As one sheikh writes, "When the sun of divine favor rises above the horizon of right guidance, the *nafs* becomes inspired and illuminated by that sun, so that it is able to distinguish between right and wrong."[21]
Inspiration not only involves hearing the inner voice of our own

heart or conscience. There are dervishes who have developed their attunement to their sheikhs who can also hear the sheikh's voice within. They are able to receive inspiration and guidance from the sheikh even when far apart. This may take the form of suddenly remembering one of the sheikh's talks or teaching stories or feeling that they are in the sheikh's presence.

In 1980, when my psychology school hosted Sheikh Muzaffer and his dervishes, we went to great lengths to be good hosts, including preparing food pleasing to Turkish palates. Some of the Turkish dervishes began to help out in the kitchen. They were excellent cooks and knew far more than we did about Turkish cuisine. However, this upset some of the students who were in charge of cooking.

In the middle of the confusion, Sheikh Muzaffer's translator came into the kitchen. He gave a wonderful short talk, packed with great wisdom, about the nature of service and the role of the ego. When it was over, I commented, "I think you have blown your cover. You can't be simply a translator. That was a marvelous talk on some of the most important principles of Sufism." The man replied, "No, I am only a translator. Those were my sheikh's words. He simply is not here now." (I later discovered that the translator was, in fact, Sheikh Tosun, the first sheikh of our order in the United States.)

The city of the inspired nafs. The city of love and inspiration is a complex place, with both positive and negative districts. Egotism, imitation, and hypocrisy are still real dangers at this stage. The traveler enters by sincerely saying the sacred phrase, *la ilaha illallah,* "There is no god but God."

> Soon I found a dervish lodge, where I saw the high and the lowly, the rich and the poor together, as if one single being. I saw them loving and respecting each other, serving each other with regard, reverence, and deference, in a continuous state of pure joy. They were talking, singing—their songs and their talk captivating, beautiful, always about God and the hereafter, spiritual, removed from all anxiety and pain, as if living in Paradise. I did not hear or see anything that resembled dispute or quarrel, anything harmful

or damaging. There was no intrigue or malice, envy or gossip. I felt immediately a peace, comfort, and joy among them.

I saw a beautiful old man, consciousness and wisdom shining through him. I was attracted to him and went over and addressed him: "O my dearest, I am a poor traveler and a sick one at that, seeking a remedy for my sickness of darkness and unconsciousness. Is there a doctor in this City of Love and Inspiration to cure me?"

He stayed silent for awhile. I asked his name. He told me his name was Guidance. Then he said, "My nickname is Truthfulness. Since time immemorial not a single untruth has passed from these lips. My duty and my charge are to show the road to the ones who sincerely seek union with the Beloved."

The guide then describes to the traveler the district of the imitators, which is within the City of Love and Inspiration. This is the district of the hypocrites, who imitate the outer forms of worship and spiritual teaching without inner understanding.

"The outer one is called the district of the imitators. The skillful doctor you seek to cure your ills is not within that district. Neither is the pharmacy that has medicine for the sickness of heedlessness, darkness of the heart, . . . they themselves are sick with the sickness of themselves. They assign partners to God, and are masters only of imitation.

"They hide their intrigue, duplicity, and malice well. Although their tongues appear to be pronouncing the prayers and the names of God, and you find them often in the circles of dervishes, . . . you will not find with them the balm to soothe the pains of unconsciousness and forgetfulness."

The dangers of the inspired nafs. This stage, the inspired *nafs*, is a critical turning point. The gross errors of the tyrannical *nafs* and the unending struggles of the regretful *nafs* are over. However, we are not yet safe. The negative ego is still very much intact and can lead us down the wrong path, as was clearly illustrated by the district of the hypocrites or imitators. In the words of one sheikh:

> At no station is the *nafs* more vulnerable or more in danger than at the station of inspiration, where it has yet to experience total liberation from self. . . . It is ever at risk of falling into the deception of having attained the station of perfection and being lured into the trap of Satan's temptation, of regarding itself with conceit, of susceptibility to flattery, of self-importance, and of self-promotion[22]

One of the important functions of the Sufi lineage is to prevent half-trained dervishes from setting themselves up as teachers. No one can set themselves up as a sheikh without formal certification from their own sheikh. A sheikh will not fail to inform overly ambitious dervishes that they have more inner work to do. Sometimes sheikhs point out the dervishes' faults directly. At other times, they tell stories or anecdotes that make clear the level of spiritual attainment it takes to become a sheikh.

This stage can be the most dangerous stage of development of the *nafs*. For the first time, we are capable of genuine spiritual experiences and insights. However, if these experiences and insights are filtered through the ego, we can become tremendously inflated.

This can be observed among creative artists, writers, musicians, and scientists. Such people may experience inspired states and creative breakthroughs. The danger is that they may think that they themselves are the source of inspiration.

Most therapists and spiritual guides have to struggle with issues of inflation and the desire for fame and fortune. In evaluating psycho-spiritual guides, we need to use our intuition and our best powers of discrimination and discernment to distinguish the sincere from the phony, the gifted from the charlatans, the knowledgeable from the half-trained. A particular danger is that people at this stage believe they are finished, done with the need for any more spiritual training. There are many charismatic but misguided self-appointed spiritual teachers who decide they are fully enlightened when they achieve this stage.

A diagram of the inspired nafs. In the oval diagram, energies and inspirations from the higher unconscious are now far more available. The area of the middle unconscious has expanded as the individual is now more aware of both the higher and lower unconscious forces in the psyche. However, the "I" still acts as if it were the center of the psyche, and the impulses of the lower unconscious are still strong. Because of this, impulses from the higher unconscious can be distorted and used in the service of the ego rather than spiritual growth and development.

Although there is, as yet, no direct connection between the soul and the "I," the sheikh serves as an indirect connection to the divine. Ideally, this experience is seen as a preview of finding the divine within; that is, the external sheikh is a necessary intermediate step prior to finding the divine within oneself. In Sufism, the stage of *fana fi sheikh,* or "annihilation" (of our negative characteristics) in one's sheikh precedes the stage of *fana fiʾllah,* or annihilation in God.

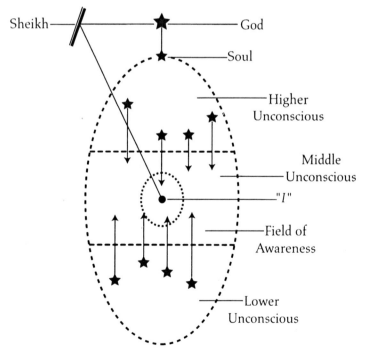

Figure 3. The Inspired Nafs

The Serene Nafs

The ruler of this stage is also wisdom and the prime minister is love. The characteristics of the serene *nafs* include trust in God, good actions, spiritual pleasure, worship, gratitude, and contentment. According to Sheikh Safer, we are safe from the major distortions of the negative ego only when we have reached this stage, and even at this and at later stages, the negative ego can still affect us, if only momentarily. God directly addresses this level of *nafs* in the following passage from the Koran: "O *nafs* at peace [serene *nafs*]/Return to your Lord,/Well pleased/And well pleasing to God." (89: 27–30)

The struggle of the earlier stages is basically over. The individual is free from heedlessness. The attributes of the tyrannical *nafs* are now seen as ugly and repulsive, and there is no desire for them left in the heart.

> The wayfarer's progress at the spiritual level of the *nafs* is downward. This is to say at first, the commanding [tyrannical] *nafs* is governed by a fiery nature. When it descends from this fieriness to become the blaming [regretful] *nafs*, it becomes governed by airiness. Once it has descended from airiness and becomes the inspired *nafs*, it becomes governed by wateriness. Once it has descended from this watery nature and becomes the *nafs*-at-rest, it becomes governed by earthiness, gaining stability, whereupon it becomes characterized by humility, dignity, meekness and submissiveness. When the Satanic, predatory and bestial characteristics have been transmuted into human ones, one comes to enjoy frequent dreams of human beings, such as believers, ascetics, doers of good works, righteous people, peacemakers, pure people, worshippers and possessors of *nafs*-at-rest [serene self].[23]

> Serenity is far different from the state we are usually in. It is a real spiritual achievement to be content with the present, with whatever is, with whatever God brings us. This serenity and contentment is rooted in the love of God. "When the commanding [tyrannical] *nafs* is jolted with

76

the shock of overpowering love, it is transformed into the *nafs*-at-rest [serene *nafs*]."[24]

One foundation for this stage is the opening of the heart. As we discussed in chapter 2, the light from the heart counteracts the negative, delusive tendencies of the lower levels of the *nafs*.

> The *nafs*-at-rest is that which is illuminated by the light of the heart to such an extent that it is purged of all blameworthy attributes and becomes characterized by praiseworthy attributes, completely centering its attention on the heart, and accompanying it in its descent to the realm of sanctity while being cleansed of all impurities and assiduous in its devotions.[25]

As an illustration of the serene self, Sheikh Muzaffer used to tell this story:

> Caliph Harun al-Rashid's favorite concubine was a very plain woman, but the caliph preferred her to all of her beautiful rivals. When he was asked for a reason, the caliph offered a demonstration.
>
> He summoned all his concubines and then opened the door of his private treasure chamber, which was filled with gold and jewels. He told the women that they could go inside and take whatever they desired. They all ran to gather up as much as they could, except his favorite concubine, who did not even enter the treasure chamber.
>
> "Why don't you take something for yourself?" asked the caliph.
>
> The woman replied, "All I want is to serve you. You are all I need. You are the one I love, and your approval is all the reward I want."
>
> The caliph turned to his courtiers and said, "Now do you see why I prefer this woman to all others? Because of her inner beauty I love her too, and her every wish shall be my command!"

When we love God in the same way this concubine loved her lord, we will be at the station of the serene *nafs*.

> One person is content with pain, another with cure;
> One is content with union, another with separation;
> I am content with whatever the Beloved desires,
> Be it cure or pain, union or separation.
>
> —BABA TAHER[26]

GREAT
⟶

The district of the serene nafs. The inner work needed at this stage is to reduce the sense of separateness from God and to begin to unify the various tendencies and identifications we have developed. In the traveler's manuscript, the guide sends him to the district of the spiritual warriors.

> I followed his advice and went to the district of the warriors. The people I met there were weak and thin, gentle, thoughtful, thankful, devoted to praying, obeying, fasting, contemplating and meditating. Their strength lay in putting into action that which they knew. I became close to them, and saw that they had left all the failures of character produced by egoism and egotism and the shadow of unconsciousness.
>
> I fought hard day and night with my ego, but still I was left with the polytheism of many "me's" and "I's" fighting among each other, even though they faced one God. This, my sickness of setting up many "I's" as partners to God, cast heavy shadows over my heart, hid the truth, and kept me in heedlessness. . . . I told [the doctors] of my sickness, the hidden polytheism, the awful heedlessness, the darkness of the heart, and asked for help. They told me, "Even in this place of those who battle their egos there is no cure for your ills." . . . They advised me to travel . . . [to] a district called supplication and meditation. Perchance there, they said, would be a doctor to cure me.

A diagram of the serene nafs. In the oval diagram, the energies of the higher unconscious are even more available than before, and the impulses of the lower unconscious are reduced in strength and effectiveness. The field of consciousness now borders on both the higher unconscious and the lower unconscious; the individual is more aware of the depths of his own psyche. Inner contentment and serenity come from this new level of awareness.

The "I"-soul axis is developed. The "I," which was originally completely occupied with temporal and finite concerns, is now identified with the infinite and eternal perspective of the soul. The inner guidance of the soul is now more available to the "I," and the "I" is no longer seen as the center of the psyche. The id impulses are weakened and the "I" is transformed. For the first time, the individual is now relatively safe from their power.

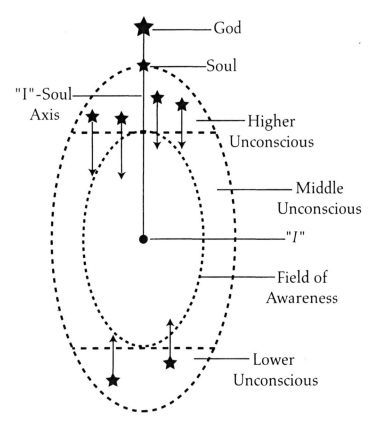

Figure 4. The Serene Nafs

The Pleased Nafs

As the sheikh's manuscript indicates, spiritual growth becomes more subtle and more inward as we progress through the higher stages. As indicated by this Koranic passage, the serene self, pleased self, and the self pleasing to God are all closely related. "O *nafs* at peace [serene self],/Return to your Lord,/Well pleased yourself,/And well pleasing to God." (89:27–30)

At this stage we are not only content with our lot, we are pleased even with the difficulties and trials of life, which also come from God. The state of the pleased *nafs* is very different from the way we usually experience the world. We realize that we are continually surrounded by God's mercy and compassion.

> Sultan Mahmud of Ghazna once shared a cucumber with Ayaz, his most loyal and trusted subject. Ayaz happily began to eat his half of the cucumber, but when the sultan bit into his, it was so bitter he immediately spat it out.
>
> "How could you manage to eat something so bitter?" The sultan exclaimed. "It tasted like bitter poison."
>
> "My beloved sultan," answered Ayaz, "I have enjoyed so many favors and bounties from your hand that whatever you give me tastes sweet."

When our sense of gratitude and our love of God are such that even the bitter tastes sweet to us, we have reached the station of the pleased *nafs*. Other characteristics of this stage are miracles, nonattachment, sincerity, contemplation, and remembrance of God. Miracles are possible because God responds to the sincere prayers of those at this stage. For example, there are many saints whose prayers for healing have been answered. Nonattachment occurs because we are no longer tempted by anything in this world. Our focus is within ourselves and on God.

The district of the pleased nafs. The traveler next reaches the district of meditation, or the district of the pleased *nafs*.

> When I came to the district of meditation I saw its inhabitants, quiet and peaceful, remembering God inwardly, reciting His Beautiful Names. To each and every one of

NON ATTACHMENT

them a son of the heart had been born. . . .

Their ways were gentle and courteous. They barely spoke with each other for fear of . . . preventing each other from deep meditation. Light as feathers they were, yet they feared most to be a burden and a load on others.

I spent many years in the district of meditation and contemplation. . . . But I was not cured of the hidden dualism of "I" and "He" that still cast heavy shadows upon my heart.

My tears ran in torrents. Wretched and wan and in total awe I fell into a strange state where an ocean of sadness surrounded me. . . .

As I stood there helpless, sad, in ecstasy, there appeared the beautiful teacher whom I had first met in these strange lands. . . . He looked upon me with compassionate eyes. "O poor slave of himself, in exile in this foreign land! O wanderer away from home! O poor wretched one, you cannot find your cure in this state of spirit. Leave this place. Go to that district yonder. . . . The name of that quarter is *Fana'*, annihilation. There you will find doctors who have annihilated their selves, who have no being, who know the secret of "Be nought, be nought, be nought, so that you will be, so that you will be, so that you will be forever."

A diagram of the pleased nafs. In the oval diagram, we are now constantly aware of various aspects of both the lower and higher unconscious; that is, we have attained a certain level of constant remembrance and self-knowledge. The "I"-soul axis has deepened, and we are now consciously aware of that which had been previously unconscious. For those who never forget God, the pains and trials of this world are like a dream. Those who attain this stage remember God and remain grateful to God no matter what happens to them.

GRATEFULL TO GOD — NO MATTER WHAT HAPPENS TO THEM !!???!!???

81

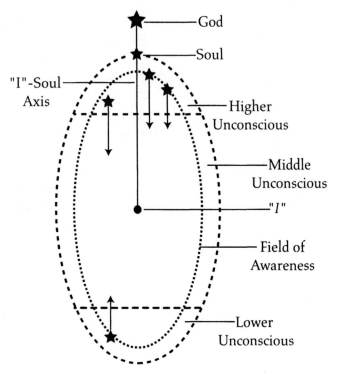

God

Soul

"I"-Soul
Axis

Higher
Unconscious

Middle
Unconscious

"I"

Field of
Awareness

Lower
Unconscious

Figure 5. The Pleased Nafs

The Nafs Pleasing to God

Ibn Arabi points out that this is the level of inner marriage of self and spirit. In Arabic, the self is feminine and the spirit is masculine. He writes that this inner marriage produces a child, which is located in the heart. The spirit inspires the self to uplift itself and then the heart follows. The inner struggles and sense of multiplicity are gone. We are no longer split between our material desires and our desire for God. At this stage, we achieve genuine inner unity and wholeness; we experience the world as whole and unified. We are real human beings.

One sheikh illustrated this state of inner unity as follows, "I choose whichever states God chooses for me and keeps me in. If God keeps me rich, I will not be forgetful, and if God wishes me to be poor, I will not be greedy and rebellious."

SupeR

NO FEAR.
NO ASKING
NO TALK

At this stage we realize that all power to act comes from God, that we can do nothing by ourselves. We no longer fear anything or ask for anything. We have no desire to talk or to communicate. Our exteriors have been destroyed but our interiors have become palaces. Our hearts are in ecstasy.

The district of the nafs pleasing to God. The traveler goes deeper within.

> Right away I went to the district of annihilation. I saw its population mute, speechless, as if dead, with no strength in them to utter a word. They had left the hope of any benefit from talk and were ready to give up their souls to the angel of death. They were totally unconcerned whether I was there or not. . . .
>
> Even in that place, among them, I felt great pain. Yet when I wished to describe the symptoms of my ill, I couldn't find a body nor any existence so as to say, "This is my body," or "This is I." Then I knew that that which was "I" turned into the owner of me. Then I knew that to say, "That being is mine," is a lie, and to lie is a sin for everyone. Then I knew that to ask the real owner for what was "mine" was the hidden polytheism of which I had wished to rid myself. What, then, was to be done? . . .
>
> In my despair, if I were to call upon Him and say, "O Lord," then there would be two—I and He, and the One from whom I seek help, the will and the Willed, the desire and the Desired, the lover and the Beloved, O so many. I knew not the remedy.
>
> The wailing attracted the pity of the angel of inspiration . . . [who] read to me from the book of divine inspiration: "First, annihilate your actions." He gave that to me as a gift. As I stretched my hand to receive it, I saw that there was no hand. It was a composition of water and earth and ether and fire. I had no hand to take with. I had no power to act. There is only One who has power, the All-Powerful. Whatever action occurs through me, it belongs

ALL POWER TO ACT COMES FROM GOD.
WE CAN DO NOTHING BY OURSELVES.

to the Absolute Actor. All power, all acts, I referred to Him, and I left all that happened to me and through me in this world. . . .

Then I wished . . . to leave my attributes—those qualities that make one's personality. When I looked, what I saw was not mine. When I talked, what I said was not mine. Neither was the content mine. Totally helpless, I was cut off from all the attributes, visible and invisible, that distinguished me, from all qualities exterior and interior that had made me "me."

With all my being and feeling and spirit I supposed myself a pure essence. Then I sensed even this was duality. . . . Then even my essence was taken away from me. Still I wished and longed for Him. I felt the meaning of "The one who longs for Me is My true servant." . . . God Who "encompasses all things," Who is "before the before and after the after and all that is evident and all that is hidden, and He is the knower of all things"—became manifest in the secret of my heart.

Even then I wished that the secret of "to die before dying," be actualized in me. O woe, again this hidden duality of I and the One I long for. This too cannot be the truth.

A diagram of the nafs pleasing to God. In the oval diagram, *nafs* and soul have merged, and there is no longer any dichotomy or duality in the psyche. As the individual becomes unified, the divine unity of the world is now apparent. As Rumi writes, the world appears to be a multiplicity, just as a shattered mirror reflects many different reflections of the same image. If we heal the breaks in the mirror and it becomes unbroken once again, it will then reflect only a single image.

MULTIPLICITY → BROKEN MIRROR IMAGE

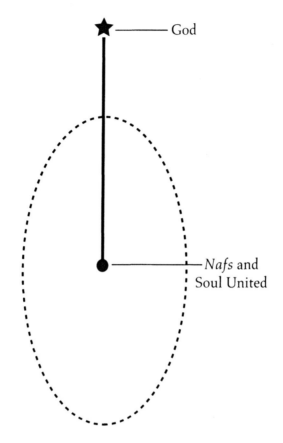

Figure 6. The Nafs Pleasing to God

The Pure Nafs

Those few who have attained this level have transcended the self entirely. There is no ego or self left, only union with God. This is the state called "to die before dying." Rumi describes God as the one who dissolves our separateness into unity:

Dissolver of sugar, dissolve me,
if this is the time.
Do it gently with a touch of hand, or a look.
Every morning I wait at dawn. That's when it's happened
before.

Or do it suddenly like an execution. How else
can I get ready for death?

You breathe without a body like a spark.
You grieve, and I begin to feel lighter.
You keep me away with your arm,
but the keeping away is pulling me in.[27]

As long as a trace of ego is left, you cannot reach this level. You
have to take out the "me" from yourself; then what is left is God. One
sheikh has eloquently described the kind of superhuman effort that is
needed to transform oneself. His path was that of love and devotion to his
sheikh. In a letter to a disciple he wrote:

> You have not tasted yet of the joy of union nor suffered the
> pain of separation from him [your sheikh]; neither have
> you experienced the awesome majesty and grandeur of his
> presence. You have not wished to die every day, a thousand
> times. . . . You have not sunk the razor-sharp tooth of the
> shark of voluntary failure into your heart! You have not
> dug up an entire mountain with your fingernails![28]

The most profound love is, in itself, transformative. One master
writes, "You may try one hundred things, but love alone will release you
from yourself." In the words of another teacher:

> My friend, the moth's nourishment is provided by his love
> for the flame, for without fire the moth is distraught. The
> moth does not obtain life through fire until fire so com-
> pletely transfigures him that he beholds the entire world to
> be fire. When the moth hurls itself into the fire, it is total-
> ly consumed, becoming itself all fire. Of self what aware-
> ness could it possess?[29]

Those at this level are in constant prayer, therefore they have no
will left. It is as if you were ushered into the presence of an infinitely
wise and infinitely powerful ruler. The best choice is to submit yourself
fully to that ruler and to dedicate yourself completely to serving that
ruler. In the presence of such wisdom and power, there is no place left for

your will. Rumi illuminates this state for us:

> If you could get rid
> Of yourself just once,
> The secret of secrets
> Would open to you.
> The face of the unknown,
> Hidden beyond the universe
> Would appear on the
> Mirror of your perception.[30]

A diagram of the pure nafs. In the final diagram of the self, there is no longer any sense of a separate self or separate identity. There are no clear boundaries between self and God; the self has become like salt dissolved in the ocean. There is only the divine.

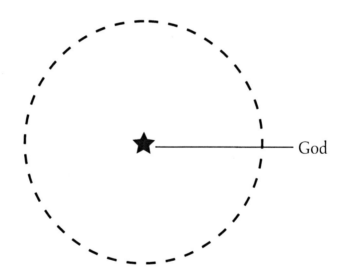

Figure 7. The Pure Nafs

The attainment of the state of the pure nafs. This stage is described by the Naqshbandi sheikh, the traveler on the path of truth, a clear example of one who transformed himself. As he is one of those few who knows this subject from the inside out, let us give him the last word.

What ill is that that gives pangs of pain when I move, when I wish, when I long, when I ask for help, when I pray and beg? What strange state have I fallen into, difficult to resolve? Helpless, I gave all these to their Owner and waited at the gate of acquiescence in agony of death, senseless, without thought or feeling, as if dead, expecting death to take me at every breath.

Following the advice "Ask your heart," I told my heart to instruct me. It said, "As long as there is a trace of you in you, you cannot hear your Lord's call, 'Come to Me.'" I felt the truth of it and wished that that trace of me in me would die. I immersed that trace in divine beatitude. An ecstasy came, from me, to me, over that which was mine, covering it all, the taste of which is impossible to describe. Without ear, without words, without letters I heard the invitation: "Come. Return to Me."

I tried to think, "What is this state?" My thought could not think it. I was made to know that thought cannot think about the sacred secret. Even that knowledge was taken away from me as fast as it came to me.

O seeker, what has been said here is not intended to show that I know. Therefore it will be made known to you only after I am gone from among you. It is for the benefit of the seekers of truth, for the lovers who long for the Beloved, so that it may help them to know themselves, so that they may find in which of the cities I traveled through they themselves are, and which of its citizens they befriend. When and if in sincerity they know their place, they will act accordingly, and know the direction of the gate of Allah's pleasure, and be thankful.

Exercises for Self-Transformation

Taming your inner gremlin. According to Sufi psychology, we are embodied spirit, and our essential nature is love, wisdom, and joy. Yet all too often we feel confused, depressed, and upset, which is nothing like our essential spiritual nature.

For practical purposes, let me oversimplify somewhat the relation of the negative ego and spirit. The negative ego is dedicated to keeping us confused and unhappy and is the enemy of our spiritual nature. For this exercise we are going to personify our negative ego and call it our inner gremlin. The dictionary defines a gremlin as an imaginary small creature who interferes with the smooth running of plans or machinery.

Your inner gremlin is the narrator in your head. It has influenced you all your life and remains with you wherever you go. Your gremlin wants you to believe it is your friend and protector and that it has your best interests at heart. It tells you who you are, *how* you are, and it interprets experience for you. However, it wants to destroy whatever happiness and meaningful relationships you have developed. Some of your gremlin's best tools are reliving the past, worrying about the future, and interpreting your experience in the worst possible light.

One of its main weapons is false imagination. It tries to get you to believe that its *interpretations* of your life are reality. Your gremlin may put you down as a failure and try to get you to believe it and act accordingly. Or it may give you an unrealistic, inflated sense of yourself, which sets you up for failure and makes you impossible to live with. Your gremlin preys on the inner fears and the hidden sense of insecurity and inadequacy that all of us experience.

Let me give you a few examples of successful gremlins and their strategies:

THE GENERAL. Jack is a thirty-two-year-old successful attorney. His gremlin is a short, stout military man, who insists that Jack live his life in obedience to a complex set of rules and regulations. Jack is convinced that without his gremlin, he would be an overweight failure and a mama's boy. As a result, Jack has developed big biceps, a black belt in karate, an ulcer and the inability to get an erection.

THE REVEREND. Katherine's gremlin looks like her grandfather with the addition of a clerical collar. He constantly preaches to her from the New Testament and likes to appear when she is making love. Thanks to her gremlin, Katherine has become good and righteous—also isolated, lonely, and incapable of orgasm.

THE COACH. Dale is a handsome, hardworking salesman. He is wealthy at twenty-seven because he has worked so hard. His gremlin resembles a feisty little coach who can never sit still. The gremlin has convinced Dale that life is a race that he has to win, and Dale has been running for as long as he can remember. He is addicted to alcohol and cigarettes and finds it impossible to relax and enjoy life.

The best way to tame your gremlin is to become aware of it. The more you become conscious of your gremlin's tactics of manipulation, the less power your gremlin will have. Can you describe your gremlin? Does it have a particular form, a favorite gesture or phrase? Close your eyes and visualize your gremlin in as much detail as you can. If your gremlin changes form or has more than one favorite guise, be sure to notice. Gremlins are notoriously tricky. Once you have gotten a basic sense of your gremlin, answer the following:

1. Describe your gremlin *in detail* and how it operates in your life. When does it appear? Are there any triggers that bring it out? Has your gremlin always been this way? Can you remember when it first appeared? What are your best guesses about the birth of your gremlin?

2. If you were to personify your gremlin, what does it look like? What would its name or nickname be? How would it dress? What would its favorite expressions and gestures be? If you like to draw, try sketching a portrait or cartoon of your gremlin. (The better you get to know it, the less power it has over you.)

3. Dialog with your gremlin. Discuss its good qualities, how it has helped you in the past, and how it has kept you from changing and growing.

4. Give your gremlin a task. What is *one* area of your life that might benefit from the attention of your gremlin? If you can keep it positively occupied, it will tend to stay with the task and bother you less in other areas of your life.

5.   Can you personify your spiritual self? Close your eyes and visu-
      alize an inner character that is the opposite of your gremlin. This
      character can be a powerful ally. To come in closer touch with this
      inner character, carry out steps 1, 2, and 3 above.

This exercise is adapted from a wonderful small book entitled
Taming Your Gremlin: A Guide to Enjoying Yourself, by Richard
Carson.[31] If you have found this exercise useful, I strongly advise you to
get the book, which provides much more detailed material on gremlins,
how they operate, and how to tame them.

UNVEILING THE TYRANNICAL NAFS. Think of a time that you
were in the grip of your tyrannical *nafs*. You may have been overcome
by anger, pride, or a hurt ego, or you were out of touch with your heart
and lost your sense of empathy and compassion. You may have said and
done things that you deeply regret.

1.   What caused you to descend to the state of the tyrannical *nafs*?

2.   How did it feel to be in this state? How did you interact with oth-
      ers? What were your main motivations? Did you feel cut off from
      your heart?

3.   How did you get out of this state? Was there an event or experi-
      ence that triggered it?

A TYRANNICAL NAFS JOURNAL. It is difficult to realize the power
and extent of the tyrannical *nafs*, because it often operates unconsciously. For one week record in your journal every time you feel the influence
of your tyrannical self. This may include instances of pride, anger, envy,
greed—occasions when you said or did something that was less than kind
or compassionate. Try and record these incidents in as much detail as possible. Observe your tyrannical self without judgment, like an impartial
observer or fair witness. (Judging and self-criticism are often tricks of the
tyrannical *nafs* and work effectively to distract us from the work of inner
change.)

EXPERIENCING THE INSPIRED NAFS. Remember a time when you
were in the state of the inspired *nafs*, in touch with your intuition and
powerful intuitive knowing as opposed to a more intellectual, less
assured kind of knowing.

1. Was there a particular experience or event that triggered this state?

2. Describe the quality of knowing and thinking you experienced. What were some of the insights that came to you? Which inspirations or insights turned out to be accurate? Were there any that were not? If so, why?

AN EXAMPLE OF THE SERENE NAFS. Do you know someone who seems to be an example of the serene *nafs*—someone who is so grounded in the love of God that the world has lost its power to disturb their equilibrium?

1. What are the most noticeable characteristics of this person?

2. Have you ever tasted this state yourself? What was it like?

EXERCISING REPENTANCE. True repentance is not merely regretting our mistakes. It is turning away from them completely. As mentioned earlier in this chapter, repentance has three parts: the past, the present, and the future.

Repentance of the past consists of reviewing our past actions. We try to see our mistakes clearly, without rationalization or self-justification. To know as clearly as possible what we have done wrong is repentance of the past.

Repentance of the present is to correct our mistakes as much as we possibly can. If we have been dishonest about money, we repay whatever we owe. If we have hurt or offended others, we apologize and admit fault.

Repentance of the future is to vow to do our very best to never repeat that mistake. If we have honestly and carefully reviewed a certain habit or mistake, it will ideally become far less attractive to us. It is said that the sign that God has accepted our attempts at repentance is that what was once so irresistible becomes unappealing or even unattractive.

For each habit or action that you repent, do the following:

1. Carefully review past instances of this behavior. Write them down as an impartial observer, without justification or blame.

2. Repent the results of your actions as much as possible. Return whatever you owe to others. Apologize for whatever you have

done to hurt others. Apologizing is not easy for most of us. If you can't apologize in person, apologize over the telephone or in a letter. If you are not sure you *can* apologize, write the letter anyhow. Later, you can always decide whether to send it or not. The act of apology is more for your own good than for others.

3. Sincerely promise yourself that you will do everything you can to avoid repeating this mistake in the future. In addition, make changes in your life to ensure that you don't keep making the same mistake. For instance, if you want to stop drinking, you might stop spending time in bars (thinking you'll order only soft drinks). Instead, begin spending time in coffee shops and remove any alcohol from your home.

Chapter Four

‹‹○››

Your Seven Souls

I died from the mineral kingdom and became a plant;
I died to vegetable nature and became an animal.
I died to animality and became a human being.
Next time I will die to human nature and lift up my head
among the angels.
Once again I will leave angelic nature and become that
which you cannot imagine.

—RUMI[1]

One day, the sultan was passing through his capital city. *Everyone bowed down to him except for an old dervish, who continued to sit and carry out his devotions to God on his prayer beads. The sultan stopped and summoned the dervish to him.*

"Why didn't you bow to me when everyone else was bowing?" asked the sultan.

The dervish replied, "Everyone else is afraid of your power and wants your wealth, so it was right for them to bow to you. I am afraid only of God, and I want only whatever God chooses to provide for me, so it was not right for me to bow."

The sultan was annoyed, but the dervish went on. "Besides, a free man should never bow to a slave." The sultan became red in the face, then white with rage. His soldiers began reaching for their scimitars.

Calmly, the dervish continued, "You see, you are still a slave to your anger and your pride, while I have freed myself

from the domination of my ego and my animal nature."
The chastened sultan waved his soldiers away. "Leave him alone. He is a man of God and far beyond my authority."

According to Sufi tradition, we have seven souls, or seven facets of the complete soul. Each represents a different stage of evolution. There are the mineral, vegetable, animal, personal, human, and secret souls, and the secret of secrets.

The Sufi model of the souls is one of balance. According to this model, spiritual growth is not a matter of developing the higher souls and ignoring or even weakening the lower ones. Each soul has valuable gifts, and in Sufism, real spiritual growth means balanced development of the whole individual, including body, mind and spirit.

There are many systems and disciplines that focus on the body—sports, martial arts, healing techniques, and a variety of other physical disciplines. Modern education focuses almost completely on the mind. Many spiritual disciplines stress spiritual principles and practices, yet they ignore mind and body. In Sufism, all of life is part of spiritual practice. Family, work, and relationships provide as much opportunity for spiritual development as prayer or contemplation.

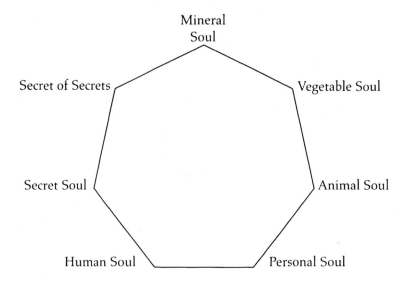

The Arabic term for soul, *ruh*, also means "spirit" and "breath." The Koran reads, "I have fashioned him (Adam) and breathed into him of My spirit (*ruh*)." (15:29) The highest level of the soul, the secret of secrets, is a spark of God's spirit.

Each facet of the soul has its own dynamics, its own needs and strengths. At different times, different souls may be dominant. Knowing which soul is most active is important information for a Sufi teacher. For example, a dream that comes from one soul will be interpreted very differently than a dream from another soul.

When the naturally healthy dynamics of the soul shift to one extreme or another, what is healthy can become toxic. For example, curare is a wonderful heart medicine, but it can also be used as a deadly poison.

If we are concerned about some of our souls and ignore others, we are inevitably thrown out of balance. For example, if we ignore our vegetable and animal souls, we lose touch with the fundamental needs of our bodies and put our health at risk. (A classic example is the stereotypical computer programmer who is so involved with her demanding intellectual tasks that she eats junk food and suffers from chronic lack of sleep and exercise.) If we neglect our secret soul and the secret of secrets and disregard our spiritual needs, our spiritual health suffers. Many people lead lives that are rich in material success and worldly activity, yet they are spiritually malnourished. Ideally, balance of all seven souls brings about balanced health and growth and a rich, full life.

The Mineral Soul

The mineral soul, the *ruh madeni*, is located in the skeletal system. In the diagram of the seven aspects of the soul, the mineral soul is adjacent to the secret of secrets, which is the place of the pure divine spark within each of us. The mineral world is close to God; it never revolts against divine will. Wherever a rock is placed, there it will stay eternally unless some outside force moves it.

Just as our physical skeleton remains hidden inside the body, there is a hidden, inner structure in our bodies that is mainly mineral—our skeletal system. The mineral soul is also hidden. If someone asked for a description of your mineral soul, you probably would not know how to begin. Yet what is difficult to know, what we frequently take for granted, often is of great value.

Most of us pay no attention to our skeletal structure unless we break a bone—then we suddenly become all too aware of it. Most people sit badly and move in a poorly balanced way. For instance, whenever I tell an audience to sit in a comfortable, relaxed position, almost everyone in the room adjusts their posture. In other words, most members of the audience were not sitting comfortably until I brought it to their attention. Our skeletal structure, especially the spine, is designed to support us in a gravitational field with a minimum amount of muscular tension. Whenever we sit or move in an unbalanced, unconscious way, we create unnecessary tension and discomfort.

Likewise, whenever we act in disregard of our deep psychological and spiritual structures, we also cause unnecessary tension and discomfort. Our deep mineral structure includes the sense of our own existence. It is the basic matter on which our material existence rests and is connected at the atomic and subatomic levels with all other matter in the universe. The subatomic particles that make up our bodies were once part of the stars. Who knows what they will become at some future date?

The skeleton itself is an amazing structure, enabling us to engage in an extraordinary variety of movement and activity. The spine, for example, combines flexibility and stability in a remarkable way. Think of the range of human movement. There is the profound stillness of the mystic wrapped in prayer or contemplation, motionless for hours. Contrast that with the amazing balance and flexibility of a gymnast, the speed of a sprinter, the dexterity and rapid, accurate finger movements of a gifted pianist or violinist.

Imbalance in the mineral soul can manifest as either extreme flexibility or extreme rigidity. We say that people "have no backbone," or are "spineless" if they are too easily swayed by influences around them. They find it hard to stick with anything or to hold a position—physically, mentally, or emotionally. One example of a lack of solid structure is the jellyfish. The boneless jellyfish is a highly successful life form that has survived and flourished for countless millennia. However, it is completely at the mercy of the tides. We would be violating our basic physical structure, which gives us the capacity for independent movement, if we behaved like the jellyfish.

The other extreme is someone who is "fossilized," calcified or unbending, rigid and unyielding, incapable of responding flexibly and appropriately to changes in the environment. Some people are "stiff-necked," too proud to bow their heads, while others are "thick skulled," or unable to take in new information.

One definition of neurosis is to continue doing the same thing even though it does not work. Some people are so rigid that they cannot change to save their own lives. Some people know they are going to die of smoking but they can't stop. In one old factory, health authorities told employees that the noise level was so high that they were gradually losing their hearing. Many of the workers stayed with their jobs and became more and more deaf, because they were unable to change. We all have some degree of inflexibility and rigidity.

> *Bahlul was considered a "wise fool" throughout Baghdad. One day he sat in the marketplace with three skulls in front of him. In front of the first skull was a sign that read, "Free." In front of the second skull was a sign that read "One Cent." The third had a sign reading "Priceless." All three skulls looked identical, and everyone who saw his booth was convinced that Bahlul was crazy.*
>
> *Finally, a man approached him and asked about the difference in prices. Bahlul took a skewer and tried to put it through the ear hole of the first skull, but it would not go through. "See," he said, "nothing goes in. This skull isn't worth anything." He then tried the skewer on the second skull. It passed easily through both ear holes and slipped out on the other side. "You see, nothing stays in. This skull is worth only a penny." When Bahlul tried the third skull, the skewer passed easily through the first hole but not through the second. He said, "This skull is priceless. Whatever goes in, stays in."*

We want to be flexible enough to adapt and assimilate new knowledge, and also solid enough to retain it. It is our deep psychic structure that enables us to do that. Unfortunately, most of us tend to ignore new ideas that contradict our beliefs. We also learn a great deal and then fail to retain it. Think of all the information we learned in order to pass high school or college courses. We generally remember less than ten per cent. Wouldn't it be invaluable to have the kind of mind that easily takes in new ideas and information and also retains them accurately, like Bahlul's priceless skull?

It is the mark of a great mind to be willing to challenge one's old beliefs by taking in new and contradictory information. Charles Darwin became a great scientist, whose theories challenged all the scientific and philosophical theories of his day. He was able to accomplish that because he was always willing to challenge his own ideas and theories. He wrote in his diary:

> I had, during years, followed a golden rule; mainly, wherever I came across a published fact, a new observation or idea which [sic] ran counter to my general results, I made a memorandum of it without fail and at once. For I had found by experience that such facts and ideas were far more apt to slip the memory than favorable ones.

When change is profound, we say it goes "bone deep." When we feel something profoundly, we feel it "in our bones." The mineral soul seems to be the least conscious aspect of the soul, yet paradoxically it is a place in which fundamental change can occur. The mineral soul is less distracted than the other souls by increasingly complex interactions with the world.

In the deep stillness of seated meditation or contemplation, we leave the awareness of our bodies and the material world as we enter into greater awareness of the divine. Without an articulated spine and supportive skeletal system, we could not remain upright. The skeletal system is a critical, but generally unrecognized, component in the prayers and meditative practices of all religions.

A relatively unchanging structure dictates the behavior of minerals; it encodes the conditions under which it was created, and its subsequent behavior continually reflects this stasis. This is the strength and the weakness of the mineral soul.

If change does occur, it is a result not of internal processes, but of outside forces such as pressure and heat. For example, a piece of coal can become a sparkling diamond, and opaque sand can be melted into clear glass. Similarly, the personality can become transformed from an impenetrable curtain that veils spirit into a transparent structure that reveals the divine. As we examine the other souls, we will find increasingly greater flexibility and capacity for change.

Soul	Location	Body System	Excess	Positive Features
Mineral	spine	skeletal system	overly rigid	inner support
Vegetable	liver	digestive system	laziness, overactivity, lack of nutrition	health, healing, nourish-ment
Animal	heart	circulatory system	anger, greed, addiction to pleasure	motivation
Personal	brain	nervous system	egotism, weak ego	intelligence, healthy ego
Human	spiritual heart		sentimentality	compassion, creativity
Secret	spiritual heart (inner heart)		world rejection	nonattach-ment, wisdom
Secret of Secrets	spiritual heart (innermost heart)		none	union with God

The Vegetable Soul

The vegetable soul, the *ruh nabati*, is located in the liver and is related to the digestive system. It regulates growth and the assimilation of nutrients, functions we share with plants. This is a new function, evolutionarily speaking, as the mineral world has no need of nourishment. In other words, there is a soul in us that is like the soul that God also gave to plants.

When we were in the womb, we functioned mainly from the vegetable soul. We were rooted to our mother's uterus by the umbilical cord through which we took in nourishment. We developed and grew larger, and that was just about all that we did. Our functioning was essentially the same as that of plants.

There is tremendous intelligence within the vegetable soul. We generally overlook this intelligence because we place so much value on the abstract learning of the head. But no matter how many college degrees we might earn, we still don't know how to digest a peach or a piece of bread. We don't know how to make hair grow on our heads. These kinds of basic physical functions are all carried out through the age-old wisdom of the vegetable soul.

The mineral soul is the place of transmitting energy (as in light passing through a crystal), while the vegetable soul is the place where transmutation begins. Plants transmute the energy of light to create food. The vegetable soul is also the first instance of nourishment and assimilation of food, and physical nourishment is a model of other kinds of nourishment, of the physical senses, for instance. There is a type of fish that lives in deep, lightless caves. Because their eyes receive no stimulation in the dark, they have lost even the capacity for sight. Overstimulation also damages the senses, as loud noise can permanently impair hearing.

Similarly, we can ask ourselves the following questions: How do we nourish our hearts? Our intellects? Our souls? We can learn a great deal from studying the process of physical nourishment. When Sheikh Tosun was about to open the first Jerrahi Sufi Center in the United States, Sheikh Muzaffer said, "First open a kitchen. A Sufi Center is really a kitchen. If you can feed people's bodies, then perhaps you become able to feed them spiritually as well."

If we have a diet deficient in vitamins or minerals, we slowly become debilitated, perhaps ill. We don't notice the deficiency immediately, but the effects add up. The same is true if we are malnourished emotionally, intellectually, or spiritually.

If we fast, the desire for food diminishes after a day or two, and our stomachs shrink. If we eat spoiled food, our appetite may suffer. We may never want that particular kind of food ever again. Unfortunately, too many people have had their appetites for spiritual nourishment ruined by what passes for soul food in many so-called religious institutions today.

The intelligence of the vegetable soul is based on millions of years of evolution. It is the intelligence that regulates all the basic operations of the body that occur outside normal conscious awareness. The vegetable soul knows how to cause and also how to cure cancer, heart disease, and all the other physical conditions beyond the control or understanding of the conscious mind.

Aspects of this intelligence can be found within our deepest brain structure, known as the first brain. It includes the brain stem, the reticular activating system, the basal ganglia surrounding the brain stem, and the spinal cord. It processes information from the outside environment through sensory and cellular feedback and interacts with the environment through impulses to and from muscles and skin. The first brain provides our most basic intelligence and deals with functions such as expansion and contraction and response to danger.[2]

One drawback in the world of plants is that their ability to respond to the environment is limited. Plants have little mobility or flexibility in their response patterns. Plants do not learn. With the evolution of the animal soul, we develop mobility, motivation, and the capacity for learning.

The Animal Soul

The animal soul, the *ruh haywani*, is located in the heart and is connected to the circulatory system. Animals have developed a four-chambered heart and a complex circulatory system that distributes blood throughout the organism. (In reptiles, the circulatory system is not yet fully developed, and the reptile heart has only three chambers. As a result, their capacity for movement is inhibited, and reptiles require warm weather to be fully active. The more developed mammalian circulatory system holds heat better, and this allows mammals to be more active in all climates.)

The animal soul includes our fears, angers, and passions. All organisms tend to move toward whatever is rewarding (passions) and to move away from (fears) or push away (angers) whatever is punishing, toxic or painful. For years behavioral psychology has concentrated on these fundamental responses to the world in studying the effects of reward and punishment.

As psychology has gotten more complex, we tend to forget the power and universality of the two basic instincts of attraction and repulsion. Even an amoeba will move away from a drop of acid placed on a microscope slide or move toward a drop of nutrient solution. If a single-celled organism has these responses, I would argue that every cell in our bodies has the same capacity.

These instincts are basic to self-preservation and species preservation, which first appear with the animal soul. In plants, the instincts to reproduce and survive are severely limited. They are built into the structure of the plants and are relatively rigid and unchanging.

The behavior of animals is far more flexible and responsive to the environment. The instinct for self-preservation moves us to avoid what is painful or dangerous. Plants may put forth seeds and orient to the sun, but there is no passion in the plant kingdom. Within the animal soul, passion is rooted in the reproductive instincts. In addition to sexual desire, it is the matrix of love and nurturing.

The Judeo-Christian tradition has devalued the body and the functions of the animal soul. Traditionally, it is considered unfortunate (if not outright sinful) to have a body, and it is even worse that this body of ours contains so many drives and instincts, fears, and passions. The drives of the body are considered antithetical to the development of the soul.

In the Sufi model of the seven souls, all souls have to be healthy for the individual to develop as a whole human being. We all have passions, fears, and appetites, and these are useful, functional parts of us. However, they should not dominate our lives. The animal soul needs to be in balance with the other souls, not in charge. When that balance is attained, a well-developed animal soul is an invaluable asset to our health and well-being.

When our passions or angers are overdeveloped, they distort our perceptions and behavior. Najmadeen Razi, a noted Sufi teacher, describes the need for emotional balance:

> If the passions exceed the limits of moderation, then mischief, greed, expectation, meanness, baseness, lust, avarice, and treachery will appear. . . . If the characteristic of the

passions is recessive and deficient in an individual's nature, then flaccidity, impotence, and abjectness result.

If the characteristic of anger exceeds the limits of moderation, then bad disposition, arrogance, rancor, irascibility, quick-temperedness, intolerance, tyranny, instability, falsity, conceit, vanity, willfulness, and selfishness arise. If one cannot expel one's anger, resentment takes root in one's inner being. If the characteristic of anger is deficient and recessive within an individual, then self-contempt, flaccidity, indifference, infirmity, depravity, and incapacity result. . . .

The virtue of the . . . alchemy of religion is that these attributes are confined within the limits of moderation, each being utilized in its appropriate domain. Religion works in such a way as to dominate these characteristics, restraining the *nafs* [lower self] from going its own way, reining it in like a horse, rather than allowing these characteristics to dominate the individual and carry him along like a captive, like a wild horse that bucks and throws itself and its rider uncontrollably into a pit, or against a wall, both becoming destroyed in the process.[3]

The animal soul has the capacity to unleash tremendous strength and vitality within us. For example, a young man was working underneath his car when the jack slipped, and he cried out for help. His mother rushed into the garage and lifted up the car so he could crawl out. When she tried to lift the car again for news reporters, she couldn't even budge it. Through her animal soul, she gained access to power she never dreamed she had.

Elizabeth Kübler-Ross, a psychiatrist who pioneered work with the dying, used to tell the story of a woman who was admitted to the hospital with advanced cancer. Nobody thought she would leave intensive care alive. However, her husband was mentally unstable and prone to bouts of homicidal rage. She knew that the life of her fourteen-year-old son would be at risk if he had to live alone with his father. The woman slowly recovered and was discharged from the hospital. For the next four years she was in and out of the hospital, but for the sake of her son, she refused to die. Finally she came back to intensive care. Dr. Kübler-Ross said to her, "You know, your son is eighteen now." The woman smiled as if to say, "I know. Now he can legally be on his own. He is finally safe." She passed away that night.

The animal soul is a great source of our motivation, strength, and power to act, and it includes the potential to do extraordinary things.

The Personal Soul

The next facet of the total soul is the *ruh nafsani*. The personal soul is located in the brain and is related to the nervous system. Just as the development of the heart and circulatory system distinguishes the animal from the plant kingdom, the development of a complex nervous system distinguishes humans from animals. This highly developed nervous system brings the capacity for greater memory and for complex thinking and planning. The intelligence of the personal soul allows us to understand our environment far more deeply than the capacities of the mineral, vegetable, and animal souls.

It also allows us to respond more effectively to the world around us. We can plan ahead and create mental models of the possible effects of our actions. For example, in one classic psychology experiment, dogs were shown a bowl of food on the opposite side of a chain-link fence. If the fence was short, the dogs quickly and easily went around it to get to the food. As the fence got longer, the dogs had to go farther and farther away from their goal to get around the fence. When the fence section became fairly wide, the dogs remained rooted to the spot directly opposite the food and tried to dig under the fence.

However, this particular problem poses no difficulty for humans, including relatively young children. Because of their inability to form complex mental models, animals tend to seek immediate gratification and to be dominated by short-term motivations. The development of human intelligence has allowed us to plan far ahead and to function much more effectively in the world. As a result, humanity has become more and more powerful, dominating all other species.

The personal soul is also the location of the ego. We have both a positive and a negative ego. The positive ego organizes our intelligence and provides our sense of self. It can be a force for self-respect, responsibility and integrity. On the other hand, the negative ego is a force for egotism, arrogance, and a sense of separation from others and God. The positive ego is a great ally on the spiritual path. It can provide a sense of inner stability during the ups and downs that inevitably occur on the spiritual path. The negative ego is an enemy. It distorts our perceptions and colors our relations to the world.

One of the major distinctions between the negative and positive egos is that the positive ego is our servant and the negative ego constantly tries to be our master. Like the story of the dervish and the donkey (chapter 3), the ego is meant to work for us, but all too often we seem to be carrying the ego on our backs and serving it.

The personal soul is located in the neocortex, the largest of our three brain systems. The neocortex is fully developed only in humans. It is composed of ten to one hundred billion neurons, capable of quadrillions of connections. One of its functions is to enable us to reflect on our thoughts, feelings, and behavior. We can develop the vast potential of the neocortex by increasing the connections between cells through practicing awareness and heedfulness in our daily lives.

Many human beings are intelligent but have little or no compassion. Mass murderers and sadists are human, but there is something critical lacking in them. They have no heart. At a less extreme level, many people have overdeveloped negative egos and underdeveloped hearts. The humanity of such people becomes stunted when the personal soul dominates and overshadows the functioning of the human soul.

Ties to the world. Animals and plants are very much *of* this world, and often they are tied to a particular place in it. For example, if we take a palm tree from Arabia and plant it in Alaska, it will die. If we take a fir tree from Alaska and plant it in Arabia, it will not survive either. At this level of existence, there is relatively little flexibility or adaptability. The same is true for animals. If we put a polar bear in Arabia, it is not going to survive (at least, not without an air-conditioned environment). Likewise, an Arabian stallion will not last at the north pole. We could, however, take a group of Eskimos to Arabia. The first thing they would do is take off their fur coats. They would sweat and suffer from the heat, but they would eventually adapt to the new climate.

Our culture is a fur coat that allows us to live in a certain part of the world. We may get very attached to our fur coats. Sometimes we keep them on when it's much too hot, which shows that we are not quite as intelligent as we think we are. However, we can change them and adopt a different lifestyle that allows us to survive somewhere else.

The Human Soul

The *ruh insani* is located in the *qalb*, the spiritual heart.[4] The human soul is more refined than the personal soul. It is the place of compassion, faith, creativity. In one sense, the human soul includes the secret soul and the secret of secrets. It is the place of our spiritual values and experiences.

Creativity and compassion first occur at this soul level. The brain, which develops in the personal soul, is like a computer, involved mainly with storage and manipulation of data, but not with the creation of new information. Creativity happens in the heart. It is unfortunate that our educational system has become so focused on the development of intellect that little attention is given to the development of the heart, which is nourished by the arts and by worship, love, and service to others.

The heart intelligence of the human soul and the abstract intelligence of the personal soul complement each other. Thinking is concerned with impersonal, logical analysis. The heart adds compassion and faith. Combining the two leads to better judgment. The head knows what is most effective, while the heart knows what is right.

Intuitive intelligence functions without the conscious use of reason. This form of intelligence is nourished by faith in God or in the existence of a larger reality; awareness of the external world and inner awareness developed through self-observation, contemplation or meditation; and compassion and a resulting sense of attunement with nature, animals and other people.

The Secret Soul

The *ruh sirr* is the part of us that remembers God. The secret soul, or inner consciousness, is located in the inner heart. This soul is the one that knows where it came from and where it is going. One Sufi teacher writes, "The inner consciousness is that which God keeps hidden, keeping watch over it Himself."[5] Another comments, "The body is completely dark, and its lamp is the inner consciousness. If one has no inner consciousness, one is forever in darkness."[6]

Before our souls incarnated, God said to them, "Am I your Lord?" and the souls said, "Indeed, truly" (see pp. 10-11). The soul that responded was the secret soul. The secret soul knew who it was then, and it still knows. For millennia, the secret souls lived in close proximity to God, bathed in the light of God's presence. Only on incarnation into this material universe did we lose this sense of connection.

> The inner consciousness [secret soul] is . . . specially bestowed on a given entity at the time of experiencing God's creative Divine Unity. . . . Hence, it has been said that only God knows, loves, and seeks God, for it is the inner consciousness that seeks, loves and knows Him. As the Prophet states, "I have known my Lord through my Lord."[7]

The Secret of Secrets

The *sirr-ul-asrar* includes that which is absolutely transcendent, beyond time and space. This is the original soul (*ruh*) that God breathed into Adam, that is, into humankind. It is at our core, the soul of the soul. It is the pure divine spark within us. For this reason, our image of what it is to be human needs to expand. We are not merely thinking animals, nor are we only our personalities. We are the divine encased in and intermeshed with the body and the personality. Our capacity for spiritual growth and understanding are virtually limitless.

The Sufi master Abdul-Qadir al-Jilani explains the relationship between the human soul, the secret soul, and the secret of secrets:

> God Most High created the holy spirit as the most perfect creation in the first-created realm of the absolute going of His Essence, then He willed to send it to lower realms. . . to teach the holy spirit to seek . . . its previous closeness and intimacy with God . . . . On its way God sent it first to the realm of the Causal Mind. . . . As it passed through this realm it was given the clothing of divine light and was

named the sultan-soul (secret of secrets). As it passed through the realm of angels . . . it received the name "moving soul" (secret soul). When it finally descended to this world of matter it was dressed in the clothing of . . . coarse matter in order to save this world, because the material world, if it had direct contact with the holy spirit, would burn to ashes. In relation to this world, it came to be known as life, the human soul.

God made bodies for the souls to enter. . . . He placed the holy spirit within the centre of the heart, where he built a space of fine matter to keep that secret between God and His servant. These souls are in different parts of the body. . . .

The place of the "moving soul" (the secret soul) is within the life of the heart. The angelic realm is constantly within its view. . . . The speech of the "moving soul" is the speech of the inner world, without words, without sound. Its thoughts constantly concern the secrets of the hidden meanings. . . .

The place of the sultan-soul (the secret of secrets) . . . is the centre of the heart, the heart of the heart. The business of this soul is divine wisdom. Its work is to know all of divine knowledge, which is the medium of true devotion recited in the language of the heart.[8]

Sheikh Muzaffer used to say, "Within you is that which completely transcends the entire universe." Each of us has within our hearts that spark of God that cannot be confined within us, or contained within this world or the thousands of universes that make up the whole of physical creation. That is also us. We all need to remember who we really are.

Once I asked my Master,
"What is the difference
Between you and me?"

And he replied,
"Hafiz, only this:

If a herd of wild buffalo
Broke into our house
And knocked over
Our empty begging bowls,
Not a drop would spill from yours.

But there is Something Invisible
That God has placed in mine.

If That spilled from my bowl,
It could drown the whole world."[9]

In one of the most famous Prophetic sayings, God states, "I cannot be contained in heaven and earth, but I can be found within the heart of the believer." The Sufi practice of remembrance is designed to lead us to rediscover the transcendent secret of secrets in us. If we could remember that everyone we meet has a divine soul, we would treat everyone with the utmost respect and compassion; all our relationships would be transformed, and our lives would be fundamentally changed.

Imbalanced Functioning

As mentioned earlier, each of the first six souls has positive and negative characteristics. (Only the seventh soul, the secret of secrets, is beyond duality.) The negative characteristics occur when the soul is out of balance. God made nothing in this universe that is bad, ugly, or useless. It is only when something is misused or out of balance that it becomes negative.

Mineral soul. When the mineral soul is out of balance, one extreme is to be inflexible, stiff, unbending, unyielding. People with this tendency find it difficult to take in new information, and without learning there is no spiritual development. The spiritual path requires growth and also radical, transformational change. This is not possible for the inflexible.

At the opposite extreme, some people are soft, mushy, or too malleable; they lack firm, clear boundaries. For such people, the constant growth and change required by the spiritual path are too traumatic, and they are likely to find themselves overwhelmed and unable to cope.

Vegetable soul. Some human beings seem to function primarily at the level of the vegetable soul. When someone is in a profound coma, for example, they are said to be in a vegetative state. There is no movement, no retreat from pain or seeking pleasure. There is only the vegetative work of growing and taking in nutrients.

At times we may consciously choose to limit our functioning to that of the vegetable soul. If we become sick or exhausted, we need to rest and regain our strength. That is a natural, temporary solution to illness or overwork. The cycle of activity and rest is natural to us, and it is built into the biorhythms of the body.

Some people, however, seem to live lives ruled by their vegetable souls. They mostly sit or lie around all day. They have little or no passion, no motivation to do anything. We often use the colloquial term "couch potato" to refer to such people. Another highly appropriate colloquialism is to "veg out," meaning to lie around doing nothing. In the movie, *What Is the Matter with Gilbert Grape?*, the mother is a clear example of this imbalance. Extremely overweight, she lives on the living room couch eating junk food and watching TV. It takes a family emergency to get her out of the house for the first time in years.

The opposite extreme is hyperactivity. Some people cannot stay still. They cannot sit and study or work for an extended period of time; they have to jump up for coffee breaks or find other excuses to move around. When these hyperactive people become ill, healing is very difficult because they find it almost impossible to let their bodies rest.

Either extreme can be spiritually detrimental. The tendency toward underactivity can manifest as laziness, one of the great enemies of the spiritual seeker. Such people find it difficult to perform their daily spiritual and religious practices. Hyperactive persons find contemplation or meditation virtually impossible. They can't slow down enough to find God hidden within themselves.

One of the great tendencies of Western culture is that of overactivity. We are surrounded by a fast-paced society, and we have to make conscious efforts to slow down and to remain in the present.

Animal soul. People whose animal souls are out of balance are often described as acting "like animals." They mainly engage in seeking immediate pleasure and avoiding immediate pain. At the stage of the animal soul, motivation is based on instinctual gratification. There is no sense of morality or compassion, and people who are dominated by their angers, fears, or passions can be as dangerous as wild animals.

In the front lines of a battlefield, for example, it is a positive survival trait to be ready to respond to a threat with immediate, violent action. Many soldiers returning from active combat develop hair-trigger tempers. However, civilian life is not a battlefield. Those who act at home as if they were on the front lines may lose their jobs, get arrested for fighting, and abuse their spouses and children. The animal soul can be extremely dangerous if it operates without intelligence.

A hunter once met a bear who was suffering from a huge thorn stuck in its paw. The hunter took out the thorn and the bear was so grateful that it brought him honey and berries. The bear followed the hunter home and continued to bring food every day. Eventually, the man moved into the bear's cave and retired from hunting. The hunter's friends tried to convince him that it was not natural to live with a bear, but he wouldn't listen. He dismissed their concerns as jealousy over his new leisurely lifestyle.

One day as the man lay napping with the bear beside him, a fly began to buzz around the man's face. The bear kept swatting the fly away, but the fly kept coming back. Finally the bear became so angry at the little fly that was annoying his friend that he went outside and brought back a large rock. The moment the fly alighted on his friend's face, the bear smashed it with the rock. So, don't fully trust your animal soul. It can easily harm you, even when it means well.

Alcohol and drugs are forbidden in Sufism (and in many other spiritual traditions as well), because they anesthetize the personal and human souls. When this occurs, the animal soul is more likely to function in an unbalanced way. Much of the physical and sexual abuse in families occurs when the abuser is under the influence of alcohol or drugs, and many lives and families have been ruined by it.

Freud's description of the human being is primarily a description of the dynamics of the animal soul, in which the main motivation is to seek pleasure and to avoid pain. Most of behavioral psychology focuses on the functioning of the vegetable and animal souls. Cognitive psychology deals with the mental operations of the personal soul. Humanistic psychology examines the complex activities of the human soul, such as creativity and compassion. Transpersonal psychology embraces the ego-transcending consciousness of the secret soul and the secret of secrets. These last two fields are not yet widely accepted in academic psychology.

Personal soul. People dominated by an imbalanced personal soul are caught in the grip of their negative egos. The ego is the core of the personal soul. At one extreme are those with low self-esteem and no self-confidence. Such people accomplish little in life, and they are their own worst enemies. No one believes in them because they don't believe in themselves. Their strong conviction that they are bound to fail at whatever challenges they face becomes a self-fulfilling prophecy.

At the opposite extreme are those who are self-centered, arrogant, and overconfident. Such people are completely egocentric; they think that the whole world revolves around them. They have no empathy, compassion, or conscience. An extreme case is the intelligent psychopath, who feels no regret for the most horrible crimes. An excellent example is Hannibal Lecter of the novel and film, *The Silence of the Lambs*. Lecter is extremely intelligent, even brilliant, but he is utterly devoid of compassion and conscience. He is so self-centered and remorseless that he appears to be more monster than human.

In real life, the trial of Adolph Eichmann, mastermind of the Nazi death camps, revealed a man who thought of his job like any petty bureaucrat. He was concerned with clear record keeping and the efficiency of death camp operations. He had no thought for the millions of lives extinguished by his well-run bureaucracy.

Human soul. If the human soul is out of balance, a person may be misled by misplaced compassion, which is actually a kind of sentimentality. Sometimes, a gentle, soft response is not what someone else needs. At times people need a kick in the pants (which should, of course, be done compassionately for maximal effect). In Buddhism, the Boddhisattva is considered to be the second highest level of attainment, because Boddhisattvas are limited by their attachment to compassion. The highest level of spiritual attainment, that of the Buddha, is beyond all attachments and therefore is able to respond effectively in all circumstances.

One evening, Sheikh Muzaffer was talking about humility and service. He spoke eloquently about putting others' needs before our own and becoming more sensitive and compassionate toward others. Then someone asked, "What do you do with the arrogant? How can you serve the arrogant?" Sheikh Muzaffer drew himself up and raised his powerful voice. "With the arrogant, you must behave arrogantly! To treat them with humility is like giving them poison. It only feeds their arrogance." Kindness and indulgence can be a kind of poison, as illustrated in the following story.

> There was once a young man who grew up to become a thief. When he was a boy he brought home eggs he had stolen. Instead of asking where the eggs came from, his mother praised him for providing food and made him his favorite egg dishes. Later, he brought home chickens, then sheep. Still later, he brought home money. Each time his mother praised him and never asked where his gifts came from.
>
> When the authorities finally captured him, the young man had become a robber and a murderer. He was sentenced to hang. His last request was that his mother be brought to him on the scaffold. He asked his mother to come close to him and show him her tongue. When she complied with this strange request, the thief bit his mother's tongue so hard he drew blood.
>
> The condemned man explained, "My last wish was to bite the tongue that brought me to this fate. If my mother had asked where I got the things I brought home, if she had scolded and punished me for stealing, I might never have become a thief. Her over-indulgent tongue was my worst enemy."

Secret soul. One form of imbalance of the secret soul is materialism. Many people treat only the material world as real and important and ignore the spiritual. The opposite form of imbalance is rejection of the world, along with a kind of laziness. It is the attitude, "I'm really concerned with higher things, so why should I pay that much attention to this mundane job?" or "I am interested only in the divine, so I don't need to pay attention to people." In fact, how else can we seek the divine unless we learn to serve consciously in the present moment? How can we love the divine unless we love our families, friends, and neighbors? Love of others is a kind of warm-up exercise for learning to love God.

Secret of secrets. Unlike the other six souls, there is no such thing as imbalance in the secret of secrets. As it is the spark of divine nature within each of us, it is by definition transcendent and beyond the limitations of the other souls.

Archetypes of Imbalance

In many cultures around the world, there is an archetype for the person whose functioning is dominated by an *unbalanced animal soul.* That archetype is the werewolf, or were-creature. In northern Europe, berserk warriors were said to be able to go into a battle rage that gave them the ferocity of the animal whose skin they wore. Berserkers traditionally disdained armor and never thought of defense. Their ferocious attack was their only defense.

The ability to plan and think ahead (coming from the intelligence of the personal soul) is submerged in the anger and rage of the animal soul. In many legends, a person turns into an animal involuntarily and in that state is unable to restrain rage or passion. There is little thought or planning and little impulse control. Action is dominated by immediate desires and drives.

In many different cultures, there is also an archetype for those who are dominated primarily by an *unbalanced personal soul.* They are less impulsive and more intelligent than were-creatures—and more deadly. That archetype is the vampire. A vampire looks human and has human intelligence, but it has no warmth or compassion. With no life energy of its own, it survives by taking vital energy from others. The vampire is dominated by the self-seeking intelligence of the personal soul, without any mitigating influence from the human soul or secret soul.

According to most vampire legends, someone dies and then comes back as a vampire. This can be seen as a metaphor for the death of the human and secret souls. This may be the result of sudden trauma or gradual atrophy resulting from years of domination by the ego and the lower self. The result is someone who appears human and might often act in a cultured and refined way, but whose essential human nature is gone. Without compassion or any sense of spirituality, a human being can easily become a monster.

Years ago, when Sheikh Muzaffer was visiting New York with a group of dervishes, I stayed with them. The dervishes got by on very little sleep, as Sheikh Muzaffer often became inspired late at night and would teach or compose poetry. No matter how late they stayed up, the dervishes were up before dawn for morning prayers. One night, I excused myself at about 1:00 A.M., and fell into bed. At 5:30 A.M., when I got up for prayer, the dervishes looked completely exhausted. I asked why they were so tired. One of the men said, "We were just about ready to go to bed at 2:00 A.M., but someone turned on a vampire movie and Sheikh Muzaffer decided to watch it. We didn't get to bed until 4:00 o'clock."

Later that morning I asked Sheikh Muzaffer about the movie. I was very curious about what could have kept him up so late. He said, "It was a good movie. They got most of the details right. You know, it's best to use wood from an apple tree for the stake through the heart." The sheikh went on to discuss the phenomenon of vampires. "A vampire is created when a person is at the edge of death, and the secret of secrets, the spiritual soul, and the human soul all leave the body. Then the personal soul and the animal soul dominate. Even worse, a master vampire is created when the personal soul leaves as well. The person becomes an empty shell, which is then filled by an outside spirit. This kind of vampire is the most dangerous." I didn't know what to make of the Sheikh's description of vampires and vampire legends, but I was struck by the way the model of the souls fitted the vampire archetype.

We are all dominated by our different souls at times. We have all been famished and thought of nothing but food. We have all been swept away by sexual feelings and thought of nothing but making love. We have all been overcome by egotistical desires for fame or fortune, or by envy of those who achieved what we did not. We have all, at times, become carried away by feelings of pity or compassion. However, for most of us, there is a basic balance among our souls, so we act appropriately most of the time. This is one of the goals of Sufism—to act effectively and suitably in the world, and also to maintain a kind of spiritual balance.

Exercises for Soul Balance

Self-identification. Ideally, we have the ability to identify or disidentify with any of our souls. This gives us the power of choice and greater psychological freedom to effectively utilize whatever aspects of our personality are most appropriate to each situation.

This exercise is a tool to give you the ability to focus your attention of each of the souls.[10] Sit comfortably, relax, and then recite the following, slowly and thoughtfully:

1. I *have* a body, but *I am not only* my body. My body may be healthy or sick, tired or energized, but *I* am not necessarily affected. I value my body as a precious instrument of healing and nourishment. I *have* a body, but *I am not only* my body.

2. I *have* emotions, but *I am not only* my emotions. I may be angry, afraid, or passionate. My emotions and motivations help make my life rich and fulfilling. An emotion may even submerge me at times, but I can observe and understand my emotions and motivations. I value my emotions as a source of energy and motivation. I *have* emotions, but *I am not only* my emotions.

3. I *have* a mind, but *I am not* only my mind. My intellect is a valuable tool of discovery and understanding. Its contents change as I learn more. I value my mind as a source of planning and understanding. I *have* a mind, but *I am not only* my mind.

4. I *have* an ego, but *I am not only* my ego. My sense of self-esteem and self-worth allows me to accomplish a great deal. I value my healthy, self-affirming ego as a source of personal power and self-confidence. I *have* an ego, but *I am not only* my ego.

5. I *have* a heart, but *I am not only* my heart. My heart provides me with a sense of compassion and allows me to see and feel more deeply. I value my heart as the source of my deeper feelings, creativity, and understanding. I *have* a heart, but I *am not only* my

heart.

6.   I *have* a spiritual center, but *I am not only* my spiritual center. I value my spiritual center as the place of remembrance and deep spiritual experience. I *have* a spiritual center, but *I am not only* my spiritual center.

7.   *I am all my souls,* and I am an infinitely rich mystery, a mystery that includes God's presence hidden within me.

Next, you can repeat the central sentence in each affirmation:

I *have* a body, but *I am not only* my body.
I *have* emotions, but *I am not only* my emotions.
I *have* a mind, but *I am not only* my mind.
I *have* an ego, but *I am not only* my ego.
I *have* a heart, but *I am not only* my heart.
I *have* a spiritual center, but *I am not only* my spiritual center.
I am all my souls.

Experiencing your souls

The Mineral Soul

1.   Think of yourself as a skeleton covered with flesh. Mentally strip away your concealing flesh and become aware of your inner skeleton. You are this marvelous structure that combines solidity and flexibility. Develop skeleton awareness as you sit and as you move. How might you become *more flexible* in your movement, and also *more solid* in your stillness?

2.   Are there some areas in your life in which you are too flexible, where you might want more stability and a sense of solidity? Are there areas in which you are too rigid, where you might want to be more responsive or more open to change?

The Vegetable Soul

1.   Recall a time when you were perfectly relaxed, a vacation where you had nothing to do but take it easy and replenish your ener-

gies. Think of a specific moment, when you were lying on a beach or sitting in an easy chair. See if you can recall that state of deep relaxation, if you can taste it even now. What does it feel like? Can you sense the healing power of deep relaxation? Take five or ten minutes a day to just relax. Listen to soothing music or a relaxation tape. Short periods of daily relaxation can work wonders for the immune system. Keep a journal record of your daily sessions and note the effects.

2.   Think of a time when you were really hungry and you ate just the right amount of delicious, nourishing food. Recall how wonderful it felt to satisfy your hunger, and how your body responded. Can you also recall times when you nourished yourself mentally, emotionally, or spiritually? What was your experience at those times?

In your journal, keep track of how you nourish your body through food and exercise, how you nourish your mind through reading and listening to provocative ideas, the ways you nourish your emotions through honest communication and expression in relationships, and how you nourish your spirit in reading inspiring material and in prayer or contemplation.

The Animal Soul

1.   Reflect on the role of anger in your life. Recall a time when you needed to push away something or someone toxic. How did it feel to use your anger to defend yourself? Do you feel that you need to develop your capacity to use your anger positively? Most of us feel we don't use anger well; either we let ourselves get taken advantage of or we upset everyone, including ourselves. A Zen master once said that anger should be like the sound of thunder, or clapping your hands: once the sound is over, there is stillness. He went on to say, "I wish I could express anger so perfectly."

2.   How about your fears? Recall a time when you moved away from something or someone toxic. How did it feel to leave a threatening situation? Were you comfortable with your actions? Do your fears serve you well? That is, are you a reasonably prudent person, one who does not needlessly or foolishly put yourself into danger?

How might you further develop this capacity in yourself? Are there some areas in your life in which you need more prudence and care? Are there some areas in which you would like to be *less* careful, to take more risks?

3.   How do your passions serve you? What are the people and activities in your life about which you feel passionate? Recall a time when you were in the grip of a passion. Perhaps it was a romance or a time you were deeply in love with art, music, or some other activity. How did you feel? What would it take to rekindle that kind of passion? What were the drawbacks of being in the grip of passion? Where in your life could you use more passion and fire? What can you do to generate it? (It may help to read inspirational biographies or passionate poetry, or to spend time with others who are passionate about some aspect of their lives.)

Personal Soul

1.   Reflect on the positive and negative aspects of your ego. Think of the times that your sense of self-worth and self-confidence helped you to succeed in spite of serious difficulties and challenges. Recall times when lack of self-confidence held you back. Were there times that you gave up too easily, or even failed to begin a challenging task because you lacked self-confidence? Do you still feel the same today?

2.   Has overconfidence or false pride been an obstacle for you? Think of a time that your overconfidence led you to underprepare or fail to appreciate the difficulties you were facing. Can you think of a time that someone criticized you for a perfectly valid reason, and your negative ego responded with anger and denial? Most of us don't take criticism well, even when it is justified, because our negative ego can't stand the notion that we are not perfect.

The Human Soul

1.   Reflect on the role of compassion in your life. Recall a time that you were kind to someone without any thought of reward. (We often feel this way with young children, who so clearly need our help and nurturing support.) What triggered your sense of com-

passion? How did it feel to help another selflessly?

2.   Can you recall a time that you refused someone who needed your help? Why did your sense of compassion close down? How did it feel afterward?

3.   Was there a time when your compassion was misplaced; that is, when you helped someone who didn't deserve or appreciate it, or you showed sympathy when the other needed a more critical response from you? How did it feel to show compassion when another response would have been more appropriate and effective?

The Secret Soul

1.   Recall a spiritual peak experience, a time when you felt God's presence within you and around you. It may have been a time when you were deeply inspired by the beauty of nature, or at time you felt transported by great art or music. How did it feel? What triggered it? How long did it last? What triggers might bring about a similar experience?

2.   Can you remember a time when your thoughts of spiritual matters led you to devalue the mundane world? Have you felt a split, a basic dichotomy between the spirit and the profane? (This dichotomy is considered a heresy in many spiritual traditions, because it leads to devaluing everyday experience.)

Secret of Secrets

God within. To develop deep inner peace, begin by calming your mind for just five to ten minutes. Do this with absolute faith that God is fully present within you, even if you are unaware of that presence. Practice with a sense of certainty and determination to realize God.

This is known in Zen as sitting with a "bright mind." It is extremely important to sit with the faith that your deepest nature is divine, that you need not add anything or develop anything within yourself to grow spiritually; you already have everything within you, and all you need to do is to uncover it.

Chapter Five

❧

HARMONIZING YOUR SEVEN SOULS

I noticed an Arab of the desert sitting in the company of
jewelers. He said, "I once lost my road in the desert and
consumed all my food. I considered that I must perish
when I suddenly caught sight of a bulging canvas bag. I
shall never forget the joy and ecstasy I felt on thinking it
might be parched grain, nor the bitterness and despair
when I discovered it to be full of pearls."

—SA'DI[1]

great

A wealthy and influential man invited many distinguished guests to a dinner party. The guests included a
Sufi sheikh who was well known for his healing powers, and also the minister of health, a medical doctor who had
been educated in France. After dinner, the host's daughter suddenly became very dizzy and had to be put to bed. The host
asked the sheikh to pray for her, and the sheikh went to the girl
and recited several prayers for her health.

Great

This incensed the minister of health, who began grum-
bling that this kind of superstition had to go. "Today," he said,
"we have vitamin injections, modern medicines, and other scientific ways to heal people. This kind of old fashioned nonsense
is holding back progress!"

The sheikh turned to the minister and said, "I didn't
know they were putting minister's uniforms on donkeys these
days! How could such a foolish and ignorant man become a doctor, much less a minister?" The minister was furious. His face
turned bright red and he became so angry he couldn't speak.

123

The sheikh immediately said, in a soft and kind voice, "Minister, please forgive me. I merely said those insulting things to make a point. See how your face is red, your blood vessels are dilated, your heart is racing, and your adrenaline level has shot up. All this was caused by a few words. If secular speech could cause such physical changes, perhaps holy words from God's scripture can help bring about physical healing."

Some words almost instantly bring out our animal soul with its capacity for anger, fear, or passion. Other words inspire us and bring out our secret soul, with its capacity for worship and remembrance of God.

We might ask, "Which of my seven souls is in charge?" The Sufi's answer is that *God* is in charge. The mineral and vegetable souls certainly cannot run our lives, nor can the animal soul and its instincts. The personal soul is very limited; the negative ego, with its self-centered arrogance, has caused more pain and killing than the greed and lust of the unbalanced animal soul. Intelligence without faith or compassion often does far more harm than good. The souls must cooperate, like a well-balanced government in which each branch has its own expertise and area of authority.

Note: before reading the following section, I suggest that you complete the exercise called "Drawing the carriage" at the end of this chapter. It will be more meaningful if you have not read the discussion first.

The Metaphor of the Carriage

There is an old Sufi metaphor that likens the souls to a horse-drawn carriage (the ultimate in transportation when this metaphor was first developed). The mineral soul is the framework and axles of the carriage. The vegetable soul is the body of the carriage. The animal soul is the horses, and the personal soul is the driver. The human soul, combined with the secret soul and secret of secrets, is the owner, sitting inside the carriage.

All the souls have to be healthy and work together for the carriage to operate properly. The frame and body must be sturdy, the wheels and axles strong. The roof and windows should be watertight in case of rain. If the carriage breaks down, the journey cannot continue.

The horses, one black and one white, must be healthy. The black horse represents fear and anger, and the white horse represents the passions. We need our animal soul and its drives, since without their motive power we won't get anywhere. In the Judeo-Christian tradition we are frequently told we should beat the horses (mortify the flesh) and starve them so they are weakened and have little influence on us. (Extremes of religious asceticism are not so far in our past as we might think. A colleague of mine served as a Jesuit novice director about twenty years ago. In exploring his office, he found in his closet several boxes of whips, chains, and hair shirts.)

In the Sufi model of the carriage, we want the horses to be as strong and healthy as possible. (We also want them to be obedient and well trained.) If all the souls are healthy, we can achieve a far better-balanced life in this world than if some souls are sick and weak.

The driver has to be strong enough and skilled enough to guide the horses and steer the carriage properly. Perhaps most important, the driver also has to be able to follow the instructions of the owner. However, the driver is not equipped to understand the journey or discover the correct destination. That is the job of the owner.

The owner must be strong and clear and able to speak up so that the driver can make the right decisions. For many people, the speaking tube between driver and owner is clogged up due to lack of use. The driver has forgotten, in fact, that there is an owner inside the carriage, and has taken charge. The ego is a wonderful servant, but a very poor master.

The Sufi practice of remembrance means, at one level, learning to hear the still small voice of the owner, in other words, the higher impulses and the divine within us. With practice, the voice of our innermost divine nature becomes clearer and louder and more easily understood.

All of the parts of the carriage must function harmoniously. If the carriage is in charge, there will be no journey at all. Nothing moves because there is no motivation to go anywhere; motivation is not present in the mineral or vegetable souls. If the horses are in charge, they will lead the carriage into the fields with the best clover, and the carriage will remain stuck there. The animal soul introduces motivation, but it is short-term motivation, determined by instinctual gratification. The driver does not have the capacity to choose the right destination either, no matter how well he can steer around curves and obstacles. The carriage will probably end up parked in front of a tavern. The intelligence of the personal soul is a wonderful tool, but it is limited and self-centered. We need the human, secret, and secret-of-secret souls to guide the carriage to its destination. These souls contain the compassion, wisdom, and divine guidance necessary to live a fulfilling life as a real human being. Ideally, all seven souls come to work together in harmony. If any one soul cannot function, the carriage cannot proceed on its journey.

Dreams and the Souls

In some Sufi orders, work with dreams is an important aspect of spiritual counseling. Dervishes are expected to bring their dreams to their sheikh regularly, and the sheikh's interpretation is an important aspect of the guidance each dervish receives. Through hearing the dervishes' dreams, the sheikh may learn what spiritual level they have attained and what spiritual practices are appropriate for them.

Dreams come from different souls. The dreams of the secret soul and of the secret of secrets need no interpretation. They are revelations or direct spiritual experiences. The most profound and spiritually significant dreams emerging from these souls generally come at dawn.

The dreams that come from the human soul can also have profound meanings. They are the kinds of dreams Jung studied, and they often include universal symbols and archetypal images. These dreams frequently contain messages of great value for the dervish, but they have to be interpreted by the sheikh.

The dreams that come from the personal soul are psychological dreams, often filled with symbols that have personal meanings. These are the kinds of dreams Freud wrote about, as are the dreams at the level of the animal soul, which are mainly wish fulfillment dreams.

Dreams that are from the vegetable or mineral soul are generated mainly by bodily sensations. According to an old Turkish saying, a hungry chicken dreams of corn. It is said that dreams are the windows of the soul. This refers to the dreams of the secret soul and secret of secrets.

Such dreams provide one of the ways we can begin to understand that highest aspect of ourselves. It is as if the soul flows out, like light from a flashlight. If you turn on a flashlight at night and point it at a book, light instantly moves from the source to the target and illuminates the writing. Similarly, the secret soul flows out from its place in the inner heart to illuminate God's book of wisdom, the source of all knowledge. Such dreams can have very important messages. The dreams of the secret of secrets need no interpretation. They are profound mystical experiences or divine revelations. The numinous quality of such dreams speaks for itself.

Of course, you have to know which soul is dreaming. The revelations of the secret soul or the secret of secrets are very different from the dreams of the vegetable and mineral souls.

The Souls in Balance

The mineral soul is meant to provide us with a strong foundation, a solid inner structure to support us in life. When out of balance, it is a source of rigidity, inertia, and inflexibility on the one hand, or flaccidity, fickleness, and vacillation on the other. The vegetable soul is meant to assist us in keeping our bodies healthy and strong. When out of balance, it may be a source of either laziness or hyperactivity. The animal soul is meant to give us the passion and drive to accomplish worthwhile service in the world. When unbalanced, the animal soul leads us to act badly, through anger, greed, or passion.

The personal soul is meant to guide us, to provide the intelligence necessary to understand ourselves, and to comprehend the world around us. The unbalanced personal soul misleads us through arrogance and egotism or incapacitates us though a weak ego and lack of self-esteem and self-confidence. Rationalization and false imagination can distort the truth, or we may misuse our intelligence to destructively criticize ourselves and others in a rigid, judgmental way.

The human soul provides compassion and the deeper intelligence and creativity of the heart. When out of balance, it can lead us to act foolishly out of misplaced pity or softhearted solicitude. The secret soul can provide real inner wisdom but, out of balance, it may lead us to reject the world and dichotomize the spiritual and material. The secret soul can also keep us at the level of our separate individuality and become an obstacle to full union with God.

Awareness of the World

With each soul, our level of awareness changes. With the animal soul the organism contacts the environment—through sight, hearing, smell, taste, and touch. This is a great improvement over the minimal perceptions of the vegetable soul or the lack of perception of the mineral soul. However, we sense only the outside forms of things, and we can be easily misled. For example, someone walking along a forest path in the dark sees a snake coiled up, ready to strike. The next day, in full daylight, the person sees the same form, but now recognizes it as only a gnarled tree root.

From a Sufi perspective, creation is one of God's holy books, and learning from it is potentially one of our greatest and most profound educational experiences. The more we understand creation and the deeper our connection with our environment, the greater our learning. The five senses of the animal soul provide us with the basic, beginning tools for this study.

With the intelligence of the personal soul, we not only perceive the outer aspects of things, we can begin to learn about their inner nature. For example, we cannot perceive the inner workings of the body with the naked eye, but we can understand how the body works through the use of microscopes and through medical and biological theories. We can come to understand through studying psychology something of how the human mind works. Over the years, human intelligence has unlocked many of nature's secrets.

At the level of the human soul we can perceive more deeply still. We can go beyond what is available to the senses and the intellect. Compassion allows us to feel what others are feeling. Compassion means "to feel with." It comes from the realization that we are interdependent, that we are not separate from each other. In the words of Christian mystic Meister Eckehart, "Whatever happens to another, whether it be a joy or a sorrow, happens to me."[2]

In Arabic, the most frequently used names of God are *ar-Rahman* and *ar-Rahim*, generally translated as Mercy and Compassion. The root of both words is *rahm*, or womb. The mother's womb protects and shelters the fetus, and the mother gives of her own flesh and blood to nourish her baby. God's love and compassion for each of us is far greater still.

We can penetrate still deeper into reality at the level of the secret soul, and deeper still at the secret of secrets. The saints, the prophets, and God's messengers operated from the deep wisdom of the secret of secrets. They plumbed the hidden depths within themselves and creation. They acted from inner knowledge. That is why we try to imitate them.

How do we develop our awareness of the inner realm? In order to understand creation we need our human, secret, and secret-of-secret souls. The Koran teaches, "We (God) will show them Our signs upon the horizon and in themselves, until it is quite clear to them that it is the Truth." (41:53)

As mentioned earlier, if someone is in a coma, the mineral and vegetable souls function while the other souls are buried. In that state there is virtually no awareness of the world. When a person is controlled by the raw, unbalanced functioning of their animal soul, they are blind to everything else. Whatever we perceive in the world around us tends to reflect who we are and what we care about most deeply, as in the old saying, "When a thief sees a saint, all he sees are his pockets."

The Inner Jihad and the Personal Soul

Some people are dominated by their negative egos; for example, pride and the desire for recognition and adulation. They are stuck at the level of the personal soul and are blinded by their arrogance.

The battle with our negative egos is an inner struggle, one we all have to fight on the spiritual path. Most people want recognition and fame. Many people who are dominated by their negative egos are seen as ambitious and enterprising and are well rewarded by society. As a result, most people view this condition as healthy rather than as something to be remedied. Many of the descriptions of the tyrannical self in chapter 3 pertain to the unbalanced personal soul.

When Muhammad and the early Muslims were returning from a major battle, he turned to his companions and said, "Now we are leaving the lesser jihad and going to the greater jihad." The warriors were stunned at his words. They were exhausted, their arrows were gone, their swords and lances were blunted or broken. The Prophet went on, "The greater jihad is the battle with what is in your breasts!"

The translation of *jihad* as "holy war" is misleading and usually inaccurate. Muslim leaders have often called their wars *jihad*, meaning God was on their side. The basic Koranic meaning of *jihad* is "struggle," and most often refers to struggle "in the path of God." The basic practices of Sufism—remembrance, service, contemplation—all involve struggle. They take energy, commitment, and will power.

Once, a Sufi saint known as Somonju-baba was lecturing on the sura Fatiha, the opening sura of the Koran. He pointed out that each line has at least seven levels of meaning. The first level is the most basic, literal meaning and is understood by anyone who knows the words. The second level can be understood by those who have reflected on the meaning of the words. The third level is understood only by scholars who have studied still more deeply, and so on.

When Somonju-baba came to the sixth level, he said, "Besides me, the only one in the room who understands this level is a man sitting in the back behind a pillar." The man behind the pillar was the grand mufti, the religious advisor to the sultan, considered one of the greatest scholars in the Ottoman Empire. Somonju-baba said that he himself was the only one in the room who truly understood the seventh level.

The grand mufti was seized with the desire to learn this seventh level of interpretation, and so he went to the Sufi master's lodge. After greeting the saint, the grand mufti said that he had come to learn the final level of meaning of the sura Fatiha. The master thought for a moment and then replied, "No, I'm afraid that you are not able to learn this final level of meaning."

The grand mufti said, "Please try me. I am considered a fairly accomplished scholar, and I am sure I will manage to learn what you have to teach." After all, he had been the best student of the finest, most accomplished scholars and was now the religious authority for the whole empire.

The saint replied, "All right. The first step will be for you to ride my donkey into town in your formal robes. Tie the don-

key's feed bag around your neck, fill it with walnuts and give
them to all the children on the street."

The grand mufti thought long and hard. "I have consulted my nafs (ego), and I must admit that I cannot carry out this
first step."

The scholar's pride prevented him from penetrating fully
the depths of wisdom of the Koran, but at least he was honest
about his limitations.

Then Somonju-baba said, "Because you have been so
kind to come here and honor us with your presence, even sitting
in the straw with my dervishes, I want you to make an interpretation of the sura Fatiha for us."

The grand mufti began to interpret the sura and was
amazed to hear the new depths of understanding coming from
his own mouth. Later, he wrote a manuscript on the sura Fatiha
and told this story in the introduction. The manuscript can still
be found in the some of the great libraries in Istanbul today.
How much more might he have understood had he been able to
ride the saint's donkey!

What is the inner nature of those select few who are guided by the
human and secret souls? What is life like when the owner of the carriage
is truly in charge of the journey? To understand, we must look at the
lives of the saints. They are the ones who have loved God, who sought
God's pleasure, served the world, and constantly remembered God.
Stories of the saints and prophets can help us realize the extraordinary
extent of our own potentials. They are the real human beings. A human
being is one who remembers God no matter what happens. That is the
inner jihad, the inner struggle. The world is designed to make us forget.
Our job is to remember.

Imagination. In Sufism, we sometimes talk about the devil. There
is an outer devil and an inner devil. The outer devil is in the world, in the
outer temptations and distractions that we have to learn to cope with. For
instance, if we are praying and a woman in a bikini or a man in a tight
bathing suit walks by, there go our prayers. But how often does the devil
send somebody in a bikini while we're praying? Not very often. Our real

INNER STRUGGLE more IMPORTANT

struggle is with our own inner distractions. The imagination that conjures an image of a woman in a bikini is the inner devil. We do have to struggle with the world at times, because there are real challenges out there, but the inner struggle is much more important.

Drugs and alcohol. One of the reasons that drugs and alcohol are forbidden in Islam is because they deaden the human and secret souls. People who use drugs or alcohol often behave like animals. Much physical and sexual abuse comes from people whose human and secret souls are anesthetized.

> There was once a wicked old man who was allied with the devil. He tried to lead astray as many people as possible. Each day a sincere, God-fearing young scholar walked past his house, and the old man decided to set a trap for him. One evening, as the scholar was returning from his studies, the old man opened the door to his chicken coop. The chickens ran out into the street. The old man ran after them, pleading for the scholar to help him round up his chickens. The compassionate young man was happy to be of service, and after the chickens were back in their coop, the old man invited him inside for tea. The scholar tried to demur but the old man insisted.
>
> Over tea, the old man asked the scholar about his studies, and then said, "Would you please do me another favor? My niece and her baby are staying with me, and the baby is very sick. Would you please recite a blessing over the baby?" The young scholar agreed, and the old man took him to the guest room, where the baby and his mother were sleeping. Once the scholar was inside the room, the old man slammed the door and locked it. "What are you doing?" shouted the scholar.
>
> The old man replied, "If you don't do what I tell you, I'll rip my clothes and scream and swear that you broke into my house, beat me up and attacked my niece. My neighbors will believe me and they will kill you for it. You must do one of three things. There is a bottle of alcohol in the room. You can drink the entire bottle of alcohol, have sexual relations with the woman, or kill the baby. Then I will let you go."

The scholar thought and realized that he couldn't possibly kill the baby or have sex with the young woman. Even though alcohol was forbidden, it was the lesser of the three evils, and so he drank down the bottle. After he finished, the young woman looked extremely attractive to him. He took off his clothes and got into the bed. As he reached for the woman, the baby woke up and began to cry. Angry at the distraction, the drunken scholar hit the baby and knocked it to the floor, killing it. At that moment, the old man ran into the street, screaming for his neighbors.

The seemingly trivial act of drinking led the naive young man to actions he would never normally have dreamed of committing. In a real sense, he was not himself when he was drunk.

Actualizing the human and secret souls. Those who attain a certain level of remembrance and guidance by the human and secret souls are not easily swayed by the world. They are not puffed up with pride if praised, or angry if their pride is hurt. They are not greedy for gain or afraid of loss; they rely on God, not on this world.

One of the great lessons that Moses received was to rely solely on God. When Moses first spoke with God, the Koran tells us that God asked him what was in his right hand. Moses answered, "This is my staff. I lean on it. I use it to knock down fodder for my flock, and I have many other uses for it." God told Moses to throw down his staff, and the staff turned into a snake. Moses was shown that he should not lean or rely on anything other than God.

Later, Moses threw down his staff before Pharaoh and his magicians, and it became a snake that devoured all the magicians' snakes. One of the lessons of this story is that whatever comes from God's command is far stronger than that which comes from human will or effort. God said to Moses, "You did not throw when you threw." Moses had become the instrument through which God acted. That is the ideal—to be worthy of becoming God's instrument and to serve creation without our will or desires distorting God's will.

Another story further illustrates this attitude of one who is no longer controlled by the characteristics of the vegetable, animal, personal, or human souls—characteristics such as heedlessness, greed, fear, ambition, and pride.

> During the time of the Ottoman Empire, there was a great Sufi sheikh in Istanbul. His fame spread until even the sultan heard of him. The sultan began to visit the sheikh's lodge every Thursday evening to hear the sheikh teach and to participate in the remembrance ceremony.
>
> After several weeks, the sultan told the sheikh, "I really love you and your teachings, and I love to participate in your remembrance ceremony. Ask me for whatever you want. If it is in my power I will grant it." Here was a blank check offered by the wealthiest and most powerful ruler on earth, the kind of opportunity most men and women would give anything for.
>
> The sheikh replied, "I do have one request of you, my sultan. Please do not come back."
>
> The sultan was baffled and troubled. "Have I offended you or violated any of the rules or traditions of your order? If so, I humbly apologize. I assure you that it was out of ignorance and not out of any lack of respect for you and your tradition."
>
> "No," replied the sheikh, "The problem does not lie with you. You have always behaved with the greatest courtesy and respect. The problem is with my dervishes. Before you came, they chanted and prayed to God. Now they chant and worship to please you. So I must ask you not to come back, because we are not developed enough to support your presence."

Charity. We bring out the human and secret souls mainly through our actions. Genuine charity is not just giving money; it is to give others what they truly need. We can give our precious time, empathy, caring, and knowledge to help others. This is the kind of action that brings out the human and secret souls. This includes remembering God in the midst of the distractions of the world. Sheikh Muzaffer was fond of saying, "Keep your hands busy with your duties in this world and keep your heart busy with God."

The believer is the mirror of the believer. The Koran says that the believer is the mirror of the believer. In the sincere believer, we can the human and secret souls. Seek those who are engaged in this inner struggle. Don't look among those who act like minerals, vegetables, animals, or selfish egotists. If we go to a hospital and look for inspiration from someone in a coma, we will find very little spiritual nourishment. Similarly, what can you learn spiritually from those who are dominated by their lust, anger, or greed? The only possible benefit would be to see those negative tendencies in yourself. That may be useful in more fully understanding your own faults, but it does not teach you anything about your spiritual nature.

When the believer becomes the mirror of the believer, the secret soul in one becomes the mirror of the secret soul in the other. Likewise, the deepest part of the soul, the divine spark, the secret of secrets, becomes the mirror of the divine in the other.

> O heart, sit with someone
> who knows the heart;
> Go under the tree
> that has fresh blossoms.
> —RUMI[3]

Remember that everybody has *all* the souls. A believer is not a plaster saint who is absolutely perfect. When we look closely at others, we can see their mineral nature, their vegetable nature, their animal nature, and their personalities. We should not ignore these souls, nor should we stop at them. We are all more than our limited motives and instincts. We can look *through* these souls to the human and secret souls.

Western psychology tends to stop with personality defects. According to Western psychology, we have to focus on examining our childhood and cleaning up all our personality problems. This will take a lifetime, if not longer, and we will never get to what comes next. That is why most of Western psychology never gets to the spiritual and tends to get stuck at the level of the personal or the animal soul.

Spiritual systems often have the opposite problem. In many spiritual groups people pretend that they are purely spiritual beings, that they have no animal nature, no ego, no limited personality. They focus on perfecting their spiritual nature and tend to ignore the need for work at the personality level. In particular, the teacher (or sheikh) is often thought to be perfectly pure and purely spiritual. But no teacher, no human being is perfect.

No one is perfect. Sheikhs are human beings who try to remain in contact with their secret souls and who work hard to act according to their highest nature. A sheikh is someone who can serve as a channel for the wisdom and spiritual blessings of his order. But a sheikh still has all the souls. These souls and their influences never go away completely. We must never forget that, and we should never put another man or woman on a pedestal and say, here is the perfect human being with no faults, who is not subject to temptation.

Spiritual attainment is not about transcending temptation, or even never succumbing to it. Spiritual attainment means to resist temptation, and if one does make a mistake, to do something about it immediately, as we can see in the following story.

Many years ago, there was a sheikh in Istanbul who was famous as a healer. The sultan's daughter was ill, and the finest physicians could do nothing for her. The sultan sent for the sheikh. The sheikh told the sultan's delegate, "I cannot go with you right now, but I will send with you one of my dervishes. Mehmet, you go with them." Mehmet was young, and he knew nothing at all about healing. Mehmet looked at his sheikh with astonishment, but all the sheikh did was to gesture for Mehmet to join the delegation.

The young dervish was escorted to the palace and brought into the princess' sitting room. She lay on a couch, pale and unmoving. Not knowing what else to do, the dervish raised his hands and with all his heart he prayed to God to heal the princess—for the sake of his sheikh's reputation and for his own sake as well as that of the princess. Three times he repeated, "Bismillah ir-rahman ir-rahim, In the Name of God, the Merciful, the Compassionate."

Within moments, color began to flush the princess' cheeks. She sat up and asked for food. The word immediately spread throughout the palace that there was a new healing saint in Istanbul. The sultan himself gave the young dervish a magnificent turban and robe, along with several bags of gold.

Mehmet left the palace mounted on a white Arabian stallion, followed by a guard of honor. Suddenly, he stopped at the entrance to the palace kitchens. He got off his horse and went inside. There he picked up a bucket of bloody entrails from a sheep that had just been slaughtered and dumped them over his head, drenching the turban and robe. The honor guard was shocked and mystified as Mehmet rode through the city in this strange state.

When he arrived back at his sheikh's lodge, he sought out the sheikh at once, bowed low, and kissed his hand. The sheikh smiled and asked him what happened. Mehmet described the princess' healing and the gifts he received from the sultan. Then, he said, as he was leaving the palace, the thought crossed his mind that he, Mehmet, must be even greater than his sheikh. After all, the sheikh could heal only with complex formulas, while he healed the princess by faith alone! He was immediately horrified by this evidence of inner pride and arrogance. He thought, "If my inside is so ugly, I will make my outside match it!"

Mehmet eventually became the sheikh's successor and a famous healer as well. His spiritual attainment did not come from inner perfection, but from his sincerity and willingness to work on his faults, immediately and effectively. Rumi writes, "O Lord, make my insides reflect my outside. And if you will not, please make my outside reflect my insides." Most of us pay a great deal of attention to our outer appearance. We make sure that we are clean and well groomed. Wouldn't it be wonderful if all our inner thoughts and feelings were just as attractive?

Because Rumi was dedicated to his own inner development, his first wish was to cleanse his insides, and if that was not possible, to have his outsides reflect his inner imperfections so that he could not hide from them. He would thus be forced continually to confront them and so eventually change.

Our outsides are relatively easy to clean up. Expensive clothing and jewelry can make any man look like a prince or any woman like a princess. Developing a beautiful inner nature is much harder and takes much longer. We need patience and perseverance to remain in touch with our human and spiritual souls and to keep *all* of them in balance. It does not mean to become perfect.

Many disciples like to think of their teacher as perfect, which may artificially boost their sense of self-worth. After all, the disciples of a "perfect master" must be very special. However, this attitude does a real disservice to the teachers, who have to struggle with their own inner limitations and imperfections just like the rest of us.

In one spiritual community I have known, when the so-called "perfect" teacher lost his temper, his disciples would say, "Ah, the master is perfect, so he *couldn't* have lost his temper. This must be a *lesson* that he is teaching us. He was only *pretending* to be angry, for our sakes." This absurd notion put a terrible burden on the teacher and everybody else. Everyone began to pretend they had no personality faults, that they were just like the false, plaster-saint image they made of their teacher. When this happens, nothing real can occur, because inner development cannot be based on pretense and unreality.

There is an old Chinese saying that the journey of a thousand miles begins with a single step. But if you pretend to be further down the road than you actually are, you can't really take the first step, and the real journey never begins.

One of the most important Sufi practices is to avoid gossip about the ego or the imperfections in others. Instead of focusing on those things, it is far better to see the divine nature in each other. However, we should not ignore those other souls either, because to ignore them is to be unreal, to pretend. The ideal is to see *through* these limitations to the positive, balanced qualities and to the divine within. That is what is truly important. When you meet other beings, the challenge is to see the spark of God in them.

As human beings, our job is to bring out the best in ourselves. We all have potential, but it has to be made conscious and developed. Anything that is not used atrophies. All the souls are like this. If we ignore our vegetative and animal souls we become sick and weak. If we don't exercise the human soul, if we don't act on our humanness, it atrophies just like our muscles. Our job is to keep the souls in balance and to keep our spiritual nature healthy and strong, by action such as charity, service, prayer, and remembrance.

Sufis traditionally come together for spiritual exercise. We can exercise at home, but it's better in a group, just as aerobics are easier when done in company. In our order, the dervishes meet together several times a week. In Istanbul, Thursday is the night for the remembrance ceremony, and Monday is the night for music and turning practice. Dervishes begin arriving late in the afternoon. By sundown the lodge is crowded. The dervishes chat, pray, and have dinner together, after which they hold either the remembrance ceremony or music practice.

After the ceremony, they relax and talk some more. If there are many guests, the sheikh may answer their questions. The sheikh comes in Saturday evenings as well. These gatherings are generally smaller and devoted to informal talks, questions and answers, and dream interpretation. In addition, dervishes often go together to a local mosque for the Friday prayers and then have a leisurely lunch afterwards.

Our most important job is the inner struggle. The goal is not to destroy the vegetable, animal, or personal soul. It is to see *through* them to the human and secret souls. We need the personal soul in order to function in society.

The function of the personality is illustrated in a classic movie, directed by Akira Kurosawa, called *Derzu Uzala*. The title character is a Tartar hunter and trapper who becomes a guide for a Russian mapping expedition led by a Russian Army lieutenant from Saint Petersburg. The lieutenant is a sophisticated city dweller who doesn't know how to handle the wilderness, and the guide saves his life several times. Derzu knows exactly how to function in the woods. For example, he teaches the lieutenant that if you take water from a pump you must leave a bucket of water to prime the pump for the next party. If you find a cache of firewood and use it to cook and to thaw out from the bitter cold, you are obligated to replace the firewood for the next traveler.

Later on, the lieutenant takes Derzu back to Saint Petersburg. It's a total disaster. At one point the police throw Derzu in jail for cutting down trees in the park. He complains, "How can you be stopped from cutting down trees? They are God's trees! Nobody owns them." Firewood in the wilderness is a necessity for survival and is available to all. Then Derzu attacks someone for selling water in the street. In the wilderness it is inconceivable and immoral to sell water.

Derzu does not understand all the strange, complicated ways that human beings have developed in order to live together in society. He is a man with an extremely simple, underdeveloped personal soul. He really doesn't need a complex personality as long as he lives in the wilderness.

We need all the souls. Our complex personalities are valuable tools, even though they can cause us great problems. Our egos and personalities may lead us astray, but we need them to in order to relate to other people and understand their personalities.

We also need our vegetable and animal souls so that we can remain healthy and fit. For example, we must know what foods to avoid and what foods are good for us. Unfortunately, our animal soul is often overwhelmed by the personality, and then we don't know what's good or bad for us. If we were more in touch with our animal nature, we would live much healthier lives than most of us manage today.

The different souls enter during the development of a human being in the womb. It is said that the first month of pregnancy, the mineral and vegetable souls come in. In the second month, the animal soul enters. In the third month the personal soul enters as the nervous system develops. In the fourth month, the human soul, secret soul, and secret of secrets come.

The mineral and vegetable souls last after death, but they remain with the body. For example, the hair and fingernails will continue to grow. It is said that the animal soul and perhaps the personal soul remain as well, since the mineral, vegetable, animal, and personal souls are all located in physical organs, while the human soul, the secret soul, and the secret of secrets are located in the spiritual heart. These first four souls are tied to the physical body, but the last three are not. They leave the body at death and they do not perish. That is why Sufis do not say that a saint "died," but that he or she "passed on." The ones fully identified with these souls do not experience death as do most people.

If we are identified with our materially based souls, it is very difficult for the human and secret souls to leave at death. The experience is described as like pulling barbed wire through the nerves. This kind of person is attached to the pleasures and life of the body, the desires of the ego, and those things that the ego needs a body to do. But if we are identified with the human soul, the secret soul, or the secret of secrets, it is said that the soul slips from the body like a hair pulled from butter. This kind of person is not attached to the experiences of this world.

It is very important to look beyond the personality, to see through the greed, the negative ego, and to find the human, secret, and secret-of-secret souls in ourselves and in each other. Each day we are presented with others' limited personalities over and over again. We need compassion, courage, and awareness to go beyond the personality and touch the human soul that lies behind it. We can keep striving to interact with others without forgetting their higher nature, no matter how they act.

Sufism has been spread by sincere dervishes who were real human beings. They saw beyond the limits of the personality and they could touch other people deeply and serve them selflessly. As a result, people changed, and many said, "Well, if that is how Sufis are, I want to be a Sufi."

> *Ali, the son-in-law of the Prophet, was known as the Lion of Islam. In one of the early battles in defense of Islam, Ali knocked the sword away from an enemy warrior. Ali raised his own sword and was about to cut the warrior's throat when the man spat in his face. Ali stepped back, sheathed his sword, and said, "You can go! Your life is unlawful to me now." The fallen warrior asked, "What do you mean?"*
>
> *Ali replied, "I was fighting for God's sake, and I would have been willing to kill you in the heat of battle, fighting for my religion. But when you spat at me, you made me angry. I will fight and even kill for God's sake, but I will not be a murderer for the sake of my nafs." The warrior was so deeply impressed that he became a Muslim.*

Ali was a great leader, a great spiritual teacher. He was the fourth Caliph of Islam. Virtually all of the Sufi orders trace their lineage back to him. The Prophet Muhammad once said, "I am the City of Knowledge and Ali is the Gate."

Yet even Ali had his ego. He did not get rid of it completely, for all his spiritual attainment. However, when his temper flared, Ali didn't become controlled by it. He fought immediately against the demands of his ego. That is the inner jihad. The seven facets of our soul will not leave us. We must recognize that they are still very much with us, work with them and struggle to balance them when necessary.

Exercises for Harmonizing the Souls

Drawing the carriage. Take crayons, pastels, or watercolors and draw a picture of a horse-drawn carriage. The carriage should have the following five elements:

- The wheels, axles, and framework of the carriage.
- The body of the carriage—roof, sides, front, back, doors, and windows.
- Two horses.
- The driver.
- The owner, seated inside the carriage.

1. Once you have finished the drawing, read over the section of this chapter entitled "The Metaphor of the Carriage." How well does your drawing represent the relationship of the different souls? For example, are any parts of your drawing either oversized or undersized?

2. Are the horses harnessed to the carriage? If not, this may indicate that your drives and motivations are not well connected to your actual physical needs. For example, many people are addicted to foods that are not good for them.

3. Did you draw reins connecting driver and horses? If not, this may indicate that you have difficulty controlling your drives, that even though you know what to do, you find it difficult to do so.

4. What changes would you make in your carriage? Are the carriage and its framework sturdy enough? Are the horses strong enough to pull the carriage throughout a long and arduous trip? Is the driver capable of guiding the carriage effectively, and can the owner direct the journey to its proper destination?

Self-examination. One of the great Prophetic sayings treasured in Sufism is, "Know yourself and you will know your Lord." Make a list of those habits and personality traits you would like to change. Be honest; it is not easy to list our faults and shortcomings. Do not identify yourself with the traits of your personality. To help you disidentify, list each trait according to the stage of self it is associated with. For example, "My ego wants recognition." "My animal self is prone to anger."

A dream diary. Keep a dream diary by your bed and write down your dreams every morning in as much detail as possible. Don't try to analyze them; simply notice what level of the self each dream seems to be coming from.

Nourishing your souls. Some years ago, I was talking about the Sabbath with an old friend, Rabbi Zalman Schachter-Shalomi. Reb Zalman is a Jewish scholar and teacher, and he is also a member of my Sufi order. (When he met Sheikh Muzaffer, he immediately fell in love with the sheikh and his teachings.)

The orthodox Jewish observance of the Sabbath forbids work of any kind. That day is devoted to prayer and study of the Torah rather than worldly activities. Reb Zalman commented that for many years he observed the Sabbath with his attention concentrated on all the proscriptions—don't carry anything, don't turn on a light, don't cook, don't drive, and so on. Then he remembered that the basic purpose of the Sabbath was to devote oneself to spiritual pursuits rather than simply avoid worldly activities. Instead of focusing on what he should *not* do, Reb Zalman asked himself instead, "How can I nourish my soul today?" This completely transformed his experience of the Sabbath.

List all seven souls and then ask yourself how you might nourish each one. If you contemplate each soul and ask what each wants and needs, you will find clear answers. Does your vegetable soul desire rest, or better food? Does your animal soul wish that you would express pent-up emotions, or spend a romantic weekend with your beloved? Perhaps some intellectually challenging books will nourish your personal soul. How might you express your compassion, creativity, or other qualities that nourish your human soul? What kinds of prayer, contemplation, or meditation will nourish your secret soul?

Chapter Six

✺

THE PRACTICES OF SUFISM: PSYCHOSPIRITUAL THERAPY

The thing we tell of can never be found by seeking,
yet only seekers find it.

—BAYAZID BISTAMI[1]

A Bedouin was traveling through the desert, carrying a filled water skin over his shoulder and weeping bitterly. When another traveler asked him why he was crying, the man replied that his dog was suffering terribly from thirst. The traveler asked why he didn't give his dog a drink from the water skin, and the Bedouin said, "I couldn't do that. I might need this water for myself."

✺

Most people prefer to listen to and talk about Sufism rather than practice it. But without practice there is no Sufism, only empty words. Sufism is like psychotherapy. However, the goals of conventional psychotherapy are to eliminate neurotic personality traits and to help the individual adapt to society; the goals of Sufi practice are to transform negative personality traits, to open the heart, to get in touch with the deep wisdom within, and come closer to God.

The basic Sufi practices discussed in this chapter are fasting, retreat, *adab*, Remembrance of God, and recollection of death.

Fasting

Fasting is found in almost all the religions and spiritual traditions of the world and is a basic practice in Judaism, yoga, and Buddhism. Partial fasting, such as refraining from certain foods, is a part of the Catholic practice of Lent.

The main Islamic fast is carried out in the month of Ramadhan. Muslims fast between sunrise and sunset each day for one lunar month, abstaining from food, drink, and sexual relations. In the Koran, God tells us, "I have prescribed fasting for you, and *I* am the reward for your fast." The Prophet loved fasting and fasted for days or weeks at a time throughout the year. This practice is still carried out by many ascetic dervishes.

What is so special about fasting? Why is it that God rewards this activity directly, or even that God Most High is our reward for fasting? For one thing, fasting is essentially private. It is between the individual and God. No one else in this world knows for certain whether you have fasted or not, and no one can tell if you swallow a little water when brushing your teeth or rinsing your mouth. Only God and you know. The ego cannot get involved in fasting as easily as it does in most other actions. (Of course, it is always possible to tell everyone around you that you are fasting, which feeds the ego and diminishes the inner value of the fast.)

Almost all of our other actions are more observable, so there is always the possibility that we will be noticed by others. With charity, for example, many people look for praise from those they are helping, or for a tax deduction or recognition as a philanthropist. For example, if a woman builds a hospital and has it named after herself, the desire for fame may have motivated her as much as if not more than the work of healing others. It is said that if you seek a reward in this world for your actions, you may receive worldly recognition, but you will get no reward in the hereafter—no real spiritual advantage.

Another benefit of fasting is that it is said to weaken the *nafs*.[2] Our *nafs* usually encourages us to do what is easy, comfortable, or pleasant rather than what is right. Often our *nafs* wins easily, without any opposition. For example, when we are hungry or thirsty, we almost immediately rush to satisfy those desires. Most businesses allow employees to take coffee breaks whenever they feel the slightest bit hungry or thirsty. The lunch break is even more important. We are convinced that we can't possibly get anything done in the afternoon if we haven't had lunch.

If people living under a tyrant immediately rush to obey the tyrant's commands, the tyrant remains in perfect control. The people even think that they are *choosing* to obey orders, because they never question or oppose them.

Fasting reveals the *nafs*. When fasting, it whispers to us that we really should eat or drink, that we won't have the energy or concentration to continue, that we might even lose our jobs if we insist on fasting. The *nafs* comes up with all kinds of reasons and excuses to break our fast, and it becomes much more visible that it usually is. We can often see our impatient and selfish side more clearly when we fast.

When the *nafs* is revealed, it loses its power to some extent. The *nafs* is a little like the wizard in the classic movie, *The Wizard of Oz*. The wizard is a charlatan, and he hides behind a curtain and manipulates a huge head that strikes fear and awe in everyone who beholds it. When the wizard is discovered, he causes the huge face to cry out, "Pay no attention to the little man behind the curtain!" The *nafs* also pretends to be far greater and more powerful than it really is. The more clearly we observe it, the more the *nafs* loses its power, just as the wizard does when he is seen as he really is.

At another level, fasting weakens the *nafs*, because as our bodies have less energy, so does our *nafs*. That is, the *nafs* is very much tied to the body, and when we fast, our *nafs* becomes less active. We don't have energy to waste. During the rest of the year, many of us will sit and work for an hour or two and then feel a need to jump up and get some coffee or talk to some people or run out for a snack. We interrupt ourselves to run to new and interesting things. We find it difficult to concentrate because we are compulsively active. We often take on all kinds of trivial projects just to keep ourselves busy. During a fast, we are much more likely to stay with the task at hand. We do not have the energy to rush our work or to run around trying to do a half a dozen things at once.

Because we don't have energy to waste, it is easier to stay in the present and focus on what we are doing. Our tendency to dwell on the

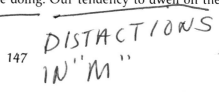
DISTACTIONS
IN "M"

past and fantasize about the future is one of the most powerful allies of the *nafs*. We can't grow spiritually or psychologically if we are always thinking about the future or the past and are never in the present. After all, the past is unchangeable and the future has not yet come. The only time we can truly work on ourselves is in the present.

Fasting also strengthens the will. Each time we feel thirsty or hungry, we exert our will and refuse to satisfy the impulse to eat or drink. In our everyday life, how often do we exert our will to achieve something spiritual instead of giving in to what feels most pleasant and comfortable? We are regularly controlled by the *nafs* without even noticing it. Fasting is a way of nurturing our souls instead of nurturing our senses or desires.

Fasting encourages remembrance of God. Each time we refuse to eat or drink during the day, we have the opportunity to remember God and to say, "I will not eat or drink now, for God's sake." In addition, fasting disrupts the habit patterns that make us unconscious. During Ramadhan, we get up and eat breakfast before dawn and dinner after sunset. We tend to stay up later and sleep less. Our whole daily rhythm and routine are altered.

Fasting teaches us that we don't have to be slaves of our habits. One of the hardest things for me in the early years of fasting during Ramadhan was missing lunch. I did not miss eating as much as the break in my work day and the lunch meetings I enjoyed. I saw how attached I was to the habit of taking long lunch breaks and socializing in the middle of my workday.

According to the Sufis, there are three major levels of fasting. The first is the fast of ordinary people, which is simply to refrain from eating, drinking, and sexual activity during the day. This simple, straightforward practice requires willpower and commitment.

The second is the fast of the dervishes, which is to watch what comes out of our mouths as well as what goes into them. This includes refraining from speech or action that might harm others. This requires far more will, awareness, and discipline than the first level. It is also a practice we can keep up throughout the year.

If I can discipline myself from eating, I can also discipline myself from getting angry. While I refrain from drinking, I can also refrain from acting in ways that cause pain to others. I can abstain from making love to my wife during the day, and I can also abstain from staring at attractive women and fantasizing about them. I can discipline myself to watch my eyes, my tongue, and my behavior. It is also another way to become more independent of the influences of our culture, which constantly bombards us with alluring advertisements and programs featuring food, drink, and sex.

The third level of fasting is that of the saints. At this level, fasting means to refuse to become occupied with worldly thoughts and to remember God constantly. The saints fast from any and all attachments to this world; from the false notion that anything in this world is independent or separate from God.

> Once, two famous religious scholars went to visit a well-known Sufi saint. They wanted to test this woman in order to see if she was a genuine saint, so they decided to quiz her on religious law. This was the field in which both scholars had attained international renown, and they were convinced that any attainment in Sufism had to be built on a solid foundation in conventional religious practice.
>
> Finally, the scholars found the saint in her isolated cottage in the woods. They asked her if she knew the laws of ablution; that is, when individuals were required to ritually cleanse themselves in order to be fit for prayers and other forms of worship. The saint answered, "Do you mean the laws of ablution for you or for me?" The scholars were taken by surprise. They had never heard that there was more than one set of laws.
>
> The saint went on, "The laws for you are that you must take ablution whenever you go to the bathroom, if you bleed more than four drops of blood . . ." She systematically enumerated all the detailed rules regarding ritual ablution. Then the scholars asked her what she meant about the laws concerning ablution for her and she answered, "For me, I have to take ablution whenever I forget God."

Retreat

One of the forty main Sufi orders is the eight-hundred-year-old Halveti Order. Halvet, or *Khalwat* in Arabic, means "retreat." In the past, one of the main spiritual practices of Sufism was that of spiritual retreat. The classic retreat lasts for forty days, following the example of Moses on Mount Sinai.

Retreat is a part of every religious tradition. All the great prophets and messengers of God had their times of retreat from the distractions of the world. They often went on retreat just before they began spreading God's message. The Buddha sitting under the Bo tree is one example, as is Moses meeting God in the midst of the desert and later going up Mount Sinai to receive the teachings of the Torah. Muhammad was on retreat in a cave on Mount Hira when the first lines of the Koran were revealed to him. The desert fathers of early Christianity made retreat their major spiritual practice. Native Americans practice the vision quest.

Retreat is a time to practice remembrance of the divine. Dervishes on retreat normally remain in silence and see no one.

> A day of Silence
> Can be a pilgrimage in itself.
>
> A day of Silence
> Can help you listen
> To the Soul play
> Its marvelous lute and drum.
>
> Is not most talking
> A crazed defense of a crumbling fort?
>
> I thought we came here
> To surrender in Silence,
>
> To yield to Light and Happiness,
>
> To Dance within
> In celebration of Love's Victory![3]

In my own order, our founder taught that dervishes on retreat were not to occupy their days with reading or complex spiritual practices.

They were not to *do* anything. Instead they were to seek deeper aware-ness of God's presence. They were basically to remain in God's presence for forty days. This is *not* an easy practice.

One danger of a practice like this is the tendency to become proud as a result of it. It is such a dramatic practice, and it is so easy to say, at least inwardly, "Well, *I* have been on a forty-day retreat. What have *you* been doing?"

The practice of retreat mirrors themes of the heroic journey found in the myth and folklore of every culture. This journey has three major parts: First is leaving home—the known, the habitual, the worldly.

Second comes entrance into the unknown, often a world of mys-tery, power, and challenge, of dramatically different experiences. We can see this in the Knights of the Round Table setting out on their quest for the grail, in the practice of pilgrimage, and in other life-changing jour-neys.

The third stage is the return home. In many ways, this is the most important part of the journey. It is about what we have learned, how we have changed, and what we bring back with us. If the retreat merely con-sists of powerful but unintegrated spiritual experiences, it is like watch-ing an interesting movie. After the film is over, we are no different than we were before, no matter how thrilling the special effects. The whole purpose of the retreat is to deepen our consciousness and awareness in the context of our everyday lives.

Adab

There is really no good English translation for *adab*. It means behaving well or good etiquette. It is acting with heedfulness, beauty, refinement, graciousness, and respect for others. The Koran teaches us the importance of acting beautifully. "Do what is beautiful. God loves those who do what is beautiful." (2:195)

You can see beautiful *adab* in how a dervish serves or receives a cup of tea. You can learn to serve tea graciously if you are trained in the right charm school, and it would look just lovely on the outside. However, what is most important is the inner sense of genuine respect and service. Without this, service is merely lifeless form. One sheikh has pointed out that outer service without inner respect is like the corpse of a gorgeous movie star; it may look beautiful at first glance, but it is dead. The heart has to be there. Beautiful behavior must be rooted in inner beauty. The Prophet Muhammad indicated the crucial importance of *adab* when he said, "I was sent to this world to teach *adab*." A common Sufi saying is, "All of Sufism is *adab*."

If you serve a cup of tea with a real sense of caring and appreciation for the opportunity to serve, your actions will reflect this inner attitude and it will naturally be good *adab*. Our inner feelings are inevitably revealed in how we act.

When you receive a cup of tea, if you are genuinely grateful to be served, then you will also be demonstrating good *adab*. As guests, many of us receive food or drink as if it were owed to us. We think, "Fill up my cup. And make sure it is good tea, too!" Instead, we might reflect, "I have done nothing to deserve this tea. How kind and caring it is for someone to have taken the trouble to brew the tea and to bring it to me. How grateful I am for this wonderful service."

The quality of *adab* often becomes truly exquisite when you see one dervish serving another. Tears have come to my eyes when I have seen such caring and conscious interactions among the old Turkish dervishes. When Sheikh Muzaffer still smoked cigarettes (he later stopped on doctor's orders), the dervishes rushed to light his cigarettes. In general, all the dervishes lit each others' cigarettes, poured each other tea, and served each other in whatever ways they could. It was, of course, a special privilege to light the sheikh's cigarette. Some American dervishes, who understood only the outer form of *adab*, would rush to light Sheikh Muzaffer's cigarette, literally elbowing others out of the way so *they* could be the ones to serve him. Sometimes it looked like a football scrimmage or basketball players fighting for a rebound.

When I was sitting close to Sheikh Muzaffer along with the older dervishes, even if I was a little late in getting out my lighter, they would inevitably allow me to light his cigarette. The older dervishes would almost always notice his need for a light before I did, because they were more heedful and conscious. The important thing was that the sheikh was served. In addition, if anyone else was ready to serve him, out of *adab*, they graciously allowed others the privilege of serving.

I still remember clearly my visits to Sheikh Muzaffer when he visited New York years ago. He traveled to America twice a year with a large group of Turkish dervishes, who assisted in the remembrance ceremony and who also gave concerts of Sufi music. Sheikh Muzaffer stayed in a lovely large house that was always filled with dervishes and guests.

One year I came out with a young man who wanted to become a dervish. Sheikh Muzaffer initiated him, and we visited the sheikh the next day and stayed for lunch. There were thirty or forty people there. As everybody got up to leave the dining room, I suggested to the young man that we wait and let everybody else go before us. After all, he was the newest dervish there and it would only be proper for him to let his seniors go first.

Everybody else filed out of the room. Most did not even notice we were waiting for them to go first. Finally, the only one left beside us was Kemal-baba, the second senior dervish in our order. He was a wonderful, sweet man who always exhibited the finest *adab*. He spoke rarely, but when he did speak, it was always short and very much to the point. Kemal-baba told us to precede him. I wanted nothing more than to show him respect and let him go before us, but he wouldn't let me. He insisted on being the last one out of the room, when he should have been the second or third to leave. It was a powerful message, one that I experienced over and over again. The older dervishes would constantly serve us better than we could possibly serve them, even though it should have been the other way around. They were wonderful models of *adab*—humility, awareness, graciousness, and service.

At another lunch at Sheikh Muzaffer's house, I noticed that one table of young men and women was not being served. The servers, who were all new to Sufism, concentrated on serving the sheikh's table and the senior dervishes. The young people were ignored. Without saying anything, Sheikh Safer, who was then the senior dervish in the order, quietly moved from his place among the older dervishes and sat at the young people's table. Immediately, the servers rushed to serve him and the other people at his table. This is one of the ideal ways to teach *adab*, by example rather than lecture.

Meal time is an excellent opportunity for practicing good *adab*. Among the dervishes, I have found myself served better than in the finest restaurants, because everyone around me is more concerned with serving their neighbors than with putting food on their own plates. Whenever anyone finished a glass of water, a neighboring dervish noticed and refilled the glass. Whenever anyone finished a piece of bread, a nearby dervish offered the breadbasket. Whenever someone finished eating their salad, a dervish passed the salad bowl. I learned to do this as well, and I found that I could pay attention to my neighbors' needs and still always have my own plate filled by neighbors who were paying attention to what I needed.

The profound humility of the great Sufis can be deeply transformative. Someone once struck a Sufi saint with his walking stick and the stick broke. Next day, the saint brought the man who hit him a new stick and a bowl of honey, saying, "Because of me your stick broke and you suffered loss. Here is a new stick to replace your old one and some honey for you to eat." Can you imagine how the man must have felt after this?

The essence of good *adab* is captured by the following dialog. One dervish commented, "All my Sufi brothers and sisters are better than I."

"Why do you say that?" he was asked.

"They all consider me more worthy than themselves, and whoever rates me higher than him or herself is in fact better than I am!"

Service. To serve others with gratitude for the opportunity of service is good *adab*. A dervish seeks opportunities to serve, knowing that service is an essential part of the spiritual path.

Some years ago, an American dervish was visiting Turkey, and he spent all of his free time in Sheikh Muzaffer's bookstore. When a boy came to the shop with tea for everyone, the American dervish immediately pulled out his wallet and paid for it. At lunch time, he rushed to pay for the lunches brought to the store. As he reached for his wallet a third time to pay for soft drinks, Sheikh Muzaffer scolded him, "Do you want to take all the benefits of serving others today? Don't be selfish; give someone else a chance to pay!" Serving others is like serving God.

One of the children of Israel came to Moses and said, "Please tell God that I want to invite Him to dinner." Moses replied that God does not eat or come to dinner. But the next time he went up to Mount Sinai, God said, "Why didn't you give me my dinner invitation from my servant?" Moses said, "But my Lord, You don't eat." God replied, "Keep what you know between you and Me. Tell the man that I will come in answer to his invitation."

Moses came down from Mount Sinai and announced that God was coming to dinner after all. Of course, everyone prepared an incredible feast, including Moses. While they were all busy cooking, an old man suddenly showed up. He was hungry and he asked for something to eat. The busy cooks said, "No, no, we are waiting for God. When God comes we will all eat. Now, why don't you make yourself useful and help fetch water from the well?" The appointed hour for the feast came, but God did not appear. Moses was terribly embarrassed.

The next day he went up to Mount Sinai and said, "God, what are You doing to me? I'm trying to convince everybody that You exist. You said You would come to our feast and then You never showed up. Nobody is going to believe me any more!" God replied, "But I did come. If you had fed my hungry servant, you would have fed me."

God tells us, "I, who cannot be fitted into all the universes, fit into the heart of my believing servant." When we serve one of God's servants, we serve God. Of course, not all of us are fit to be called God's servants, but the general principle is that when you serve the created, you serve the Creator. Sincere intention gives meaning to our service.

Once there was a devout woodcutter who lived in the woods near a primitive tribe who worshiped a giant tree that grew in the middle of their village. One day the woodcutter decided to cut down their tree. He wanted to show them that what they worshiped was nothing but a part of God's creation and that they needed to worship God rather than a tree.

As he walked through the forest, a man stepped in front of him and asked him where he was going. "For God's sake, I am going to cut down the tree that is worshiped by the tribe who lives in the forest."

"That would be a mistake," warned the man.

"Who are you to tell me what to do?" asked the wood-

cutter.

"I am the Devil and I will not let you cut down the tree."

The woodcutter became angry. He grabbed the Devil, threw him to the ground, and put his ax to the Devil's throat.

The Devil said, "You are being very unreasonable. The tribe will never let you cut down their holy tree. If you take even one swing at it, they will probably kill you. Your wife will be a widow and your children orphans. Besides, even if you managed to cut down the tree and escape with your life, they will simply choose another tree to worship. Be reasonable."

The Devil often talks with the voice of logic and reason. We have each heard an inner voice, persuasively arguing against our doing good or doing what we know to be right. There is something within us that can always find reasons to do what is easy rather than what is right.

The Devil went on, "I will make a bargain with you. I know that you are a poor but devout man with a large family, and that you like to help others. Every morning I will put under your bed two gold coins. Instead of getting yourself killed and accomplishing nothing, you will get two gold coins every day. You can spend the money on your family's needs and also help the poor."

The woodcutter agreed. The next morning he found two brand new gold coins under his bed. He bought food and new clothing for his family and he distributed the remainder to the poor. The next morning, the woodcutter found nothing. He searched all over the bedroom but found no gold coins.

Furious at the Devil's treachery, the woodcutter took up his ax and set off to chop down the tree. Again, the Devil stepped into his path, smiling, and asked, "Where do you think you are going?"

"Cheat, liar! I'm going to chop down that tree!"

The Devil tapped the woodcutter on the chest with one finger. The woodcutter fell to the ground, senseless with the force of the blow. Then the Devil put his finger on the woodcutter's chest and pinned him to the ground. The Devil said, "Do you

*want me to kill you? Two days ago you were going to kill me.
Promise not to touch that tree."*

*The woodcutter replied, "I promise not to harm the tree.
Just tell me just one thing. Two days ago I defeated you easily.
Where did you get this tremendous power today?"*

*The Devil smiled again. "The other day you were going
to cut down that tree for God's sake. Today you were fighting
with me for the sake of two gold pieces!"*

The woodcutter's sincerity was only a temporary state and was
easily disrupted by the Devil. How many times have we fooled ourselves
into thinking we were acting with perfect sincerity, when in fact our
motivations were not quite so pure?

Brotherhood and sisterhood. The sheikh is like the head of a
family, and the other dervishes are our brothers and sisters. Relationships
among dervishes can have a great influence on their spiritual progress.
Sometimes we can learn a lot from our siblings. Rumi emphasizes the
transformative effects of spiritual companionship:

> Acts of spiritual combat are of many kinds, the greatest of
> which is mixing with companions who have turned their
> faces toward God and their backs toward this world. No act
> of spiritual combat is more difficult than to sit with sound
> companions, for the very sight of them wastes away the
> ego and annihilates it.[4]

According to the Sufi sage al-Ghazzali, real friendship includes
the following eight responsibilities:[5]

1. MATERIAL AID. Help your companions with food, money, or
other needs. One of the great goals of Sufism is to develop generosity. Ibn
Arabi writes, "Spend from what God has given you. Do not fear poverty.
No one who has been generous has ever died in destitution."

Al-Ghazzali distinguishes three degrees of sharing among
dervishes. The lowest degree is to treat other dervishes the way you
would treat servants; that is, to handle their needs out of your surplus.
The second degree is to place other dervishes on the same level as yourself. You treat them as partners in your property, to the point of sharing

equally whatever you have. The third degree is to prefer the others to yourself and set their needs before your own.

As you read over the above descriptions of generosity, pay close attention to the objections of your *nafs*. An inner voice may say, "How could you possibly be so absurdly generous," or "This kind of teaching certainly isn't meant for today's modern society!" I'm sure that for centuries the *nafs* of the dervishes have made the same objections.

2. PERSONAL SUPPORT. "If they are sick, visit them; if they are busy, help them; if they have forgotten, remind them."[6] Generosity includes emotional support as well as material help. To be a dervish is to have a safety net, which includes the security of the traditions of one's order and the support of one's dervish community.

According to an old Sufi saying, if one dervish has a stomachache, all the other dervishes feel pain in their stomachs. The opposite is also true. One great sheikh said, "If I feed a piece of food to another dervish, I find the taste of it in my own throat."

3. RESPECT. Do not complain of another's faults, either to them or to others. Do not give advice when you know it cannot be acted upon. It is often a challenge to go beyond others' faults and to see and respect the divine within them. The more we can do this, the more we lead each other along the path to God.

4. PRAISE AND ATTENTION. Praise the good qualities of your companions and let them know that you care for them. We all need the strengthening power of praise and attention. The path is long and it is easy to become disheartened. The warmth of companionship among the dervishes goes back to the beginning of Sufism.

> One day a prince was out hunting and he saw two men greet each other warmly, then sit down and share a meal. The prince was struck by the affection these men showed, so he called to one of them and asked who his friend was. The man replied, "I don't know." The prince was astounded. "Then why do you feel such affection for each other?" he asked.
>
> The man replied, "We follow the same Path."
>
> The prince said, "Let me build you a place where you can meet together," and he did. This was the first Sufi lodge.

5. FORGIVENESS. Forgive others for their failings. It is said that if we forgive others God will forgive us. It is much easier to overcome our failings in the atmosphere of a forgiving community.

6. PRAYER. Pray for the well-being of your companions with the same fervor as you pray for your own. In learning to love each other, we learn to love God.

Mansur al Hallaj, a Sufi saint, made the following prayer: "Forgive the people and do not forgive me. Have mercy on them and do not have mercy on me. I do not intercede with You for myself or beseech You for what is due to me. Do with me what You will."

7. LOYALTY. Be firm in your friendships so that you can be depended upon by those who put their trust in you. Loyalty is easy in the first flush of enthusiasm for the path. It is a real achievement to maintain loyalty and friendship when we begin to see each others' faults.

8. RELIEF FROM DISCOMFORT. Do not create awkward or difficult situations that involve your companions. Do not be a burden to others. We all need to learn to stop thinking only of ourselves, to think of others' needs and circumstances, and even to put their needs before our own. If everyone does this, a marvelous, incredibly sensitive and supportive group atmosphere develops.

Sufis are extremely scrupulous in observing the rights of others. This brings about an atmosphere of love and trust among the dervishes.

> *Ali, the son-in-law of the Prophet, was walking with a group of companions on a hot day. As they passed the orchard of one of his close friends, one of his companions suggested that they sit for a while in the shade of the trees. "I cannot," said Ali. "You see, my friend has borrowed some money from me and I don't want him to think that I feel I have the right to shade from his orchard because he owes me money."*

A sheikh explained the importance of brotherhood and sisterhood as follows:

> If you wish to draw near to God, you must seek God in the hearts of others. You should speak well of all, whether pre-

sent or absent. If you seek to be a light to guide others, then, like the sun, you must show the same face to all. To bring joy to a single heart is better than to build many shrines for worship, and to enslave one soul by kindness is worth more than the setting free of a thousand slaves.[7]

A man said to Junaid, "True companions are scarce these days. Where am I to find a companion in God?" Junaid replied, "If you want a companion to provide for you and to bear your burdens, such are few and far between. However, if you want a companion in God whose burden you will carry and whose pain you will bear, then I have a multitude I can introduce you to."[8]

Remembrance of God

One of the great Sufi practices is that of remembrance. The full name of this practice is Remembrance of God. We can see the importance of remembrance in the Prophetic saying, "The People of Paradise will regret but one thing alone: the hour that passed them by in which they made no remembrance of God."

Remembrance has four basic meanings.[9] First, it is an act of constantly striving to be mindful of God. In this sense, it is the opposite of heedlessness. Prayer is also remembrance. When we pray, we are invited into God's presence. We try to keep our mind focused on the prayer and to feel God's presence.

Second, remembrance is the repetition or invocation of a mystical formula or divine name. The practice of invocation requires instruction and authorization or initiation into the practice, as well as sincerity of intention, awareness, and concentration. This is the remembrance of the tongue.

Third, remembrance means a temporary, inner state (*hal*) in which awareness of God and fear of displeasing God overwhelm us. We become completely divorced of all concerns for the world, at least for the moment. This is the remembrance of the heart.[10]

Fourth, remembrance is a stable inner station (*maqam*) in which invocation and mindfulness have become constant. We have attained the state of constant inner prayer. This is the remembrance of the soul.[11] In the words of one Sufi saint, "Before this there was one heart but a thousand thoughts./Now all is reduced to: There is no god but God."

The dervishes of my order meet weekly to perform the remembrance ceremony together. In this ceremony we invoke God by singing devotional Sufi music and by repetition of God's Names. There are ninety-nine names of God revealed in the Koran. These are also called divine attributes, and they include Merciful, Eternal, Ever Living, Peace, Strength, Glory, and Power. Each Sufi order has been given, through dreams and visions, the right to use some of these names. As we call on God's attributes, we also remember the divine within us.

In the remembrance ceremony, we seek unity of breath, sound, and movement. Unity among the dervishes can bring us closer to God, who *is* Unity. Ideally, we move as if there were only one dervish moving, chant as if one dervish were chanting, and breathe as if just one dervish were breathing. The ceremony is designed to carry us away from our usual concerns with daily life, to transport us to another state in which we can feel God's presence in our own hearts.

Remembrance is a deepening process. It descends from the tongue to the heart, and from the heart to the soul. In Arabic, the term *dhikr* means both "repetition" and "remembrance." The remembrance of the tongue is the beginning and is often just mechanical repetition. As the meaning and power of the words begin to sink in, our hearts are filled with joy, longing for God and other spiritual feelings. This is the remembrance of the heart. Our longing for God is also a sign of God's presence within us. As this longing, it becomes the remembrance of the soul. The founder of the Halveti-Jerrahi Order said that real remembrance is to never ever forget God for even an instant. According to an old Sufi saying, "At first, you act as if you're doing the *dhikr*. Then you do the *dhikr*. Finally the *dhikr* does you."

Sheikh Muzaffer taught that the remembrance ceremony recapitulates creation:[12]

> The remembrance ceremony is symbolic of the very creation of the universe. The beginning of creation was light, which God created from Divine Light. . . . This first aspect of creation contains the total knowledge and total mind found in creation, and so we first recite in the remem-

brance ceremony the prayers celebrating the birth and the life of the Prophet Muhammad.

God created Adam and blew Adam's soul into his body, and so within the individual soul is hidden a spark of the universal, divine soul, the secret of secrets. God activated Adam's heart to beat, and it beat in rhythm with creation, and then God gave Adam a voice, and Adam sang aloud the praises of God and God's creation.

This is the essence of all music and it is this essence that the sacred music of Sufism still retains. . . .

The sheikh also explained:

The hymns we sing contain all the secrets of the universe. The music is the joy of the soul who has heard the voice of God in the universe of the souls. It is the confirmation of the souls who will come and the souls who have come to the universe.

The reason we are so touched by music is that it helps us remember our connection with our origins and our time in the Universe of Souls.

The traditional Halveti-Jerrahi ceremony of remembrance opens with the dervishes bowing to the sheikh. The sheikh and the dervishes kneel in a circle, on sheepskins, and bowing, they kiss the floor. The sheikh then chants the traditional opening invocation.

Sitting in the circle, the symbol of unity, the dervishes join the sheikh in chanting the opening invocation. They take refuge in God's compassion and mercy, pray for the Prophet's intercession, and express dedication and salutations to Hazreti Muhammad. Then the dervishes make a declaration of intention, a vow to leave the limited self.

The first action in creation was the remembrance of that first light. The light pulsated, saying, "La ilaha ilallah," ("There is no god but God"). This is the first of the holy phrases we recite in the remembrance ceremony. The dervishes begin to chant in unison, *"La ilaha ilallah."* . . .

The *dhikr* momentarily stops at this point. The dervishes sit motionless as they listen to the chanting of the Koran or to a hymn glorifying Hazreti Muhammad. The Word of God, the Holy Koran, came into being after the Light. The Koran is both the first word of God and also the last revealed of the great scriptures.

Before the creation of the physical universe, God created the Universe of Souls. . . . [T]hen bodies were created, and then the souls entered the bodies. When they found themselves embodied, they started calling upon God, with the recitation, "Allah, Allah, Allah."

The next recitation is the divine attribute *Hu*. In Arabic this means "He" or "Thou." It represents God without any attributes. The repetition of this name means, "There is only You; there is only You; only You, only You." Every human breath repeats this name. All creation vibrates with this name, and every atom performs this remembrance.

Next, everything in creation materialized, and the dervishes stand up. As all bodies separated from each other when the total divine soul entered into them, we get up and hold hands. This symbolizes the unity of the multiplicity in creation.

With the joy of that unity of the individual with the divine, the dervishes start swinging and begin turning. As everything turns around its axis in the whole universe, we start turning also.

The dervishes form a circle, hand in hand, a sign of having lost our individual identities. The circle slowly begins revolving clockwise, moving . . . in the direction of our hearts, symbolizing the placing of God into the heart. We chant divine names to the accompaniment of the beat of the drum and the background chanting of traditional hymns and poems. . . .

The Divine Name *Hayy*, The Ever Living, is

chanted next. The circle of dervishes revolves around the sheikh. . . . At the end of the *dhikr*, the dervishes join in sounding once again the name *Hu*, signifying that we desire nothing but God, only God.

In general, the remembrance ceremony symbolizes the movement from the immaterial to the material, and from material existence back to the immaterial. The breath is an important part of the remembrance. . . .

When the dervishes recite *"La ilaha illallah,"* we turn our heads from right to left. *La* is negation. We turn to the right saying, "There is nothing" to the environment, to the world around us. We turn our heads down and to the left as we recite *"illallah"* ("but God"). . . .

First we clean, by saying *La*, negation, "There is nothing." We throw everything away. . . . The negation of all existence, which is symbolized by *la ilaha* on the right, is the cleansing of the heart. Then, by saying *ilallah*, we are putting God in His house, because God, Who doesn't fit in all the universes and the heavens and earth, is housed in the human heart. . . .

All of creation, whether living or seemingly unliving, is calling upon God. . . . When we chant the Name *Hayy*, the Ever Living, we refer to those things in creation that are visibly alive. Then *Hayy* becomes a rhythmic breath, symbolizing those things that are alive yet beyond our senses. The inhalation is matter becoming essence, and the exhalation is the Ever Living. Even those who deny God, who even curse their Creator, by the very act of their breathing, however, are still calling upon God.

A dervish was a guest at NASA, and they demonstrated for him instruments that could record the sounds of subatomic particles. The electrons in an atom whirl around the nucleus several hundred thousand times a second. They spin like the dervishes turn in the remembrance, and they also make a sound. When they whirl, they say, *"Hu."* ("Thou"). In the same way the earth turns and also whirls around the sun, and the earth too says, *"Hu."* Everything in the universe calls out to God, each in its own way. The ones whose ears are open can hear these sounds.

> Adam was the first Sufi.[13] Allah taught Adam all the
> Names. In the *dhikr* we are painting the image of the beau-
> tiful Names of God and tracing the Creation of the
> Universe, its development, its breakdown and destruction,
> and finally its joy.
> The music of the *dhikr* is symbolic of the sound
> of the Creation. It is the sound of the falling of the leaves
> in the Garden of Eden.

> *Years ago one of the sheikhs of Istanbul sent his dervish-*
> *es out to gather flowers for their lodge. They all returned with*
> *large bouquets, except for one dervish who brought back only a*
> *single withered flower. When asked why he didn't bring back*
> *any beautiful blossoms, he answered, "I found all the flowers*
> *busy remembering the Lord. How could I stop their constant*
> *prayer? I kept looking and finally one flower finished its recol-*
> *lection, and this is the one I brought." This dervish became the*
> *next sheikh.*

The dervishes have been turning and chanting "*Hu*" for a thousand years. Only now, in the second half of the twentieth century, have
we developed subatomic physics, and we realize that electrons and other
subatomic particles turn, as do planets, solar systems, and whole galaxies,
around a center. In traditional Sufi movements there is an exchange of
energy. We generally think that our actions use up energy, but in spiritual activities like this, we actually recharge our spiritual energies.

The practice of the "whirling dervishes" is called the *sema*, and
the movements are actually referred to as "turning." Turning is a formal
ceremony in the Mevlevi Order, which was founded seven hundred years
ago by Jelaladdin Rumi, the great Sufi poet and sage. His son, Sultan
Veled, created the ceremony based on the spontaneous movements of his
father and the first Mevlevi dervishes. Music as well as movement is an
essential part of the ceremony. There are other orders that also use the
sema as a formal practice.

> *The first one to turn was Hazreti Abu Bakr, the first*

Caliph of Islam. When the Prophet asked all of his followers to give whatever they could for the good of their religion and community, Abu Bakr gave all he owned. He and his wife kept only one long cloth between them, so that one of them at a time could go outside to shop or handle business obligations. As a result, Abu Bakr was not able to go to the mosque for prayers.

One morning before dawn, the Prophet sent someone to summon Abu Bakr to prayers. His wife had taken their one cloth and so Abu Bakr hid himself so that his visitor would not see his nakedness. When he was told that the Prophet had personally summoned him to prayer, Abu Bakr knew he had no choice. He grabbed some leaves and wove them into a skirt to cover himself.

While the Prophet waited in the mosque he saw the angel Gabriel dressed in a very peculiar costume made entirely of leaves. He asked Gabriel why he was dressed so strangely and Gabriel replied, "God has ordered all the angels in heaven to dress this way in honor of Abu Bakr." Then he told Muhammad the whole story. When the Prophet saw Abu Bakr, he exclaimed, "God is pleased with you, are you pleased with God?" Abu Bakr was so thrilled with this wonderful news that he went into a state of ecstasy and began turning and spinning.

I am happy even before I have a reason.

I am full of Light even before the sky
Can greet the sun or the moon.

Dear companions,
We have been in love with God
For so very, very long.

What can Hafiz now do but Forever
Dance?[14]

The practice of remembrance today reflects the love of God and the joy of feeling God's presence. Lovers of God have all felt that God was pleased with them; they were transported with joy or ecstasy. Each form of the remembrance ceremony was developed by a different saint from that saint's deep sense of God's presence. Dervishes who have not yet reached this spiritual state practice in order to develop this feeling in themselves. Some of the dervishes turn or move spontaneously; some call or cry out to God. Although the ceremony begins with a strict form, at a certain point, there is no form, no control.

In the Halveti-Jerrahi remembrance ceremony, we try to stay aware of each other and to keep our attention focused on the sheikh. We attempt to remain grounded and centered in the present moment. Paradoxically, we make an intention to enter into a state of ecstatic closeness to God, yet we have to be "taken" by the practice of remembrance, in spite of our efforts to remain grounded. The purpose of the ceremony is to leave our bodies, to leave what is material. Then all kinds of seemingly miraculous things are possible, such as piercing the body with needles or holding hot coals.

In contact sports we see something similar. In the middle of a game we may get hit or kicked and not even feel it: we lose ourselves in the action. But once the game is over, we become aware of all kinds of bruises and aches. In a far deeper sense, those who lose themselves in God cannot feel their bodies. In real Remembrance of God, we are transported to God's presence, and we completely leave our everyday state of consciousness.

All orders do only two basic kinds of remembrance ceremony—sitting or standing. The basic form of sitting *dhikr* is always the same. The dervishes form a circle around the sheikh. Some orders do only a sitting *dhikr*, some do both sitting and standing.

When we turn in a circle we begin by moving to the left. That is because the heart is on the left side. It is said that the angels turn toward the left and circle the throne of God.

When we sing and chant, the pitch is gradually raised and then lowered. This is called raising the veil. We raise the veils one by one, so that what is between us and God is removed. The ideal is to attain the state of constant remembrance. The poet Kabir wrote, "The breath that does not repeat the name of God is wasted."

It is said that the Prophet also turned out of a spontaneous sense of spiritual joy.

> *Kaab was one of the great Arab poets at the time of the Prophet. He was jealous of the beautiful poetry of the Koran, and he disliked the teachings of Islam. He still worshiped the idols his family had always worshiped. Kaab was famous throughout Arabia in a culture that placed great value on poetry and literature.*
>
> *Kaab went to Medina to visit his brother, who had become a Muslim. His brother convinced Kaab to go to the mosque and just sit in the corner and hear Muhammad for himself. When Kaab heard the Prophet and his eyes met Muhammad's, Kaab was transported into an ecstatic state. He spontaneously recited an extremely beautiful poem on the spot. The poem was filled with Kaab's newfound love of God and God's Messenger.*
>
> *When the Prophet heard this poem, he stood up and began to turn. As he spun around, his cloak fell off his shoulders and onto Kaab. Later he insisted that Kaab keep the cloak.[15]*

The Prophet's right hand was turned palm up to heaven, and his left hand was turned palm down to earth. This symbolizes receiving inspiration and divine blessings with the right hand and the teaching and spreading of these blessings with the left hand. This is the same hand position that the Mevlevi dervishes use today. Then dervishes take what they receive from God and give it to others.

Every person has these two qualities of receiving and giving, of being both a student and a teacher. A dervish is always a student, always open to learning and growing. In addition, dervishes should be willing to pass on what they learn. The right hand symbolizes the student and the left hand symbolizes the teacher. Both studying and teaching work only with love. To study deeply, you have to love your subject. To teach or to do anything else in the world, you will be successful to the extent that you love what you do.

All prophets were students when they were learning from God. They became teachers when they spread God's truths to others. The same is true of us. We have to learn and then teach others what we've learned. Many people do not teach in a formal or conscious way, but rather by example. Those who learn and live by what they learn are teachers in this way.

Recollection of Death

When the Prophet knew that he was nearing the end of his life, he confided in his closest disciples. They were extremely upset; many felt that they could not get along without his guidance and example. The Prophet consoled them, saying, "I will leave two teachers behind. One is a speaking teacher and the other is silent." The disciples began to speculate about the identity of these teachers, and then the Prophet added, "The speaking teacher is the Koran and the silent teacher is death."

Contemplating death can be a powerful tool in releasing us from old habits and attitudes. Thinking about our death is an exercise in becoming more aware of the present, and it is one way of beginning the process of personal growth.

> Some years ago, two patients were scheduled for surgery in a major hospital in Istanbul. One was a young man with appendicitis and the other was an old man with cancer. The same surgeon operated on both. The appendix operation was extremely simple and was over quickly. When the doctor opened up the man with cancer, he saw that the cancer had spread so much it was inoperable. He simply closed up the incision.
>
> The doctor commented that the young man probably had many more years to live, but that the old man would not last very long at all. That night, the young man died, and within a few days, the old man left the hospital. Months later, he returned, bringing the doctor fresh fruits and vegetables from his garden, apparently in good health.

We don't know how much time we have. We may think that we are strong and healthy and have many years left, but we should always remember that death can come at any time. And even if we have a serious illness like cancer, we should remember that if God wills we may have many years to live.

We need to develop two important attitudes toward death. One is that death is inevitable. If we remember that, we will live more consciously and responsibly. The second attitude is to remember that we don't know *when* our time will come. It might be in the next moment or many years from now, but we don't know and we have no guarantees.

When Sheikh Muzaffer was visiting New York, a young woman said to him, "I feel so inspired whenever you and the Turkish dervishes are visiting, and I know at these times that God is real and that our prayers and spiritual work are the most important things in our lives. But after you leave, the world slowly comes back, and all that you have taught begins to seem unreal. How can I maintain my love of God and keep the world from distracting me when you are gone?"

Sheikh Muzaffer laughed and said, "I'm glad you didn't ask me something difficult! The cure for your attachment to the world is to remember death. Once a man came to Abu Darda, one of the most spiritually advanced companions of the Prophet, and asked him a similar question. Abu Darda told the man to visit those who are on their death beds in hospitals, to attend funerals, and to visit graveyards. You should do the same.

"When you visit the hospital, see yourself in that bed and remind yourself that one day you will get into bed and never get out again. When you attend a funeral, see yourself in the coffin and think that there will inevitably come a day in which the funeral service will be for you. When you visit the graveyard, imagine your own grave marker and know that your grave will be the final resting place of this body of yours."

Exercises: Basic Sufi Practices

Fasting

In Sufism, the traditional practice of fasting is to abstain from all food, drink, and sexual activity from dawn to sunset. Try this practice for one week. Every day, get up an hour before dawn for a prefast meal. Be sure to drink one or two cups of water or juice and also to have some protein. (I personally prefer cottage cheese or protein powder with juice.) This makes the fasting much easier.

When you have finished eating, at least fifteen minutes before dawn, brush your teeth and make intention to fast for the coming day, for God's sake. Whenever you are hungry or thirsty during the day, remind yourself that you are fasting for God's sake, that you have chosen this exercise in self-discipline not to lose weight or for any worldly reason, but to please God. Also, fasting brings us closer to the angels, who have no need of food.

At sundown, break your fast, if possible feed others or eat in the company of others. It is said that we are closest to God at the moment we take our first bite. Do not practice fasting without consulting a doctor if you suffer from low blood sugar or a similar physical condition. If you develop bad headaches or some other strong reaction to fasting, stop the fast or switch to a partial fast by drinking water or sweetened fruit juice during the day.

Retreat

You can perform a retreat at home, at the house of a vacationing friend, or even in a motel or hotel room. Unplug the telephone and the TV. Remove books, magazines, and other distractions. Close the curtains or cover the windows so that you can't see out. Cover the mirrors as well, so you won't become distracted by your reflection.

To begin the retreat, formally seal yourself in the room, visualizing that your energies and consciousness will remain contained and concentrated within your place of retreat. Say a prayer and formally state your spiritual intention for the retreat. At the end, unseal yourself by praying that your intentions have been realized and that you are able to carry into your daily life the blessings of the retreat.

Take a shower each morning, praying that God help you cleanse yourself within and without. Eat lightly or fast from dawn to sundown. Don't let your meals take up too much time and energy.

You can try a retreat for as little as twenty-four hours, but a minimum of three or four days is preferable. You can pray, sit still and contemplate your life, or meditate on some aspect of the divine. You can read scripture or the writings of a great saint, but don't let reading fill all your time; read for ten or fifteen minutes and then contemplate what you have read for at least thirty minutes to an hour.

The essential part of retreat is to become more and more quiet and still inside. Slow down and let your mind focus on God instead of being distracted by the sights and sounds of the world. In the words of one saint, "Let go and let God."

Prayer

Formal prayer is one of the fundamental practices of Sufism. The form of prayer we use today is virtually identical with the way the Prophet himself prayed. I have slightly simplified this complex practice but I have attempted to preserve its essential beauty and power.

Prayer has been called the *miraj* of the believer. The term *miraj* refers to the Prophet's most profound mystical experience, in which he traveled through the seven heavens and spoke directly to God. For us, formal prayer provides an opportunity to come into God's presence.

ABLUTION. Outer cleanliness is a requirement for prayer. For Sufis, the act of outer cleansing is a metaphor and also an aid to inner cleansing.

1.   Wash your hands three times.

2.   Rinse your mouth and your nose three times. (To rinse your nose, hold some water in your cupped palm, raise it to your nose and gently inhale, then exhale the water.)

3.   Wash your face three times.

4.   Wash your arms from wrist to elbow, three times.

5.   Wet your right hand and run it over the top of your head, from front to back, and then on the back of your neck, once.

6   With wet hands, gently clean in and around your ears, once.

7.   Wash your feet, up to your ankles, three times.

As you wash your hands, ask God to make your hands clean, pure instruments to serve God's creation. May your hands reach out only to take what is rightfully yours.

As you wash your mouth, pray that you will use your mouth for prayer and praise of God, and not for gossip or hurtful or untrue words.

As you rinse your nose, ask God to let you smell the heavenly perfume of Paradise.

While washing your face, pray that your face is always turned to God and that you look only to God for help and satisfaction.

In washing your arms, pray that your arms work only for God's pleasure, and not to injure anyone or for any evil ends.

In wiping your head, thank God for crowning your head with faith. In wetting the neck and ears, pray that God lets your ears hear only words of truth, and that God does not set on your neck the yoke of sin and rebelliousness.

While washing your feet, ask God to set your feet firmly and constantly on the path of truth. Pray that your feet never stray from the path that leads to God and pleases God.

The steps of prayer. You can pray in any clean place, except a graveyard or a bathroom. Face northeast, the shortest direction toward Mecca from most parts of the US. A prayer carpet (a clean carpet or cloth on which no one has walked with shoes) or a clean towel should be used. Men must be covered from navel to knee, and women from neck to ankles and wrists. Your clothing should be clean. Shoes may not be worn.

1. INTENTION. Making intention is one of the basic requirements of prayer. Before beginning prayer, say silently, "I intend to perform two *rakats* (sets) of morning (or evening) prayer, for the pleasure of Allah."

2. STANDING. Begin by standing, prayer carpet in front of you, facing northeast. Raise your hands up to your ears, palms forward. Say, *"Allahu ekbar"* ("God is Great"). Next, place your hands, right over left holding the left wrist, just below your navel (for men), or chest height (for women). Repeat three times, "Allah, Allah, Allah," or if you prefer, "God, God, God." (Traditionally you would recite the sura *Fatiha*, the opening chapter of the Koran, plus another sura or other verses from the Koran. However, Sheikh Muzaffer taught that those who are just beginning prayer, who have not memorized any of the Koran, can stay with the essence of prayer, which is remembering and calling upon God.)

3. STANDING BOW. Bend at the waist and place your palms on your knees, fingers spread. Try and keep your back parallel to the

ground. Look down and slightly ahead. Again recite three times, "Allah, Allah, Allah."

4.   STAND UP. Place your arms at your sides.

5.   KNEELING BOW. Place your arms on your knees and slowly and easily lower yourself to a kneeling position, then bow, touching your forehead to the ground, hands on the ground on each side of your head. Recite three times, "Allah, Allah, Allah."

6.   KNEELING. Sit up, resting on your knees.

7.   SECOND KNEELING BOW. Repeat step 5.

8.   SECOND KNEELING. As in 6. (This completes one *rakat*, or set, of prayer. For the next set, repeat steps 2–8.)

9.   FINAL KNEELING. At the end of the last set (two sets for morning, three sets for evening), remain kneeling and recite a final time, "Allah, Allah, Allah."

10. PERSONAL PRAYERS. Remain kneeling, or if that is too uncomfortable, sit cross-legged or in a chair. Hold your hands palms up and ask God for whatever help or support you need—for yourself, for friends or loved ones or for the world. You can pray for peace, for the alleviation of suffering, for health, strength, or patience. Pray with the words of your heart. God knows what is in our hearts, but it is important for us to ask.

Prayer practice. Perform this practice for one month, two prayers a day, morning and evening. The morning prayer can be carried out from twenty to forty-five minutes before sunrise. (Check your local paper for times.) The time for evening prayer begins just after the sun has set below the horizon.

Make a firm and clear intention that you will do this every day for a month. It may become difficult some days, and all kinds of excuses may come to mind, but there is great value in setting this goal and sticking to it.

Remembrance

La ilaha ilallah. To remember implies recalling what we already know. Sufis believe that there is a spark of the divine spirit in each of us, and that this spark always was and always will be a part of God. To practice remembrance is to unveil the knowledge and power and beauty of this spark of God within us. Christian mystic Meister Eckehart writes, "The seed of God is in us. . . . Now the seed of a pear tree grows into a pear tree, a hazel seed into a hazel tree, the seed of God into God." Through remembrance of God, we can grow this divine seed within us.

One classic practice of remembrance consists of the repetition of the phrase of unity, *la ilaha illallah*, "There are no gods but God." This phrase literally means, "No gods, there is God." It has also been interpreted to mean that there is nothing worthy of worship but God. Our worship of money, fame, power, sex, and so on, is really idol worship. That is, we have confused limited aspects of God's creation with God. All our sustenance, all good that comes to us, all our power to act—comes from God and not from the world.

It is said that if you say this phrase even once with complete sincerity and concentration, all your past sins and misdeeds are forgiven and you are completely cleansed spiritually.

> *At the time of the Prophet, an extremely handsome and powerful desert chieftain came to the mosque in Medina to embrace Islam. The Prophet rose to greet him and even spread his cloak for the chieftain to perform his first prayers. Afterward, the chieftain repeated the phrase,* la ilaha illallah *and burst into tears. The other worshipers, jealous of all the attention this man had received, began to whisper that he regretted becoming a Muslim. With a stern glance at the congregation, Muhammad asked the chieftain why he was weeping. The chieftain replied that as he repeated* la ilaha illallah *all his past sins passed before him. He realized how many men and women he had killed on raids, how many widows and orphans he had made. The Prophet looked at him with great compassion and said, "With your sincere repetition of the holy phrase,* la ilaha illallah, *all your past sins have been forgiven."*

To practice remembrance, kneel on the floor or sit in a chair. Put your hands on your thighs, close your eyes, and with great reverence begin to repeat *la*. As you utter *la*, turn your head to the right and down, and begin to bring up the words *la ilaha* from your belly. As you pronounce *ha*, bring your head to the middle with your chin raised slightly, your attention at the point between your eyebrows. With *illallah*, move your head down and to the left, and direct the words *illallah* down to your heart. Your head moves in a half circle, from right and slightly down, up and to the middle, and finally down and to the left. This creates a flow of energy up from the navel to the forehead and down into your heart. This is similar to the flow of *kundalini* energy in yoga or the circulation of light in Taoist meditation.

In pronouncing these words, do not raise your voice, but keep your voice focused and low, so someone would have to be standing fairly close to you to hear you. You may also practice silently.

The following is another variation on this practice, taken from a modern Sufi master. Sit with your hands on your thighs, concentrate your heart, and close your eyes. With total reverence and complete concentration, begin to recite the formula *la ilaha illallah*. Bring the words *la ilaha* up from the navel and direct the words *illallah* down to the heart so that the power of the invocation reaches all parts of the body.

Keep your voice low, barely loud enough for you to hear the words yourself. In your heart, meditate on the meaning of this phrase. *La ilaha* negates any passing thought that may enter your heart. You are saying in effect, "I desire nothing, seek nothing, and have no aim or love but God." Then with *illallah* you affirm that God is your only goal, purpose and beloved.[16]

One classic Sufi medicine for the heart is to repeat *la ilaha illallah*. Your heart is a temple built to house God's presence within you. Unfortunately, most of us have neglected this temple and have even placed within it the idols of our various worldly ambitions. Sheikh Muzaffer used to say that the first half of this phrase, "There are no gods" or literally "Not gods," helps to sweep clean our neglected heart temple. The second half of the phrase, "There is God," serves to sanctify the temple, to place God on the altar of the heart as the only one worthy of our worship.

Say the phrase *la ilaha illallah* in your heart, "*la ilaha*" ("other than You there is nothing"); "*illallah*" ("only You are God"). As you recite this phrase, keep your attention on your heart.[17]

Practice this one hundred times a day for a month.

Working with the Names of God. Another basic practice of remembrance is to repeat one or more of the ninety-nine names of God, or Divine Attributes. In order to understand the names, it is not enough to repeat them or to memorize them. We can connect with the divine by finding and nurturing within ourselves the Divine Attributes.

The ninety-nine names can also be called divine truths or even divine commandments. In the Koran, God says, "I have not created *jinn* and man but to know me." Also, according to the famous Prophetic saying, "Those who know themselves know their Lord." One interpretation is that to know God by knowing ourselves is to find the divine attributes within us.

Everything is from God. Sight, speech, power, will, generosity, compassion, love, and the ability to forgive are all divine qualities hidden deeply within us. It is our task to raise them to consciousness and to live according to them.

We also have to realize that whatever qualities of the Divine Attributes are within us are but a tiny fraction of those qualities in God. For instance, if we find in ourselves an ability to be compassionate, we can realize that this is, at best, a tiny fraction of one percent of God's compassion. It is important for us to remember that the Divine Attributes, reflected in creation and in each of us, are not God. Nor are they other than God.

Each day, for ninety-nine days, study one of the ninety-nine names by doing the following:

1. In the morning, repeat the name of the day one-hundred times (use prayer beads or any kind of counter).

2. Contemplate the meaning of this name, or Divine Attribute.

3. Look within and contemplate the ways in which the name is present within you. Think of one or more times in your life that you have strongly and clearly experienced this name in yourself or in others.

4. Seek to act in accord with the divine attribute—at least once during the day you are working on that name; for example, helping others is a way of expressing *Ar-Rahim*, the Merciful.

We often connect most deeply with God when we realize how much we *need* God. When we are feeling lost, we call out to God as *Al-Hadi*, The Guide; when we are impatient, we call to God as *As-Sabur*, The Patient, the source of all patience. In looking over the list of names, you will also notice that a number of names are paired, as God brings both life and death, pain and joy.

Pronunciation Guide

dh   the soft *th* of "this"

th   the hard *th* of "thing"

gh   a gargled, throaty *g*, close to a French *r*

kh   as in German *ach*, or Yiddish *Chassidic*

ʻ   a stop in the back of the throat

q   a sharp *k* sound, made deep in the throat

Allah   God—the greatest name, which contains all the divine attributes

Ar-Rahman   The Beneficent—who wills mercy and good for all creation, at all times

Ar-Rahim   The Merciful—the source of infinite mercy to all believers, here and hereafter

Al-Malik   The King—the owner and absolute ruler of all creation

Al-Quddus   The Holy—most pure and devoid of all blemish or shortcoming

As-Salaam   The Source of Peace—God is the only security, because only God is free of all faults or weakness; whatever else we might lean on may break or fail us, except God.

Al-Mu'min   The Guardian of Faith—who illuminates faith in our hearts and protects our faith

Al-Muhaymin   The Protector—who sees and guards the evolution and growth of all creation

Al-'Aziz	The Victorious—whom no force can overwhelm, whose power is always victorious
Al-Jabbar	The Forceful—whose will is enforced without any opposition, whose power repairs the broken and completes whatever is lacking in us
Al-Muakabbir	The Majestic—the greatest, whose greatness is seen in everything, at all times
Al-Khaliq	The Creator—who creates from nothing
Al-Bari	The Evolver—who orders creation with perfect harmony
Al-Musawwir	The Maker of Beauty—who gives everything the most unique and beautiful form
Al-Ghaffar	The Forgiver—who accepts our repentance
Al-Qahhar	The Conqueror—who dominates everything with irresistible power
Al-Wahhab	The Giver—who gives without conditions or limits, without asking for any return, giving everything freely to everyone
Ar-Razzaq	The Sustainer—who maintains all creation, with both physical and spiritual sustenance
Al-Fattah	The Opener—who opens all doors, all that is locked, tied, or hardened; God opens our hearts, which hold the treasures of divine secrets
Al-'Alim	The All-Knowing—who knows all past, present, and future
Al-Qabid	The Constrictor—who constricts and releases, brings pain and joy, who opens the heart and constricts the heart
Al-Basit	The Expander
Ar-Rafi	The Exalter—who raises us up to honor and fame, and casts us down to the lowest of the low
Al-Khafid	The Abaser

Al-Mu'izz	The Honorer—who gives us pride and dignity or shame and disgrace
Al-Mudhill	The Humiliator
As-Sami	The All-Hearing—who hears all that is spoken and unspoken, audible and inaudible
Al-Basir	The All-Seeing—who sees all that has passed and all there is and will ever be, who sees both the exterior and also what is hidden in everything
Al-Hakam	The Judge—who brings order, justice and truth; who judges perfectly and executes perfect justice
Al-'Adl	The Just—who is absolute justice and secures peace, balance and harmony
Al-Latif	The Subtle—the most delicate, fine, gentle, beautiful one; who creates the most delicate beauty of the rose and the rainbow
Al-Khabir	The All-Aware—who is aware of the most hidden inner occurrences in everything, everywhere, whose awareness penetrates all things actual and potential
Al-Halim	The Forebearing—who delays the punishment of the guilty, giving them time to realize and repent
Al-'Azim	The Great—whose greatness is absolute and perfect, and beyond all comparison
Al-Ghaffur	The All-Forgiving—who hides our faults and relieves our conscience, which suffers from our actions
Ash-Shakur	The Thankful—who repays good deeds with a much greater reward
Al-'Ali	The Highest—who is higher than the unimaginable heights, yet close to every atom in creation, "closer to you than your jugular vein"
Al-Kabir	The Greatest—whose greatness stretches from before the beginning to after the end
Al-Hafiz	The Preserver—who remembers and protects and pre serves all that was and is and ever will be

Al-Muqit	The Nourisher—of everything in all creation
Al-Hasib	The Reckoner—who takes account of all and every-thing
Al-Jalil	The Sublime—Lord of Majesty and Might, the source of all good and perfection
Al-Karim	The Generous—whose rewards and forgiveness surpass all expectations
Ar-Raqib	The Watchful—who scrutinizes every detail in all creation and who protects whatever is rightful
Al-Mujib	The Responsive—who responds to all prayers and all needs
Al-Wasi'	The Limitless—limitless vastness, whose knowledge, mercy, power and all other attributes are infinite
Al-Hakim	The Wise—who is perfectly wise in knowledge and in action, with no doubt or uncertainty
Al-Wadud	The All Loving—the only one worthy of love, who gives us the ability to love God, the Beloved
Al-Majid	The Glorious—who is majestic and who cannot be affected by any power, and whose state of pure perfection reflects perfect glory and honor
Al-Ba'ith	The Resurrector—who has raised us from the dust and who will revive us from the dust after death
Ash-Shahid	The Witness—the one who witnesses all that happens everywhere at all times
Al-Haqq	The Truth—who is ever unchanged and uninfluenced by anything
Al-Wakil	The Trustee—who faithfully completes all things, leaving nothing undone, whom you may trust to do for you better than you can possibly do for yourself
Al-Qawi	The Strong—who possesses all strength, whose strength is inexhaustible
Al-Matin	The Firm—whose power cannot be opposed or weakened, whose force is all-pervasive

Al-Wali	The Friend—who helps, enlightens and protects those who have faith
Al-Hamid	The Praiseworthy—who is praised by all existence, the only one worthy of devotion and praise
Al-Muhsi	The Calculator—the possessor of all quantitative knowledge, who knows the number of all that exists in creation, who counts and weighs our good and bad deeds
Al-Mubdi	The Originator, who creates without model or material, creator of all creation
Al-Mu'id	The Restorer—who recreates and restores all that was created and then destroyed, who will perfectly recreate all creatures on the day of judgment
Al-Muhyi	The Giver of Life—who gives life to all things
Al-Mumit	The Creator of Death—who has destined a time for each being to come into existence and a time to leave
Al-Hayy	The Ever Living—the source of all aliveness, all action and all awareness
Al-Qayyum	The Self-Existing—whose existence depends on no others, and upon whom the existence of all others depends
Al-Wajid	The Finder—from whom nothing can hide; all things are in God's presence at all times
Al-Majid	The Noble—who is infinitely generous and glorious
Al-Wahid	The Unique—who is one without equal
As-Samad	The Eternal—who satisfies all needs, who is the only one without needs
Al-Qadir	The Infinitely Able—who is all-powerful and whose will is never deflected
Al-Muqtadir	The All-Powerful—who creates all power and has total control over all power
Al-Muqaddim	The Advancer—who brings forward, who advances whom God wills

Al-Mu'akhkhir	The Regressor—who leaves behind, who regresses whom God wills
Al-Awwal	The First—there is nothing prior; all comes from God, who is before the before
Al-Akhir	The Last—who has no end, who is eternal; all existence returns to God
Al-Zahir	The Manifest—who can be seen in the beauties and wonders of creation, and who can be found within each of our hearts
Al-Batin	The Hidden—who is hidden within all things, whose essence is unknowable
Al-Wali	The Governor—who effortlessly manages all creation
Al-Muta'ali	The Supreme—whose greatness never wanes, who is free of any defect or lack
Al-Barr	The Source of All Good—all good and bounty, spiritual and material, come from God
At-Tawwab	The One Who Brings Repentance—God awakens through love the hearts of believers from the sleep of heedlessness
Al-Muntaqim	The Avenger—who punishes those who insist on revolting and harming creation
Al-'Afu	The Forgiver—who eliminates or erases our sins
Ar-Ra'uf	The All-Clement—who sees all and chooses to forgive
Malki Al-Mulk	The Eternal Owner—who does not share the ownership, power, or guardianship of the universe with anyone
Dhul-Jalali-Wal-Ikram	Lord of Majesty and Bounty—who owns all perfection and honor
Al-Muqsit	The Equitable—who distributes the bounties of creation in justice and fairness
Al-Jami'	The Gatherer—who has gathered together galaxies and also the cells of the body
Al-Ghani	The Wealthy—who needs not nor needs to earn,

whose riches are independent of all others

Al-Mughni	The Enricher—who gives material or spiritual riches to whomever God chooses
Al-Mani	The Protector—who averts harm from creation
Ad-Darr	Creator of Harm—who has created both what is harmful and what is beneficial; what is poison to one may be medicine to another
An-Nafi	Creator of Good—who has given the greatest of gifts to creation
An-Nur	The Light—that makes creation apparent and makes the conceivable known
Al-Hadi	The Guide—who creates guidance and leads us to good and truth
Al-Badi	The Originator—who has invented the first of everything in creation
Al-Baqi	The Everlasting—whose existence is without end
Al-Warith	The Supreme Inheritor—to whom all things return
Ar-Rashid	The Teacher of Righteousness—who leads us on the straight path
As-Sabur	The Patient—who loves patience

Contemplating Death

A visit from the Angel of Death.

The following exercise is designed to deepen your awareness of death:

You have died. Azrael, the angel of death, appears before you to take your soul from your body. Azrael looks deeply at you and says, "Because of the good deeds you have done in your lifetime, I will give you a little more time." Then he disappears from your sight. You realize that Azrael did not say what he meant by "a little more time." What is an angel's conception of time? How do you begin to live the rest of your life knowing that Azrael may come for you at any moment?

A meditation on death. Think of your contemporaries who have already passed away. They were your age or younger when they left this earth. Recall the honors they received, the fame they earned, the high positions they held, and the wealth they enjoyed. What is left of all that now? Remember how they left widows and orphans behind. Remember their strong, active bodies, which now lie in dark holes underneath the earth. At the end, your contemporaries were foolishly trying to provide for twenty years, when less than a day of their lives was left. They never expected that death would come to them as it did, at an unexpected hour. Do not fix your hopes on your wealth or strength or knowledge. Look on death as inevitable, as much a part of life as birth.

Chapter Seven

SHEIKH AND DERVISH:
SPIRITUAL GUIDANCE IN SUFISM

The hardest hazard facing disciples of "great" teachers: that
each and all tend to worship the teacher and not live
according to the principles he or she announces.

—JAMI[1]

Whoever travels without a guide
needs two hundred years for a two-day journey.

—RUMI[2]

A young man became the student of a sheikh and was
given the job of cleaning the latrines. His mother, a
wealthy physician, asked the sheikh to give her son
some other task, and sent the sheikh twelve Ethiopian slaves to
clean the outhouses. The sheikh replied, "You are a physician. If
your son had an inflammation of the gall bladder, should I give
the medicine to an Ethiopian slave instead of giving it to him?"

The practices of Sufism are medicines, and the sheikh is the physician. We are all spiritually ill, to the extent that we are not living up to
our potentials as dervishes or as human beings. To be a real human being

is to remember God in all circumstances and to serve creation as God's representative. Most of us are far from that ideal. The root of our sickness is our separation from reality, from God.

According to Chinese medicine, we become ill when we are out of balance. Medical treatment is designed to restore balance so that the natural healing powers of the body will bring us back to health. Likewise, the practices of Sufism are meant to bring us back to a healthy spiritual balance so that our inner wisdom and spiritual nature can naturally assert themselves.

With a physical illness, it is foolish to attempt to diagnose and treat oneself or to run from doctor to doctor and take a treatment prescribed by one doctor along with treatments prescribed by others. That is why each dervish has one sheikh.

The Relationship between Sheikh and Dervish

There is an old Sufi saying that it is easy to be a sheikh but difficult to be a dervish.

> Two Sufi saints were sitting together in a teahouse when someone came running in to announce that one of the sheikhs the first saint had sent to India was dead. Would he please send a new sheikh? The first saint turned to his companion and said, "I'm glad they asked for only a sheikh, because if they had asked for a dervish, either you or I would have to go!"

To be a real dervish is to exist at the threshold of the divine, to follow the path of Sufism fully and completely, with absolute sincerity, and to manifest the ideals of Sufism in one's life. Very few attain this level. Some dervishes become teachers or sheikhs, just as some university students eventually become professors. As teachers, sheikhs pass on what they have learned. As spiritual guides, they must be observant, knowledgeable about their dervishes, and skilled in giving the right guidance at the right time.

To be an effective guide, the sheikh must know the territory the dervishes are exploring. The sheikh who has already experienced the trials and tribulations of the path has the firsthand knowledge to guide dervishes through their trials. Just as a fine coach can bring an athlete to levels of performance far beyond the coach's own abilities, sheikhs can lead their students beyond their own spiritual level.

A sheikh is like an automobile battery that can hold a charge. At first, the dervish gets charged—inspired by the remembrance ceremony and by being in the sheikh's presence. However, this charge generally dissipates all too quickly. Over time, the dervish can maintain the charge for longer periods. Those who can sustain a strong charge develop the capacity to recharge others as well, and they become sheikhs.

On this path our main asset is love—love of the sheikh and love of God. Sufism is the path of opening the heart and deepening our capacity for love, which is the quickest way to grow spiritually. It is also extremely important to develop sincerity, lack of willfulness and selfishness, and obedience to the path.

The following is from Sheikh Muzaffer:

The relationship between sheikh and dervish is a complex, mystical, living process. It is in some ways like the relationship between a husband and wife. However, in this profound teaching relationship, the act of love is not physical; the connection occurs between the mouth of the sheikh and the ear of the dervish. If the relationship is pure and loving, it is said that a child is conceived in the dervish's heart
. . . .

The love between dervish and sheikh should be a hundred thousand times more than the highest form of love between a man and a woman. When the love between a man and a woman is consummated, often the two parties turn their backs and forget about each other, at least for the time being. When the love between a sheikh and a dervish is consummated, they never separate. Their hearts remain together, always, and this love never ceases. . . .

Although the sheikh is often referred to as the sun and the dervishes as planets, the sheikh is also like a mirror or transmitter. That is, the light and blessings that flow from a sheikh are not his or her own. They come from God.[3]

In another metaphor, God is the ocean, the dervish is a drop of water, and the sheikh is a river linked to the ocean. The drop learns to become one with the river and eventually becomes one with the ocean. In order for this process to occur, the drop must be in intimate contact with the river and then with the ocean until it becomes absorbed into the greater whole. This contact is achieved through remembrance.

Why is a guide necessary? A guide, out of his or her own personal understanding and depth of being, teaches students to move closer to realizing their inner nature. That teaching is in itself an expression of the divine will. "With a Guide you may become a real man, without one you will remain an animal."[4] Mohammed Shafii, a psychiatrist and student of the Sufi tradition, suggests:

> The Sufis feel that maturity cannot be achieved alone. They feel there is a need for guidance and discipline. The . . . road is full of danger, includ[ing] preoccupation with selfishness, false visions, misinterpretations of mystical states, arrest in development, fixation in a particular state, appeal to various drugs to create false mystical experiences and, not infrequently, overwhelming anxiety and insanity.[5]

Ideally, the sheikh has the capacity to give each disciple what is needed at each stage of development. Sheikh al-Shabrawi was described by a disciple.

> [He was] a mentor of exceptional quality, a guide to the path of the Truth whose style was ever courteous. He protected his disciples from all tiring and wearisome things; whenever a spiritual state threatened to overwhelm a disciple he would bring him to a halt, and whenever a disciple surrendered to indolence, the neglect of his acts of worship, and the attraction of his appetites, the Shaykh would take him by the hand and make him move.[6]

Eight duties of a sheikh. Although the teaching techniques and personal styles of teachers vary widely, the following outline, based on the writings of Al Ghazzali, is an excellent guide to understanding the complex role of the sheikh:[7]

1. "The first duty of the teacher is to be sympathetic to students and treat them as his [or her] own children." Generally, the group of dervishes who works with a sheikh form a study circle or fellowship. This group is like a family, in which the dervishes are brothers and sisters and the sheikh is father and mother. In our order, any romantic or sexual involvement between sheikh and dervish is absolutely forbidden.

Much of the spiritual growth in Sufism is based on the love and support of the dervishes for each other, their love for the sheikh, and the sheikh's love and understanding of each dervish. Tremendous change is possible when the dervishes find that the sheikh is fully aware of their faults and weaknesses and still loves and respects them. Without this loving and supportive atmosphere, little or nothing can be accomplished.

2. "The second duty of the teacher is to follow the example of the Lawgiver: he should seek no remuneration for his services . . . and accept neither reward nor thanks." This is related to the ancient tradition in both Judaism and Islam that one does not take money for teaching God's scriptures or divine truth.

Neither should a sheikh seek nonmaterial rewards, such as praise. A psychology colleague of mine said the same thing about therapy. He emphasized, "If you need praise from your clients you shouldn't be a therapist. Get your praise from your colleagues and your family, and make sure that your clients feel that any growth they experience comes from their own efforts. Otherwise, instead of healthy clients, you will be creating clients who are dependent on you."

3. "[The teacher] should not withhold from the student any advice, or allow him to attempt work at any grade unless he is qualified for it." The teacher is open handed with his or her teaching. At the same time, overly ambitious students need to be discouraged from taking on duties or practices that are beyond their capacities. Sheikh Muzaffer used to say, "Don't increase your spiritual practices and duties too quickly. But whenever you begin a practice, commit yourself to keeping it."

4. "The teacher, in dissuading the student from his evil ways, should do so by suggestion rather than openly, and with sympathy rather than with odious upbraiding. . . . Open dissuasion destroys the veil of awe, invites defiance, and encourages stubbornness." My teachers have almost always refused to give direct advice, even when asked for it. This

forces students to make up their own minds, to take credit for their own achievements and responsibility for their mistakes.

The sheikh often sees faults or bad habits in the dervish, but getting the dervish to see his or her own faults and to do something about them requires skill, compassion, and patience. According to Sheikh Tosun, before a sheikh brings a fault to a dervish's attention, three conditions must be met.

First, the dervish has to understand the nature of the fault. Second, the dervish must also be ready to acknowledge that this fault might be his. Third, if a dervish understands the fault and can acknowledge that the fault is his, the sheikh must still refrain from bringing it to his attention unless he is ready to do something about it. At times, a dervish may be caught in the grip of an addiction or habit and incapable of doing anything about it. To point out this fault at such a time only makes the dervish feel guilty.

When the sheikh's insight is combined with love and acceptance, a dervish is far less likely to deny the insight or to rebel. Knowing he is seen clearly and loved in spite of his faults gives the dervish new strength and motivation to change.

5. "The person who is teaching a certain science should not belittle or disparage the value of other sciences before his [or her] students." A wise teacher praises the strengths and advantages of other teachers and schools and says nothing about their faults. Ideally, the teacher finds something positive to say about everyone and every tradition. I have occasionally criticized others to my sheikh, and he has always found something positive to say in reply, even when their behavior seemed to me to be completely in error. I have learned a tremendous amount from his patience and tolerance and his faith.

6. "The teacher should limit the students to what they are able to understand, and should not require anything which their minds cannot grasp for fear that they will develop a feeling of dislike for the subject, and their minds will become confused." An older man came to Sheikh Muzaffer one day and said that his doctors told him he had a terminal illness. He had not been particularly religious, but now he wanted to begin reading the Koran. Sheikh Muzaffer said, "Don't start reading the Koran now. Begin with Rumi's *Mathnawi*, which is really an extended com-

mentary on the Koran." He knew that the man would quickly become discouraged trying to understand the Koran without a substantial period of preparation.

7. "The teacher should give his [or her] backward students only such things as are clear and suitable to their limited understanding, and should not mention to them anything about the details . . . that he [or she] deems fitting for the present to withhold. . . . Even the most foolish and most feebleminded . . . is usually the most pleased with the perfection of his [or her] mind." Those who are truly intelligent are not usually proud of their intelligence; they know their intellectual strengths and weaknesses. Those who are truly beautiful rarely brag about their looks. Those who are convinced of their intelligence or beauty are usually considerably less gifted than they think they are. The basic problem is that we don't see ourselves as we truly are. The teacher's job is to lead students back to reality. At the early stages in particular, the teacher has to be fully aware of the distortions in the minds of each student.

8. "Teachers must do what they teach and not allow their works to give the lie to their words." In the West we often put on a pedestal those who write or speak beautifully about great truths. It is hypocrisy to talk about the truth and not live it. It can weaken or even destroy students' faith to realize that their teacher does not practice what he or she preaches. Empty words have no weight.

> One day, a sheikh was asked about patience. He spoke beautifully about patience with words full of wisdom. Just then, a scorpion stung his foot, not just once but repeatedly. However, he did not interrupt his talk, despite the pain. When his listeners became aware of what had happened, they wondered why the teacher had not moved his foot away. "I was discussing patience," he explained. "I could hardly give you advice on that subject without setting an example myself. I would have felt ashamed before God."

The four attributes of a sheikh. According to Shafii, a psychiatrist and student of Sufism, there are four major attributes of a true sheikh—maturity, patience, awareness of the student, and being in the world while free of the world.

MATURITY. A Persian phrase beautifully illustrates this aspect of a teacher—the sheikh is a mature or "cooked" (*poukhte*) person who knows the world. That is, a teacher is an experienced and mature human being who knows the attractions and pitfalls of the world, understands others, and knows the spiritual path. Such teachers can understand the dervish's trials, troubles, and temptations.

Rumi describes in his own inimitable way what it is like to be *poukhte*, and how the personality complains as it is becoming transformed:

A chickpea leaps almost over the rim of the pot where it's
being boiled.
"Why are you doing this to me?"
The cook knocks it down with the ladle.
"Don't you try to jump out.
You think I'm torturing you,
I'm giving you flavor,
so you can mix with spices and rice
and be the lovely vitality of a human being.
Remember when you drank rain in the garden.
That was for this."

Grace first. Sexual pleasure,
then a boiling new life begins,
and the Friend has something good to eat.[9]

PATIENCE. The great Sufi sage Ibn Arabi was asked by his teacher to explain the meaning of the verse from the Koran, "I require no provision from them, nor do I need them to feed Me." Ibn Arabi thought for a while and then left without a word. Four years later he returned to his sheikh. The first thing his teacher said was, "Give me your answer. After four years, the time is ripe for it."

Patience is essential for both teacher and student. It is one of the Divine Names or Attributes, and it is mentioned more often in the Koran than any other. A common Sufi metaphor for patience is that of ripened fruit. Unripe fruit tastes bitter and may cause indigestion. If we wait until the fruit ripens, it becomes sweet and nourishing, and its ripened seeds have the potential for rebirth.

AWARENESS OF THE STUDENT. Real teachers know their students' habits and personalities and are also intuitively aware of their inner states and thoughts. If a student misunderstands what is taught and acts according to that misunderstanding, it is said that the student is charged with one error, but the teacher is charged with two. The teacher must know what the student is capable of understanding and how each is likely to misunderstand.

One day someone asked a dervish to write down some of the stories of his sheikh's miraculous powers. The same day he received a summons from his sheikh. The master asked him what he was doing. When the dervish told him, the sheikh advised him not to become a storyteller but to strive to reach the point where others would tell stories about him.

IN THE WORLD BUT NOT OF IT. In most orders today, sheikhs are expected to have jobs and families and also to serve their Sufi communities. In some orders, celibacy was encouraged, at least during the early stages of training, so that individuals could devote themselves fully to Sufi practice.

A man once complained to Sigmund Freud that almost all Freud wrote about were neurosis and mental illness. He asked Freud to describe the characteristics of a mature, normal, healthy human being. Freud answered simply and elegantly, "Love and work." To describe a sheikh we might add, "service and remembrance of God."

The teacher knows how to deal effectively with daily reality, yet not lose sight of the divine. Sufi teachers have been artisans, merchants, fishermen, and shopkeepers. Many of the greatest teachers have had lowly jobs, such as porters, water carriers, and janitors.

The Sheikh and the Path

The sheikh and the Sufi path are two halves of the same whole.

Know that the requirements of the Path are six. First is giving up—possession and position and the love of them. It is also giving up sins. . . . Second is making peace with all the creatures of the world; hurting no one with deeds or words, and withholding help and kindness from no one. . . . The third is developing the ability to be alone and not dependent on others. The fourth is practicing silence . . . in med-

itation and other situations. The fifth is the ability to experience and tolerate hunger and thirst by fasting and by
decreasing one's preoccupation with food and eating. The
sixth is wakefulness—sleeping less and developing the
ability for self-observation. . . .

The fundamentals of the Path are also six. The
first is finding a guide, *pir* [sheikh]. . . . The second is devotion and love toward the *pir*. . . . The third is obeying the
guide and following him. . . . The fourth is giving up one's
previous beliefs and will. . . . The fifth is giving up protest
and denial of the *pir's* advice. . . . The sixth is stability and
persistence.[10]

As a physician of the soul, the sheikh has personally suffered the
sickness of separation and knows first hand the effectiveness of the remedies of Sufism. Just as only an addict understands the trials and temptations of another addict, the sheikh understands the states and the challenges of the student. We can bandage ourselves but we can't operate on
ourselves. Similarly, we can make minor changes in ourselves, but we
need the help of a sheikh to carry out the far more difficult and demanding process of inner transformation. We often cannot even begin to see
what changes are necessary because we lack perspective regarding our
own personalities. Obedience and complete trust in the teacher are
important steps for the beginning student.

*Sultan Mahmud sat with his closest friends and advisors,
drinking out of a magnificent gem-studded crystal goblet, one of
his most valuable possessions. When everyone admired the
beautiful goblet, he handed it to his grand wazir and said,
"Throw it to the floor and break it!" The wazir replied, "I cannot, my sultan. It is far too precious, and I would not dare to
break one of your greatest treasures." The sultan handed the
goblet to each of his advisors with the same instruction, and
each one refused to break it.*

*Finally, he gave the goblet to Ayaz, his most loyal and
trusted companion. Ayaz immediately smashed it to pieces. The
others were amazed and annoyed. When the sultan asked him*

why he broke the goblet, Ayaz replied, "My sultan, I knew that the goblet was very precious, but far more precious to me than any cup is your command. I would not dream of refusing your wishes, and so I immediately did what you told me to do." The sultan smiled and said, "You see why I love and favor him."

Ideally, our obedience to our sheikh is like that shown by Ayaz to Sultan Mahmud.

When a dervish has attained the station of the serene *nafs*, he or she may feel the inclination to teach others. At this station, the individual is fit to become a teacher. A wise teacher generally has the dervish wait even longer before initiating him as a sheikh. I am particularly fond of the following description of the role of the sheikh.

> You may also experience, in this station [of the serene nafs], the desire for leadership, fame, guiding others and for being a shaykh, in order to gather the people so that they may be guided at your hands and that you may be recompensed by God. Beware of this, for it is a trick of the ego. However, if it is God who thus establishes you in this station, causes you to become known and clothes you in the garb of a shaykh without any effort on your part, no desire, and no pursuit, then carry out God's will, for it shall then be better for you than isolation. The sign of this is that your brothers [and sisters] love and obey you, while you do not perceive yourself as better than they, but perceive them as better than you, and you are indebted to them for their belief that they are lower and for their respect for you. If this is how it is between you, then guide them gently, respect them, teach them to love the path, be humble with them, and thank God who has made you qualify for this position of which you are unworthy.[11]

The training of a new dervish. Generally, a sheikh does not accept someone as a dervish immediately. The Sufi path requires patience, commitment, sincerity, and devotion. Not everyone is ready to enter it.

In our order, people who want to become dervishes begin by regularly attending our weekly meetings. They are encouraged to ask questions of the sheikh, which gives the sheikh an opportunity to assess their sincerity and their inner state. They are also expected to begin reading some of our order's books on Sufism. Often prospective Sufis will be assigned an older dervish who will answer their questions privately and teach them how to perform prayers and carry out other basic practices.

Before becoming a dervish, the sheikh generally makes the individual a *muhib*, an intermediate status sometimes defined as "friend of the order." *Muhib* literally means "lover," and one cannot deeply study Sufism (or anything else for that matter) without loving it. In the past, it was a common practice in some orders for a student to be tested for at least three years before initiation as a dervish.

> The Sufi Shaykhs observe the following rule. When a novice joins them with the purpose of renouncing the world, they subject him to spiritual discipline for the space of three years. If he fulfills the requirements of this discipline, well and good; otherwise, they declare that he cannot be admitted to the Path. . . . The first year is devoted to service of the people, the second year to service of God and the third year to watching over his own heart.[12]

> *A young man named Shibli came to Junaid and wished to become his student. Shibli had been the governor of an important region of Persia and had renounced his position to become a student of Sufism. He said to Junaid, "You have been recommended as an expert on pearls [of wisdom]. Please give me one or sell it to me." Junaid replied, "You could not afford the price if I sold it, and if I gave you one for nothing, you would not realize its value. You must do as I have done. Dive into the sea and wait patiently until you obtain your pearl."*

> *Shibli asked Junaid what he must do to become his student, and Junaid told him to go and sell sulphur for a year. When Shibli returned, Junaid told him that his work brought him only notoriety and commerce, and that now he should go and beg for a year. Shibli returned a year later, and Junaid said, "Now you realize your own worth. You have found that you count for*

nothing in the eyes of others. Return to your former province and seek the forgiveness of those you ruled as governor."

Shibli went from house to house until only one man he had wronged remained. He kept trying but he could not trace the man. Finally, Shibli distributed one hundred thousand dirhams in charity, but still his heart could not find rest. After four years, Shibli returned to Junaid. The sheikh pointed out that a trace of pomp and pride still lingered in him, and so Junaid told Shibli to beg for another year.

Every day Shibli brought Junaid all he received from begging and Junaid gave it to the poor. After another year, Junaid finally accepted Shibli as a dervish. He then told Shibli to serve all the other dervishes. After a year of this service, Junaid asked Shibli what he now thought of himself. Shibli replied, "I regard myself as the least of God's creatures." "Now," said Junaid, "your faith is complete."

Junaid prescribed the most difficult of remedies to eradicate any tendencies of pride and conceit in Shibli. It took many years for Shibli to free himself of these traits, but Shibli eventually became one of the greatest Sufi sheikhs.

True and False Sheikhs

Throughout Sufi history there have been a few great sheikhs, many sincere sheikhs, and also some who were corrupt. In medicine as well, some physicians exploit their patients or mistreat them due to ignorance or arrogance. However, the exploitation or ignorance of a few does not mean that the entire field of medicine should be ignored or discarded.

Those who know say that a sincere student will find the truth, even through an ignorant or false teacher. Of course, a false teacher can be spiritually or even physically dangerous. Seekers must use their best powers of discrimination and intelligence in choosing a teacher.

Rumi writes, "True teachers knock down the idol that the student makes of them. One of the signs of sincere teachers is that they will not allow students to put them on a pedestal. "

Ideally, the prospective dervish spends time visiting a Sufi group, keeping an open and critical mind. Only after they are as certain and confident as possible should they ask for initiation and accept someone as their sheikh. Even then, the founder of our order insisted that the door always remain open, and that people feel free to leave if they make a wrong choice.

Hazrat Inayat Khan, founder of the Sufi Order of the West, writes:

> Then there arises the question of how to find the real guru [or spiritual teacher]. Very often people are in doubt, they do not know whether the guru they see is a true or a false guru. Frequently a person comes into contact with a false guru in this world where there is so much falsehood. But at the same time a real seeker, one who is not false to himself, will always meet with the truth, with the real, because it is his own real faith, his own sincerity in earnest seeking that will become his torch. The real teacher is within, the lover of reality is one's own sincere self, and if one is really seeking truth, sooner or later one will certainly find a true teacher. And supposing one came into contact with a false teacher, what then? Then the real One will turn the false teacher also into a real teacher, because Reality is greater than falsehood.[13]

Dream Interpretation

In the Jerrahi tradition, the sheikh's interpretation of the dervishes' dreams is considered a gift from God. There is no school where dream interpretation is taught. It is a secret between the interpreter and God, who inspires in the interpreter the meaning of the dreams.

Once, a man told his sheikh a dream. The sheikh instructed him to go to a particular shop where he would find three people talking. Their conversation would contain the interpretation of his dream. The man found that, in fact, there were three men in this shop and that their conversation was a clear interpretation of his dream. Some sheikhs have told dervishes to go to a particular mosque on Friday and to find the interpretation of their dream in the sermon.

There are three basic kinds of dreams. In the first type, God sends the dream images directly, and the dream needs no interpretation. It is just like one person speaking to another. People of all nations and religions have such divinely inspired dreams.

The second type of dream is angelically inspired. These dreams need interpretation or clarification. The sheikh may interpret the dream or make commentary on the dream symbolism in a way that provides guidance for everyone present. Or the sheikh may give an interpretation that is highly personal and for the dreamer alone.

The third kind is a dream inspired by Satan, or by the *nafs*. This kind of dream is not interpreted. Instead the sheikh will say, "May God protect us." A sheikh can help avert negative possibilities in this way, so it is important for dervishes to tell all of their dreams to their sheikhs.

When one is given the gift of dream interpretation, the first step is to become capable of knowing what kind of dream it is, whether divinely inspired, angelic, or satanic. When a dervish tells a dream to his sheikh, the sheikh can tell the spiritual development of the dervish. He does not need to know the past history and experiences of the dervish, or whether he is saying his prayers or sinning. Dreams are the language of God, which the sheikh is inspired to understand.

When the sheikh discovers the state of the dervish, he will not reject that person. In fact, he might not even criticize the dervish directly. In order to help the dervish, the sheikh may speak to everyone gathered around him. The dervishes who need to change, if they are sincere and heedful, will understand that they are being spoken to directly.

> There was a young student who loved the Prophet very much. He prayed that God would help him study very hard and be successful, because he wanted to become the judge for the city of Medina, the Prophet's city. He even promised that if he ever became the judge of Medina, he would give everything in his pockets to anyone who asked him for money. The young man did extremely well in school, and some years later he was chosen as chief justice of Medina. On his way to Medina, he stopped in Damascus. There he saw a beggar who stretched out his hand and said, "For the sake of God, give me some money." The newly

appointed judge put his hand in his pocket. He took out five gold pieces, all the money he had. He gave it all to the beggar.

When the judge finally arrived in Medina, he went to see the tomb of the Prophet. When he entered the Prophet's mosque, he saw a man sleeping there, his feet pointing toward the tomb. The judge was incensed that someone would be so disrespectful, so he kicked the man and scolded him. The man looked sad as he gathered himself together and left the tomb.

The judge went home and slept. He dreamed that the man he kicked complained to the Prophet. The Prophet turned to the judge and asked why he had kicked the man. The judge replied that he was upset that someone should be so disrespectful. The Prophet suggested that he could have been gentler and told the two men to embrace and forgive each other.

When the judge woke up it was almost time for prayer. He went to the mosque and there he found the man once again asleep with his feet pointing to the tomb. This time the judge kissed the man's feet and said, "Please, I beg you to forgive me." The man replied, "What are you fussing about? Just moments ago, in the presence of the Prophet, didn't we make up and hug each other? And besides, here are the five pieces of gold you gave to me in honor of your promise. Last night, I did what I did deliberately so that you might dream about the Prophet."

The prophet Joseph was one of the greatest dream interpreters. As a young man, he dreamed that eleven stars and the moon bowed down to him. His dream was angelically inspired, and the meaning was not immediately obvious. Years later, his eleven older brothers and his one younger brother bowed down to him after he had risen to power and high position in Egypt.

When Joseph was imprisoned, he interpreted the dreams of two other prisoners, who had both worked in the palace of Pharaoh. To one man he said that he would be pardoned and given back his old position. He told the other he was to be executed. According to one tradition, the men laughed and said that they had not really dreamed those dreams, that they were just

joking. Joseph replied that even so, they had asked for his inter-
pretation and God would make his words come true. In fact, as
Joseph had predicted, the first man was pardoned and the other
was executed.

We can learn two important things from this story. One is that we
should not recount made-up dreams. The other is that we should not ask
just anybody to interpret our dreams. You can't learn to interpret dreams
by studying, no matter how hard you work, as this ability comes only
from God through inspiration.

In an atmosphere of love and trust, we can begin to heal our
hearts of the pain and wounds we have experienced in this world. With
God's help, the guidance of a sheikh, and the support of one's brothers
and sisters along the path, we can transform ourselves into real human
beings.

∽o∽

Exercises in Learning

Working with a teacher. For one day, choose one of your friends
or family members to be your spiritual guide. Pick someone that you
normally spend time with for most of the day.

Pray that God guides the one you've chosen to give you the support and advice that you need. Also, don't say anything to anyone about
this practice until it is over.

Resolve to treat whatever your guide says as if it came from a
genuine sheikh. Promise yourself that you will act on their advice, unless
it clearly contradicts the law or your own moral and ethical principles.

Notice your inner reactions to this exercise. What kind of resistance is there within you? Do you think you would have the same resistance if you were actually in a dervish-sheikh relationship? What other
thoughts and feelings came up during the day?

Working with Sufi stories. For centuries Sufi sheikhs have used
stories to teach their dervishes. The tradition of using stories and parables to point at subtle spiritual truths goes back to Jesus and beyond. In
some modern groups, working with Sufi stories has become one of their
central practices.

After reading the story below, do the following:

1. Does the story have relevance to your own life experience? Does the story speak to you directly? If so, what does it say? Don't intellectualize or theorize about the story's meaning. Stay with its direct relevance for your own experience.

2. Read through the story several times. Each time, take on the perspective of a different character. This can include even animals or objects. Again, without abstract theorizing or intellectualizing, notice how the experiences and the actions of the different characters relate to your own life. Do any provide a new perspective on your life experience?

In addition to the following story, you can try this process with any of the stories you find in this book. (I recommend you begin with the story of Hasan from chapter 1.) There are also a number of excellent collections of Sufi teaching stories. Among the best are the books of Idries Shah, especially his *Tales of the Dervishes*.

> *There was once a country in which all men were kings and all women were queens. The people there were content in every way, and the country was wonderful beyond our ability to describe in words. One day, the parents of young Prince Adhem told him that he had to leave his homeland. Each prince and princess was required to go into the world as a trial. This trial would prepare Adhem for kingship. Through developing his will and his vigilance, he could develop himself as a real human being. This tradition had always been a custom in their land and it would last as long as their country existed.*
>
> *Prince Adhem prepared himself for the journey. His family provided special food and other resources to guard him. He had to travel to a certain country in disguise and bring back a certain jewel, which was guarded by a great monster.*
>
> *On his way, Adhem met someone who was on a similar mission. Together they kept alive the memories of their wonderful country and their royal origins. However, the air and the food of the new land began to change them, and they both forgot their origins and their mission. For years Adhem lived in this*

new country, working to earn a simple living.

The people of his homeland eventually became aware of his predicament, and they worked together to get Adhem to remember his past. Through means that we cannot understand today, they sent him a message saying, "Awake! You are a prince and you have a mission to complete and a homeland to return to."

Once Adhem remembered, he set out to get the jewel. He used special sounds to make the monster fall asleep and he took the priceless jewel. Then Adhem traced back the sounds of the message that had awakened him and found his way back home.

Learning how to learn. Everything and everyone can teach us, if we are open. For one week focus your daily journal on what you have learned each day. Include *how* you learned and from whom (or from what).

A sheikh once asked a dervish, "Who are the intelligent and who are the truly wise?" When the dervish said that she did not know, the sheikh replied, "The intelligent are those who learn from their own mistakes and the truly wise are those who learn from the mistakes of others." Try and learn from everyone you encounter.

Chapter Eight

∽∘∾

DROPPING THE VEILS

You will not be a mystic until you are like the earth—
both the righteous and the sinner tread upon it—and
until you are like the clouds—they shade all things—and
until you are like the rain—it waters all things, whether
it loves them or not.

—BAYAZID BISTAMI[1]

The first step is to say, "God," and nothing else;
the second is intimacy; and the third is to burn.

—ATTAR[2]

In order to remain a living tradition, Sufism must be both practiced and interpreted differently in each generation and in each culture. Throughout this book, we have examined Sufism through a psychological lens, one that is particularly appropriate for modern Western culture. Although certain fundamental ideas and basic practices still remain, contemporary Sufism has changed in many ways from the Sufism of two hundred years ago. In addition to new practices, we need today new approaches to the analysis and evaluation of Sufi theories and disciplines.

Sufism Today

As a path, Sufism implies a beginning, a middle, and an end. The beginning is generally an attraction to the words of a great Sufi poet or writer, or to the presence and personality of a sheikh. The next step is to associate with dervishes and become familiar with their customs and practices. Eventually, the sincere seeker is granted initiation.

The middle of the path is the daily life of the new dervish. Remembrance of God and other Sufi practices, and association with a Sufi community, serve to transform the dervish. Sincerity of effort and patient perseverance are essential in this psychospiritual process. Also essential is the guidance of a wise sheikh.

Finally, the advanced dervish reaches the higher levels of attainment in Sufism. The external sheikh becomes less necessary as the inner sheikh becomes more available. The outer rules and regulations of the Sufi path become less important as the wisdom of the heart begins to provide more precise guidance. Eventually, as internal unity develops within the personality, inner struggle ends. Conscious of being in God's presence, the dervish can do only what is pleasing to God. The final stage is the dropping away of all veils between individual and God. The very last veil to go is the sense of an individual, separate "I."

The goal of the dervish is to become less and less—eventually to become nothing. However, this is a very special nothingness, a state that leads to union with the infinite. There is an old story often told as a joke, but it reminds us that the *nafs* can find pride in anything.

> *Once, a sheikh was praying alone in a little mosque. Overcome with a sense of God's greatness, he cried aloud, "O God, You are Everything and I am nothing. I am like a speck of dust before You." The sheikh's senior dervish heard this and came into the mosque as well. Inspired by his sheikh's example, the dervish cried out, "O God, I am nothing. All power is Yours; everything belongs to You. I am nothing and I can do nothing without You." A beggar was passing by and entered the mosque. He heard the sheikh and the dervish and he too began to pray aloud, "O God, I am nothing." Startled by the new voice, the dervish turned to look at the beggar and then said to his sheikh, "Who does he think he is, calling himself nothing!"*

From the viewpoint of the ego, the Sufi path makes no sense. The ego wants to achieve more and more; the dervish wants to become less and less. The ego wants fame and fortune; the dervish seeks to lose all worldly ambition (although he or she may still remain extremely active in carrying out worldly duties). The ego wants freedom; the dervish wants to submit to a teacher and a path leading to complete submission to God. Our desire for God has to be stronger than the desires of the *nafs* in order to persevere on this path.

During its thousand-year history, Sufism has been in a constant state of change. Outer forms of practice reflect different cultures and historical periods. Many Sufi groups have functioned like families. Dervishes lived with the sheikh, and they worked together daily and shared their meals. Some lodges grew until they housed hundreds of dervishes. There have also been sheikhs whose dervishes have numbered in the thousands or more, spread over many cities and towns. In such cases, individual dervishes rarely met their sheikh. Their spiritual progress was guided by one of the sheikh's representatives.

Both forms can still be found today. There are still small Sufi groups in which new dervishes live in the lodge and work in whatever businesses or crafts that support it. In contrast, I once met a sheikh from Bangladesh who has over 2.5 million followers. His dervishes virtually shut down the capital city of Dacca when they gather from all over Bangladesh to celebrate his birthday each year.

In the West today, the most common form is that of a group that meets together two to three times a week. Some dervishes may live in the lodge, and others may have duties that bring them to the lodge more often. Generally, the one most involved with the lodge is the sheikh. Some dervishes also serve the sheikh in various ways and so spend a considerable amount of time with him or her. The sheikh typically receives phone calls or visits from dervishes every day, as well as visits and phone calls from those outside the order who want the sheikh's spiritual blessing and support.

Sheikh Muzaffer had a religious bookstore in Istanbul, located next to the famous covered bazaar. He had a constant stream of visitors. Some simply came in to buy books, while others came to see their beloved sheikh. Sheikh Muzaffer greeted each visitor differently, depending on the visitor's attitude and intentions. In addition to the visitors, there were always a handful of dervishes who managed to find the time to hang out, often sitting quietly in the bookstore for hours, content to be in their sheikh's presence. There was a core group of several hundred who lived in Istanbul, and Sheikh Muzaffer also had many dervishes throughout Turkey, in other Middle Eastern countries, as well as Europe and the United States.

Today, the Jerrahi dervishes come to our Istanbul lodge for the remembrance ceremony on Thursday evenings and for Sufi music practice on Monday evenings, often arriving between five and six o'clock and staying until one or two o'clock in the morning. Several hundred people show up each evening along with an inevitable handful of foreign visitors. A smaller number come on Saturday evenings, which are shorter and more informal. In addition, a small group of senior dervishes attends Friday noon prayers with the sheikh and spends the afternoon with him.

Adab toward the Sheikh

In the Jerrahi Order, the dervishes generally kiss the sheikh's hand in greeting. This is a traditional sign of respect throughout the Middle East, but it is difficult for some Westerners. Also, we are not used to showing our respect to others and raising anyone else above ourselves. Because of this, hand kissing is an excellent test for prospective dervishes. It is a sign of humility and a symbol of the deep respect that must be felt for one's sheikh if the relationship is to work. My late master, Sheikh Safer, often asked the dervishes not to be too demonstrative, quoting the founder of our order. "Whenever you kiss my hand, I [inwardly] kiss your feet."

One of the core principles of *adab* toward the sheikh is to come to the sheikh with an "empty cup"; that is, ready to learn, having let go of our preconceptions and prior opinions. This allows for a rich and effective teaching relationship. I heard the metaphor of the empty cup from a Turkish Sufi teacher, although it comes from an old Zen story.

A professor went to visit a Zen master. The Zen master poured tea for the two of them, and the professor, who had read many books about Zen, began to talk about what he had read. As the professor went on talking, the Zen master picked up the tea pot again and began to pour more tea into the professor's cup. The tea overflowed and began to run onto the table. The professor cried out, "Stop! Can't you see the cup is filled? It can't hold any more tea!"

"That's right," replied the Zen master. "First you have to empty your cup. Only then can you take in anything new."

In the teaching relationship between sheikh and dervish, the dervish is expected to be quiet and attentive to the sheikh's words and actions. It is considered rude to chat with others while the sheikh is teaching or to interrupt with questions or comments. It is also considered rude to perform individual remembrance practices in the sheikh's presence. In fact, in our order, it is said that the sheikh should never see dervishes using their prayer beads. The dervishes are supposed to learn directly from the sheikh when they are in the sheikh's presence and to reserve their individual practices for those times when he or she is not present.

Part of the respect shown for the sheikh is not for the sheikh as a person, but for his position as the representative of the order. The sheikh represents not only his or her own sheikh, but also the founder of the order and the other great saints in the order's lineage. The sheikh is a channel through whom the wisdom and blessings of the order can flow. Sheikh Muzaffer used to say, "If I talk from my gut, from my personal opinions or experiences, you need not bother listening. However, if I *don't* talk from myself, then you should listen." At that time, many of us were involved with different forms of therapy and group work. We had been struggling to learn to express our feelings, to talk from our gut. It took us a long time to understand what Sheikh Muzaffer meant.

Interrelationship of Heart, Self, and Soul

The stages of heart, self, and soul range from the extremes of separation from God and domination of the urges of the personality to union with God. This range is perhaps clearest in the descriptions of the tyrannical *nafs* and the pure *nafs*. The tyrannical *nafs* contains all those forces that impel us toward evil or wrongdoing. At this level we are completely dominated by these negative forces and unable to do anything other than pursue our desires, no matter how base. At the other extreme, the pure *nafs* is a state in which there is no individual personality left, not even a trace of "I-ness" to interfere with complete union with God.

The heart contains a similar range. The breast, the outer level of the heart, has the potential to become infected by the negative traits of the tyrannical *nafs*. However, the breast can be filled with light and become a great ally in the struggle with the negative traits of the *nafs*. The innermost level of the heart is beyond all negativity or duality. It contains the pure spark of the divine and is at the core of our being, although paradoxically, it transcends the entire universe.

The first six aspects of the soul—mineral, vegetable, animal, personal, human, and secret—are like the breast. They can become either negative (unbalanced) forces in the psyche or they can be positive (balanced) influences. The seventh aspect of the soul, the secret of secrets, is like the pure *nafs* and the innermost heart. It is beyond duality, the place of the divine within us.

Self and souls. The tyrannical *nafs* might be defined as the level of the domination of those inner forces that lead us away from truth, that impel us toward evil. The issue of evil is a perennial problem in psychology and philosophy. If God is good and omnipotent, where does evil originate? If the human psyche is basically good and healthy, where does harmful or evil behavior come from?

One tendency in clinical psychology is to concentrate on the negative aspects of the psyche, as Freud did. This creates a picture of the human being that focuses primarily on the distortions and harmful influences of the negative ego and the selfish tendencies of the instincts. This picture has no place for genuine altruism, compassion or spirituality. Freud dismissed religion as an illusion, in part because his theory of human nature was so one-sided.

We can divide the negative inner forces into two major categories—the instinctual impulses and the negative ego. The instinctual impulses are found in the vegetable and animal souls, and the negative ego is located in the personal soul. The Koran describes the tyrannical *nafs* as "the self that incites to evil." When our powerful instincts and ego tendencies push us to do *whatever* it takes for their fulfillment, they often incite us to wrongdoing.

The fundamentally positive traits of the vegetable and animal souls can become negative influences when they are unbalanced and extreme. For example, the process of healthy nutrition can turn into addiction to food and gluttony on the one hand, and rejection of food, poor digestion, or malnourishment on the other. The natural process of rest, healing, and recuperation can turn into the extremes of either laziness or hyperactivity.

Our vegetable soul's instinctual impulses are relatively straightforward, for example, when we are hungry. We might decide that we can't eat right away, but the impulse keeps repeating itself, like a child nagging a parent. Once we decide we are going to eat, to have some bread perhaps, the impulse may escalate to, "Let's have bread with jam and also something to drink." Eventually this may turn into, "We need cake with ice cream and a double cappuccino."

Fasting is an excellent way to learn how to combat these impulses. When we deny the initial impulse, the demand for food does not escalate. Handling the impulse then becomes a relatively straightforward exercise of will.

The impulses of the animal soul are more complex. According to Sufi psychology, most people *look* human, but inside, they are more like a zoo filled with animals. The impulses of the animal soul can be divided into three classes. First is the tendency to move toward whatever is positive or pleasurable (the passions), which, at the extreme, turns into greed or lust. Second is to move away from the negative (the fears), which can develop into fear or anxiety. Third is to push away the negative (the angers), which can turn to rage or hate.

Any of these animal soul impulses can impel us toward evil. The stronger and more extreme the impulse, the more it can blind us to alternative solutions, and the more we are likely to act like animals rather than intelligent human beings who behave according to good judgment and higher ideals.

Fear and anxiety are more prevalent than most people realize; the lives of many people are dominated by constant low-grade anxiety—an unfocused fear that something bad is about to happen, that life will get worse in some unspecified way. They become conditioned to seek whatever reduces their anxiety, and they may easily become addicted to TV, work, a hobby, or some other distraction.

Faith and remembrance of God are a basic cure for fear and anxiety. There is a saying of the Prophet that those who fear God fear nothing else, and all others fear them. Without trust in God, we can easily become afraid of almost everything, especially death. Sufis fear displeasing God, not because they fear punishment but because they do not want to become estranged from the beloved. If our relationship with God is the most important thing in our lives, the ups and downs of everyday existence will not trouble us. We will not fear losing our jobs, our money, or even our health, because we realize that all these things are impermanent and relatively unimportant. Only our character and our relationship with God remain with us in the end. Sufis learn to contemplate death and to accept it as an integral part of life.

The passions are a major obstacle for many people. Our consumer culture feeds the passions through widespread advertising and merchandising. Passion for truth and healthy activities is good for us, but all too often passion becomes distorted and we get addicted to what is not healthy, or we seek only what is pleasurable. As with all the instincts, the middle ground is best. Desires are a normal, healthy part of life unless they go to the extremes of either no motivation at all or uncontrollable craving or addiction. Ideally, we eventually convert our passion for the things of this world to passion for God.

Anger can also impel us to evil. We do and say things that deeply hurt those we love. Many people are anger addicts, and regularly explode into anger and often violence as well. If we injure the hearts of those who are close to us, we damage the divine temple within them. This causes our own hearts to harden and close down. The Prophet said, "The strongest among you are those who control their anger, and the most patient among you are those who forgive others when they are strong enough to wreak revenge on them."

There is an old Turkish saying: "The one who gets up with anger sits down with loss." Anger brings instant loss; instead of rationalizing it, we have to learn to control our temper.

> One day, some people insulted Jesus. He responded by praying for them. A disciple asked, "Why did you pray for those men? Didn't you become angry at their treatment of you?"
>
> Jesus answered, "I could spend only what I had in my purse."

In addition to the instinctual impulses of the vegetable and animal souls, the tyrannical *nafs* includes the pride and egotism of the personal soul. This represents a qualitative jump from the basic instincts of the vegetable and animal souls. Like the instincts, the ego is fundamentally healthy, neither too strong nor too weak. A weak ego, or lack of self-esteem, inhibits us from acting or from seeking worthwhile goals. A strong ego results in pride and selfishness. Paradoxically, most people suffer from self-doubt and then cover it up with an overblown negative ego.

Negative egos keep us separate from others and from God. If we look inside ourselves deeply enough, we can see that our negative ego wants everyone to obey us and accept our judgments and opinions as truth. If we look deeper still, we see that our negative egos want everyone else to worship us as if we were God, just as the pharaohs were worshipped in ancient Egypt. This is at the core of the dynamics of the tyrannical *nafs*.

The negative ego has access to the developed nervous system and the intelligence of the personal soul, so it has certain tools that are not available to the instincts. These tools are well described in Freud's discussion of the ego defenses—projection, rationalization, denial, repression and the like. As a result, the negative ego exerts a more subtle and intelligent influence than the instincts.

For example, while we are fasting, the instincts simply repeat their basic demands: "Feed me. I'm hungry." In contrast, the negative ego argues, "You won't be able to do your work unless you eat," or "You *need* food, otherwise it's too dangerous to drive or operate machinery." Another clever argument often tried by the negative ego is, "Fasting is for those who *need* it, but you are beyond that." If the individual succeeds in fasting, the ego often tries another trick. "You are really a very holy person, and certainly better than all those who are not fasting." An old Sufi story beautifully illustrates these tricks.

> *Sheikh Abdul Qadir al-Jilani was traveling with a group of his dervishes during the month of Ramadhan. He stopped to fix a broken strap on his sandal but asked the others to go ahead. The dervishes came upon a pillar of white light, and a beautiful voice spoke to them: "You are the elite among the*

believers, and you no longer need to fast. You, the blessed disci-
ples of the world's greatest sheikh, have gone far beyond the
need for this elementary discipline. Go ahead and eat and drink
freely, my beloved ones." As the dervishes reached for their food
and water, Abdul Qadir al-Jilani arrived and recited the holy
formula, "I take refuge in God from Satan the accursed."

At these words the pillar turned black. The dervishes
dropped their food containers and water skins. An ugly, mis-
shapen creature emerged from the pillar and said to the sheikh,
"I have tried this trick on hundreds and you are the first I have
failed to catch with it. How did you know it was not God speak-
ing directly to you?"

Abdul Qadir al-Jilani said, "I knew who you really were
by my study of three disciplines—religious law, theology, and
Sufism. First of all, it is very clear who can be exempted from of
fasting; for instance, pregnant women, nursing mothers, or
those suffering from illness. None of us fell into those clearly
specified categories. And I know that God does not change the
law, which is meant for all time.

"Second, God's voice never comes from a single source.
Whenever the prophets write about hearing God's voice, they
describe it as beyond location. So I asked myself who would imi-
tate God's voice, and I figured it must be you."

"Finally, whenever anyone comes close to the divine
presence, they fall into states of awe or ecstasy. Yet everyone
here simply listened to you as they would to any another
human being. So it could not have been God addressing us
directly. It had to be you."

The creature replied, "I heard that you were great, but
you are truly fantastic, certainly the greatest sheikh in the
world. Instead of this handful of followers you should have
thousands of dervishes. Kings and sultans should be among
your disciples."

At this point, Abdul Qadir al-Jilani interrupted and
repeated, "I take refuge in God from Satan the accursed."

As this story points out, we *need* knowledge in order to distinguish the voice of the negative ego from the voice of intelligence or conscience. The moral and ethical principles of religion are our first line of defense. If we feel a strong impulse to act counter to basic moral principles, we need to stop and double check ourselves or even consult with others before we act. The Prophet said, "If you are sure that an act is lawful, you may go ahead and act; if you are sure it is unlawful, then do not do it. And if you are unsure, do not act until you are sure." The example of the great prophets and saints is another guide. In general, the more we learn and the more we are aware, the less we are influenced by the negative ego.

As we enter the realm of the human soul, compassion can lead us astray. As with all the other tendencies, there can be either too much or too little compassion. Too little compassion leads us to be selfish and insensitive to others. If we are so compassionate that all we can do is commiserate with others and pat them on the back, we will not be able to serve those who need a more tough-minded, no-nonsense response.

The spiritual soul can also become unbalanced. Too little spirituality leads us to focus on material goals and rewards. We have little faith and therefore little capacity to understand spiritual teachings and spiritual truths. On the other hand, spirituality without regard for any of the other souls can cause us to undervalue the world, to look on it as merely an illusion and not worthy of our time and energy.

Sufi psychology reminds us that the world is a place for us to grow. As one of my teachers commented, the world may be a dream, but as long as we are in that dream, we have to take it seriously, because whenever you get hit by a dream club, you are going to suffer from a dream headache.

Negative elements in the nafs. The distorting elements associated with the various souls—instincts, negative ego, unbalanced compassion, or spirituality—operate at each of the first five stages of the *nafs*. At the stage of the tyrannical *nafs*, we are unconscious of these impulses and blind to their operation, and so they tend to control us.

Many people who have gained self-control and self-insight in certain areas may still have blind spots. When particular buttons are pushed, they are overwhelmed by anger or passion, for example, and descend to the level of the tyrannical *nafs*.

At times, we may become angry or otherwise unbalanced, and in the middle of our response, realize that we are doing something stupid. That is a sign that we are operating at the stage of the regretful *nafs*. We know that we are in the grip of an addiction or an unbalanced negative tendency and we regret our actions. Even though we still act out that impulse, there is hope: we recognize what we are doing and we want to change. After a period of struggle, which may include many cycles of wrong action followed by regret and self-blame, we eventually change.

There are also positive buttons that can uplift us. A real spiritual teacher is someone who can push this second kind of button. Through the presence of a great sheikh, many people are inspired to follow the Sufi path. This kind of enthusiasm and inspiration are only temporary, however. After the honeymoon with the sheikh is over, the real work of self-transformation begins. Old habits are still strong and there is a great deal of inner work ahead.

There is an almost inevitable see-saw experience at the beginning of Sufi practice. In the presence of the sheikh and the older dervishes, everything is wonderful, the heart is open, and the new dervish experiences at least a taste of the stage of the inspired *nafs*. Unfortunately, our negative tendencies are still as strong as ever, because the stage of the inspired *nafs* has not yet truly been attained. If we keep up with prayers and other practices and attend Sufi meetings, we will feel better again as our hearts open once more. However, old habits inevitably return, the heart closes and the individual feels down once again. In fact, the struggle may seem even more difficult now, because the illumination of the heart has revealed our negative tendencies. As a result, we become more aware than ever of our negative traits.

The ideals of worship and conscious behavior are beyond our capacity at this early stage of the inspired *nafs*. In fact, we may say, "Oh, I know that is how I *should* be, but I don't know that I can possibly be that way. I've never been able to act that impeccably before." But we still have to try, to attempt what is still beyond us. That is one of the great challenges of the Sufi path.

It is important to honor the inner knowing that comes from the heart and to do our best to act accordingly. If we don't even try, the intuition of the heart is taken over by the *nafs* and turns into hypocrisy and phony role playing. The solution is to realize that we have not fully attained those higher levels that we may have heard of or even briefly experienced, and that we still have considerable work to do. To pretend that we are done with our base impulses, that we are free of all negative tendencies is the root of hypocrisy. That is the danger at this stage, and entire spiritual groups can succumb to it. One sign of this spiritual illness is that everyone seems to be quoting some spiritual authority as if the words were their own. It is important to acknowledge the ideal and also to acknowledge that we have not yet fully attained it.

One of the important functions of a sheikh is to combat our tendency to inflation and hypocrisy by reminding us that we still have to work on our negative impulses. Those who say they don't need a sheikh generally underestimate the power of these forces in their own psyches. In the words of Rumi, "Whoever travels without a guide needs two hundred years for a two day journey."[3] Jung points out that those who believe that they are free of their shadows are the ones most controlled by them. In many ways, our real work occurs at the stage of the inspired *nafs*.

After this, we move to the stage of the serene *nafs*. We are not really safe until we have reached this stage. Serenity and contentment do not mean that there are no negative impulses left. We can still become unconscious under unusual circumstances, but fundamentally, we are happy with who and where we are and what we are doing. We have established a balance of spirituality in our daily lives, and we have developed healthy relationships with friends, colleagues and family. This is a stable, solid foundation that makes it possible to go on with the deep work of self-transformation that ends in unity with God.

At the stage of the pleased *nafs* we begin to take genuine pleasure in spiritual practice. We touch, for the first time, the deepest levels of the heart, and the divine soul within us becomes the source of our real joy and ecstasy. Personality problems are finally resolved, the seeds of wrongdoing are now unlikely to sprout. The *nafs* is still present, but it has basically come under God's command. The poet Hafiz describes this stage beautifully:

> I bow to God in gratitude,
> And I find the moon is also busy

Doing the same.

I bow to God in great happiness,
And I learn from where the suns
And the children
And my heart
All borrow their Light.

I bow to the Friend in deep reverence
And discover a marvelous secret carried in the air:

This whole Universe is just as blessed
And divinely crazed as I,
And just as lost in this Wonderful Holy Dance.

My dear,
After such a long, long journey,
God has made another soul
Free![4]

There is no longer a dichotomy between the *nafs* and the divine soul within. The inner struggle is finally over—except for a single problem, which is our sense of "I." This is the last separation between us and God; it is like a thorn embedded in our flesh, a source of deep pain. Sufis describe this final transformation of the pure *nafs* in the phrase, "to die before dying," and from the point of view of the individual psyche, this does feel like death. Just as in physical death, we die to all that is temporal in ourselves, leaving only that which is eternal.

At this stage, God speaks through our tongue, acts through our hands and feet, and sees through our eyes. This happens only when there is nothing left in us to get in the way, nothing left to interfere with divine will. The personality still remains; however, its negative aspects are now like roasted seeds. They cannot sprout or interfere with the divine. Only the great saints and spiritual teachers attain this final stage.

In reviewing the spectrum of the transformation of the self, it is important to remember that nothing is possible without God's will. A Prophetic saying reminds us that God changes only those who change themselves. In a similar vein, the Sufi saint Bayazid Bistami wrote, "The thing we tell of can never be found by seeking, yet only seekers find it."[5]

Nafs and heart. As mentioned earlier, the breast is a battleground between the positive and negative tendencies of the *nafs*. The deeper levels of the heart are the allies of the positive tendencies of the *nafs*, and the more in touch we are with these levels, the more power there is to transform the *nafs*.

Level of Self	Level of Heart
tyrannical	breast
regretful	heart proper
inspired	inner heart
contented	
pleased	innermost heart
pleasing	
pure	

As illustrated in the above diagram, the traits of the tyrannical *nafs* battle with our positive traits in the breast. We are stuck at the level of the tyrannical *nafs* when the breast is closed and there is no light available from the heart proper. When light from the heart begins to illuminate the breast, we enter the stage of the regretful *nafs*; we begin to see what we are doing and to regret our mistakes.

When the light of the heart proper is more fully available and joined with illumination from the inner heart, we begin to access more fully our inner wisdom and intuition, and we enter the level of the inspired *nafs*. We begin to take real pleasure in prayer, remembrance, and other spiritual activities. This is the level that most people have attained when they first become interested in Sufism. At the earlier levels, Sufism simply does not make sense, or else people are interested in Sufism because they think they will gain some kind of financial or material benefit.

Before this stage of the inspired *nafs*, all of our knowledge and learning came from the outside. Now, for the first time, we can be guided by the wisdom and intuition of the heart. It is essential to act on our wisdom and insight, or else our connection with the heart diminishes.

The struggle between our positive and negative tendencies is now tipped in favor of the positive. However, the ego still has a few powerful tricks left, especially pride in one's new attainments. For this reason, the inspired *nafs* is considered by some sheikhs to be the most dangerous stage, one in which the wisdom and insight of the heart may become misappropriated and misused by the negative ego.

At the stage of the serene *nafs*, we have become more fully conscious of the wisdom and riches of the inner heart. Serenity and contentment with whatever comes to us from the material world become possible when we realize that our greatest rewards and treasures lie within.

As our access to inner light and wisdom deepens, we move to the stage of the pleased *nafs*. We get a tiny glimpse of the infinite light of the divine spark located in our innermost heart. We take pleasure in whatever comes, because the world is no longer a veil between us and God. It is now a source of remembrance of God, a place of deepening our love for God, and an opportunity to practice service for God's sake.

At the stage of the *nafs* pleasing to God, we finally transcend completely the struggle between positive and negative tendencies within ourselves. Our personality is unified and we are more deeply in touch with the infinite light and wisdom of the innermost heart. Only one veil remains to obscure the innermost heart; it is the sense of "I," the sense of our separate individuality, which drops away at the stage of the pure *nafs*. At this final stage, we are fully united with the divine in the innermost heart.

Heart and souls. The first four souls operate in the breast, the level of our interaction with the world. Here we practice charity, service, and other religious and spiritual activities. If the souls are in balance, these actions are effective in moving us along the path of truth. If the souls are unbalanced, our practice may become distorted or sabotaged by traits such as laziness, greed or egotism.

The human soul is located in the heart proper and is illuminated by the light of faith. Sheikh Muzaffer used to say that a real human being is one who remembers God at all times, no matter what happens. Remembrance engages and brings out the human and secret souls.

Compassion is one of the basic characteristics of the heart and the human soul. The heart proper is the site of the light of faith. The Prophet teaches, "Your faith is not complete until you wish for your neighbor what you wish for yourself."

The secret soul is found in the inner heart and is illuminated by the light of gnosis, or spiritual knowledge. It is also called the angelic soul, and just as the angels are in constant remembrance of God, the secret soul is also in constant remembrance.

The secret of secrets is located in the innermost heart, the heart of hearts. This is the place of self-transcendence and unity with the divine.

Practices for Refining the Nafs

The rules and principles of religion and the disciplines of Sufism provide clear guidelines for behavior and restraints for the negative ego and the impulses of the *nafs*. Commitment to live by these standards keeps our negative tendencies in check. Any impulse to violate them is likely to come from the *nafs*, which alerts us to the operation of our negative tendencies. The more conscious we are of the dynamics of the *nafs*, the less powerful they are.

The sheikh is an enemy of the *nafs*. There is an old Arab saying that the enemy of your enemy is your friend. The sheikh's duty is to oppose our *nafs*, but this is often a thankless task, because so many people identify with the characteristics of their *nafs*. As a result, they may oppose the sheikh or even begin to think of the sheikh as their enemy.

The sheikh models how to live and act. Ideally, the sheikh is a mature human being, one who is conscious and relatively free of negative tendencies. Through talks, stories, and answers to questions, the sheikh teaches the dervishes about the dynamics of the *nafs* and the deeper significance of religious law and the Sufi path. Through personal guidance, the sheikh also advises the dervishes and steers them away from the influence of the tyrannical *nafs*. Through obedience to the sheikh, dervishes are freed from the tyranny of negative habits and traits.

Some years ago, Sheikh Muzaffer and a group of the dervishes from Istanbul visited France to give a concert of Sufi music and to present the remembrance ceremony. The young man who was their French guide fell in love with the sheikh and the dervishes. He traveled everywhere with them and spent all his spare time in their company. After a powerful and inspiring remembrance ceremony, the young man asked whether he could become a dervish. The sheikh indicated that he would consider favorably the young man's request. Then the man asked, "But what about my freedom?" As soon as he heard those words, Sheikh Muzaffer slowly turned his back on the young man. As he began to walk away, the sheikh said, "Freedom? Keep your freedom." It was a sight that the dervishes who were present never forgot.

What seems like freedom to most of us is merely freedom to follow the *nafs*. It is the illusory freedom of prisoners who insist that they are not in prison. We need to look closely and honestly at our own resistance to achieving real freedom and closeness to God.

> We should make all spiritual talk
> Simple today:
>
> God is trying to sell you something,
> But you don't want to buy.
>
> That is what your suffering is:
>
> Your fantastic haggling,
> Your manic screaming over the price![6]

The rules of each order stress humility, service, and obedience to the sheikh. These are all antidotes to the traits of the *nafs*. In addition, many orders and sheikhs stress the principle of avoiding ego inflation by seeking anonymity or even blame in one's public life.

Brother and sister dervishes also help in the struggle with the *nafs*. Senior dervishes are excellent role models, similar to the sheikh. Ideally, the new dervish can learn something different from the examples of each of the other dervishes. Some model exquisite service, and others are examples of devotion, heedfulness, or humility. They mirror the best potentials as well as the faults and shortcomings in ourselves of which we manage to remain unconscious.

Remedies for the Souls

One of the basic goals in working with the souls is to create a healthy balance within each soul and among the souls. Moral and ethical principles and the rules of the Sufi orders are meant to provide a middle way, a self-disciplined way of life that supports this ideal. The dervish seeks to avoid the extremes of either life-rejecting asceticism or addiction to pleasure and materialism. Religious and spiritual practices are meant as support rather than a heavy burden. For example, fasting is not mandatory if we are ill or traveling. We can make up missed fast days at a time when we are in good health and enjoying a normal routine.

We can learn a great deal from the vegetable soul's function of nutrition. The unbalanced extremes of physical nutrition are malnutrition and gluttony. We have similar spiritual extremes. Spiritual malnutrition comes from lack of spiritual nourishment, often brought about by preoccupation with the world or choosing "empty calories" that are not really nourishing (for example, reading pseudospiritual "junk food" instead of the great scriptures or spiritual classics). Spiritual indigestion can come from reading too many spiritual books without assimilating and practicing their contents. Some people are spiritual gluttons who run from teacher to teacher and technique to technique, always seeking a bigger high. They are like the farmer drilling for a well who, instead of digging a single hundred-foot hole in the most likely spot, digs twenty five-foot holes. Which approach is more likely to yield water?

Similarly, the animal soul's instincts of passion, fear and anger can become distorted and unbalanced. These distortions make it more difficult to serve the world for God's sake, or to be in the world and still remember God. Someone who is afraid of everything gets nothing done, while one who fears nothing is likely to get badly hurt, like an infant playing with a hot stove. Those with no desires or passion are also likely to achieve nothing, while those with overdeveloped desires become tyrannized by them. The Sufi ideal is to develop a balanced life of work, service, family duties, worship, and Sufi practices. Ideally, a balanced outer life leads to a balanced inner life.

In many ways the voices of the first four souls are louder than the last three. That is, we generally pay instant attention when our physical needs are frustrated. We also pay prompt attention to the ego demands of the personal soul. Unfortunately, the demands of these souls tend to absorb most of our time and energy because they are rooted in the material world.

Our spiritual needs are far more easily ignored. Our main spiritual needs are to express our compassion by serving others and to remember God. Sincere service is a form of worship. These practices can deepen until eventually we are in a state of constant prayer and remembrance.

The Sufi lodge provides a place for the spiritually minded to gather, an atmosphere that supports the satisfaction of both our spiritual and our material needs. In a Sufi lodge, generous meals are served in addition to inspiring talks and spiritual practices.

Remedies for the Heart

The breast houses the light of practice. Every positive action serves to open the heart and make the light and wisdom of the inner stations of the heart more available. Every negative action tends to close down the heart and veil the light and wisdom within.

One day a man asked a sheikh how to reach God. The sheikh replied that the ways to God are as many as there are created beings. "The shortest and easiest is to serve others," the sheikh continued, "not to bother others and to make others happy." The heart is softened and healed by remembrance, by the dervish's love for the sheikh and the sheikh's love and compassion for the dervish.

Conclusions

Every spiritual tradition has a psychology, a model of human nature, either implicit or explicit, because every spiritual discipline must describe the problems and issues people face when they begin to work on themselves. A spiritual model also needs to include the changes people undergo as they pursue their path and the new problems and issues they face as they change and grow.

The path of Sufism. The Sufi path begins with an initial call. Sometimes this happens when we fail in our worldly pursuits or the death of a loved one leads us to reevaluate our priorities. For many, the call occurs when we meet a sheikh and discover a new world of spiritual experience. Newcomers quickly learn the importance of perseverance.

The middle of the path begins with a sincere commitment to Sufism, often symbolized by initiation as a dervish. Once or twice a week, new dervishes meet with their Sufi community. At these times, we often feel inspired and uplifted, but old habits and attachments are still strong, and we soon discover how long and difficult the path is. We begin to realize the truth of the old Turkish saying, "Sufism is like chewing an iron peanut." It seems to be an impossible, endless task, and our teeth may wear down before the peanut does. Patience is essential.

The end of the path begins with the serene *nafs*, an advanced stage that may take many years to attain. At this stage, we are content with our life, job, and family, and the wild animals of the self are fairly well tamed. From the point of view of the ego, life has gotten boring. This is actually a good sign—we no longer need outer excitement, and this state becomes the foundation for the transformation of consciousness.

As we go deeper and deeper, our hearts open more fully, and we begin to touch the divine spark in the innermost heart. Profound joy and pleasure, rooted in the innermost heart, begin to permeate our lives. As we go deeper still, we finally reach self-unification. The wild animals of the self are tamed and the inner struggles are over. Finally, the last veil, the sense of separate existence, is dropped, and nothing remains but the divine.

Remembering the divine within. The core of Sufi psychology is to know that God is within the heart of every human being. Within this context there can still be disagreements or even conflicts among the dervishes. The challenge is to remember the larger context, to remember that we are all sparks of God clothed in human form.

We can also see our own and each other's faults *within* this context. Some people are stingy, others don't keep their word, some have bad tempers. If we see beauty in someone else, we do them and ourselves a service. When we focus on another's faults, we make those faults more real both in the other person and in ourselves. For example, if someone is an alcoholic, and I talk about their addiction and how terrible it is, I harm both them and myself. Their addiction to alcohol may be a fact, but that is not who they truly are. The negative traits of the personality are less important than the fundamental truth that we all have temples in our breasts built by God to house God.

Once, a sheikh saw a distinguished-looking beggar on the street. The sheikh thought to himself that this man looked too cultured and intelligent to have to beg for a living. That night the sheikh dreamed that an angel came to him with a platter of meat. Although the angel urged him to eat, the sheikh thought that the meat looked very strange. He asked what it was, and the angel replied that it was the flesh of the beggar. When the sheikh expressed horror, the angel said, "Why do you turn down his flesh now when you ate it yesterday?"

For the spiritually advanced, even thinking negatively about someone is unlawful. Luckily, at our level, we are judged only by our actions. Each human being has the full range of possibilities, from the demonic to the divine. If we see people in this divine context, we don't have to ignore their negative impulses, but we have to remember where we are all going. Sooner or later, God removes everything in us except for the pure spark of the divine. If we remember the divine in ourselves and in each other, then a kind of sympathetic vibration occurs in each person. A good Sufi group provides this atmosphere.

The archangel Gabriel was curious to see who on earth was the greatest devotee. With his angelic powers he quickly traveled throughout the world, seeking out all the saints and ascetics. Finally, he came to the cave of a man who was reputed to be the greatest worshiper of all. This man was said to sleep only an hour or two a night and to spend all the rest of his time in prayer and meditation. He ate only one sparse meal a day, from food left for him by local villagers.

Gabriel was deeply impressed by the man's efforts. He felt sure that he had finally found the greatest devotee on earth. As he left the cave, he saw a man building a fence. The man was so drunk that he could not even get the fence post into the hole he had dug. He muttered, "God help me with this! Oh Lord, I can't do anything without You. Help me get this fence post in." Gabriel was shocked and offended that this man was calling on God with each drunken breath. When the drunk looked up and saw Gabriel, he said, "No, don't try to help me. I don't want your help. I want God to help me with this."

Amazed at the contrast between the heedless drunk and the disciplined ascetic, Gabriel returned to heaven. As he told God about his trip, God asked, "Did you see my friend with the fence post?" Gabriel was astonished. He replied that he had seen him, but that he was truly impressed by the ascetic living in the cave. God said, "What ascetic? I don't know him." Gabriel was even more astonished.

Then God told Gabriel to test the two men. "Tell each of them that I will be with them as soon as I have finished passing one hundred elephants through the eye of a needle," He said. "Then you will understand."

First, Gabriel went to the ascetic and repeated God's words. The ascetic threw down his prayer beads in disgust as he exclaimed, "That means that God is never coming. It's impossible to fit even one elephant through the eye of a needle. And if God isn't coming, I might as well stop this stupid way of life and go to town and enjoy myself."

Deeply disappointed, Gabriel went to the field where the drunk still struggled with his fence post. The man shouted, "I told you I don't want your help. Go away!" Gabriel revealed himself as God's angel and relayed the message. The man cried out, "Then God is coming any minute now! It will take Him no time at all to pass one hundred elephants through the eye of a needle." He dropped his fence post, grabbed Gabriel's hands, and began spinning with joy and ecstasy. As Gabriel turned and spun with the man, he felt God dancing with them as well.

This is one of my favorite stories. It is a wonderful reminder that, first of all, we don't know who is who. We have no way of knowing whose worship is accepted by God. Second, it reminds us never to be proud of our practice. The outer form of spiritual practice is not guaranteed to open the heart, and if our hearts remain closed, we may end up like the impatient ascetic. It also reminds us of the transcendent power of love of God.

The role of the sheikh. There are as many strategies to remove the veils between us and God as there are human beings. Sheikhs have different styles, based on their personalities and on the traditions of their orders. For example, Sheikh Muzaffer was an incredibly powerful teacher, yet he rarely exercised his power, probably because most of his dervishes could not handle it. However, he freely raised his voice to his personal assistant, a wonderful old dervish named Ragip Baba. When Sheikh Muzaffer scolded him, the rest of us trembled, but Ragip Baba would simply smile and run to Sheikh Muzaffer, happy that his beloved sheikh was talking to him. In fact, Sheikh Muzaffer was never really angry with Ragip Baba. Their whole interaction was play, which showed us how a real dervish acted.

The job of the sheikh is to help dervishes along the path. At each stage we meet different obstacles. Some of us may need more devotion at certain times; others may be deeply devotional by nature and need more self-insight. For still others, selfishness or an inability to serve may be a major problem.

Three or four basic processes occur within virtually everyone along the path. One is the opening of the heart, which happens through the feelings of love and joy that occur in prayer, remembrance, and devotion to our sheikh. Another basic spiritual process is the cleansing or transmutation of the *nafs*, which requires being able to see oneself clearly. The more conscious we become of our inner tendencies, the better this process works. As mentioned earlier, the tyrannical *nafs* is distinguished by basic lack of consciousness. We have no idea of our negative habits and traits, so we are run by them. The more conscious we become, the more free we are.

Cleansing the *nafs* requires different practices at different stages. In order to preserve its own power, the ego tries to convince us prematurely that we are done with our inner work. When we experience real joy in worship and can feel our hearts open, there is a strong tendency to believe that the inner struggle with negative tendencies is over. In reality this does not happen until much later.

A sheikh reminds us that we are still somewhat less than perfect, which is why having a living sheikh is important. As one Sufi teacher points out, some people prefer a dead saint as their sheikh. This is very convenient because that way there is no chance of being challenged or criticized by the teacher. Often the sheikh inspires us by example or by other indirect methods, because very few of us can take direct criticism without rebelling against the critic.

Self-awareness. The ego wants to pretend that we are beyond our faults, and we can all see this tendency operating whenever we make a major mistake. We realize, "I've done it again!" and our inner blinders are temporarily lowered as we realize how strong those negative tendencies are. It is very helpful to hold onto this critical self-image, but we generally find that within an hour or a day or two, the image fades and our faults become obscure again.

Some people are more naturally self-critical and remain clearly aware of their faults. For them, opening the heart may be an even greater challenge. These tasks—opening the heart and connecting to the divine, and the cleansing of the personality—are complementary processes.

Paradoxically, I have found that many people who are highly self-critical condemn themselves over their mistakes and thus focus their attention on feelings of guilt and self-blame instead of looking clearly at the underlying faults. As a result, they are left with a heightened sense of guilt without any greater understanding of their problems. They are likely to repeat their mistakes and feel worse and worse about themselves. As a result, the *nafs* wins again.

It is critical to continue the discipline of the path and to deepen our practices. Each day we can try to be a little more conscious in prayer and remembrance, a little more aware each time we read scriptures and the writings of the great Sufi teachers.

In a famous *hadith*, the Prophet taught that if you are the same for two days, then you are at a loss. This means not only to learn new things each day, but also to deepen and improve what we already know and what we practice. The dervish's goal is to seek spiritual progress every day.

Service. If we remember that God is within each of us, then we find it a privilege to serve others, knowing that we serve the divine. When we are served, we can be truly thankful and treat the service as a gift from someone who embodies a divine spark. *Adab* comes from the context of remembering who is serving whom. The senior dervishes are the best examples of service because they remember this. In spite of their higher rank, they realize that there is no rank at the level of the divine within, and so they naturally serve novices far better than the novices serve them.

Dervishes do not have to go into a monastery or isolate themselves in the mountains, because every interaction with another person provides them with the opportunity of remembering God, serving God, cleansing themselves, and opening their own hearts. What makes Sufi psychology so powerful and so inspiring is the divine lens through which we perceive humanity. Through it, we can see the divine in everyone, no matter what problems they have. It doesn't matter whether someone is an addict, a neurotic, or a criminal—every human being has the capacity for infinite growth and union with God.

Remembering the heart. If you remember your heart, everything becomes easy. Your heart attracts the hearts of other lovers of God. You know what to say and what not to say; you know what to do and what not to do. Even the way you talk and act is changed. There is a beautiful old Sufi saying, "If words come out of the heart, they will enter the heart, but if they come from the tongue, they will not pass beyond the ears."[7] As you act from your heart, from awareness of your divine soul, other people respond accordingly—they begin to remember that they are a divine spark in a physical body. Even self-doubt can be remedied by learning to trust your heart.

God has put this divine spark within us. It is not as if you had to go half way around the world to get the spark and bring it home. You have already tasted those states in which you were guided by your heart and effortlessly said and did the right thing.

Prayer is a practice and it is also an end. Remembrance is also both a practice and an end. The goal is a state of continuous prayer and remembrance. At our present state, we get just a taste of this, but it can deepen and increase over time.

To be a believer is to remember that God created our souls long before He created the material world. The souls existed in close proximity to God, bathed in God's light and love. Then God came to *your* soul and said, "Am I your Lord?" And you replied, "Yes, indeed." In that state, you knew that you were a cherished child of God.

After material creation came into being, the souls entered into bodies one by one. However, your soul is no different now than when it was close to God. It is just covered with the personality, which is not real.

In spite of our personality limitations, we have nothing to fear, because nothing in creation can harm the soul. No one can take anything of real value from us, because who we truly are is divine and infinite. The dervishes meet each week in order to remember this basic fact. When one dervish forgets, another may serve as a reminder by acting as a soul instead of a limited, self-centered personality. Then the believer is the mirror of the believer, and the dervish who has forgotten remembers. In the state of remembering who we are, we cannot behave badly. We realize that we are all souls, and we would not dream of doing anything to injure the heart or be disrespectful of our own or others' souls.

So, theoretically, it is easy. It is to be who we are. All the rest is who we are not. To be a *fakir*, a poor one, is to get rid of what we are not—all the useless baggage that separates us from God. What is left is pure, shining, and perfect.

Exercises

Learning to surrender. Sit still and focus your attention in the center of your chest. Slowly surrender yourself and realize that instead of seeing, you are being seen. Instead of touching, you are being touched. Instead of tasting, you are being tasted, and so you should do whatever you can to make yourself delicious.

Finally, instead of breathing, allow yourself to be breathed.

Surrender yourself completely in trust, and in the realization that you are powerless, that the only doer is God.[8]

How to talk to God. A sheikh asked his dervish if he wanted to talk to God. When the dervish replied that he did, the sheikh taught him that whenever he was by himself, he should recite the following:

> Without You, O Beloved, I cannot rest. I cannot count the blessings You have showered upon me. Even if every hair on my body became a tongue, I could not recite a thousandth part of the thanks due to You.

NOTES

Preface

1. A title of respect.

2. J. Fadiman and R. Frager, *Essential Sufism* (San Francisco: HarperSanFrancisco, 1997), 200.

Chapter 1

1. al-Ghazzali, *The Alchemy of Happiness*, trans. C. Field (Lahore, Pakistan: Muhammad Ashraf, 1964), 17.

2. Hafiz, *I hear God Laughing: Renderings of Hafiz*, trans. D. Ladinsky (Walnut Creek, Cal.: Sufism Reoriented, 1996), 109.

3. Ibid., 141.

4. J. Rumi, *Open Secret*, trans. J. Moyne and C. Barks, (Putney, Vt.: Threshold Books, 1984), 74.

5. *Yunus Emre and His Mystical Poetry*, ed. T. Halman (Bloomington, Ind.: Indiana University Turkish Studies, 1981).

6. These stages of development have been taken primarily from the work of al-Ghazzali, whose work has provided the basis for most of the other descriptions of stages.

7. Hafiz, op. cit., 43.

8. Author's translation.

9. For the foregoing discussion, I am indebted to Charles Tart's chapter, "Some Assumptions of Orthodox Western Psychology" in *Transpersonal Psychologies*, ed. C. Tart (New York: Harper & Row, 1975).

10. This material is adapted from a translation/adaptation from an unpublished Turkish manuscript by Sheikh Tosun Bayrak al Jerrahi.

11. Author's translation.

12. J. Fadiman and R. Frager, *Essential Sufism* (San Francisco: HarperSanFrancisco, 1997), 198.

Chapter 2

1. J. Fadiman and R. Frager, *Essential Sufism* (San Francisco: HarperSanFrancisco, 1997), 124.

2. Hafiz, *I Hear God Laughing: Renderings of Hafiz*, trans. D. Ladinsky (Walnut Creek, Cal.: Sufism Reoriented, 1996), 69.

3. Cited in J. Nurbaksh, *The Psychology of Sufism* (New York: Khaniqahi Nimatullahi Publications, 1992).

4. Lahiji in Nurbaksh, 1992.

5. Najmaddin Razi in *Classical Persian Sufism: from its Origins to Rumi*, ed. L. Lewisohn (New York: Khaniqahi Nimatullahi Publications, 1993), 528.

6. Fadiman and Frager, op.cit., 102.

7. Ibid., 201–2.

8. This analysis of the four stations of the heart is based on the work of al-Tirmidhi (1940), a Sufi teacher who lived in the eighth century A.D. The original Arabic terms for the four stations are *sadr* (breast), *qalb* (heart), *fu'ad* (inner heart) and *lubb* (innermost heart).

9. This row names the four levels of Sufis corresponding to each area of the heart.

10. Here al-Tirmidhi changed the traditional order of the levels of the self and places the inspired self lower than the regretful self. I have kept the more traditional order in this table.

11. Rumi in W. Chittick, *The Sufi Path of Love* (Albany: State University of New York Press, 1983), 35–36.

12. J. Rumi, *We Are Three*, trans. C. Barks (Athens, Ga.: Maypop Books, 1987), 21.

13. Cited in Lewisohn, 321.

14. See note 2.

15. Many Sufi authors list only the first four levels of the self. Others have described seven levels, which is the model discussed in chapter 3. In a sense, the last three levels of the self (the pleased self, self pleasing to God, and pure self) can be seen as enfolded within the fourth level (the serene self).

Notes

16. This interpretation is adapted fairly freely from al-Ghazzali, *Innvocations and Supplications* (Cambridge, England: Islamic Text Society, 1990 (1924).

17. Fadiman and Frager, op cit., 232.

18. The following section is based on al-Tirmidhi's description of the state of unity.

19. Hafiz, op. cit, 63.

20. Adapted from Laura Huxley, *You Are Not the Target* (North Hollywood, Cal.: Wilshire Books Company, 1963).

Chapter 3

1. J. Fadiman and R. Frager, *Essential Sufism* (San Francisco: HarperSanFrancisco, 1997).

2. The original Arabic for each of the levels of the self is *ammara, lawwama, mulhima, mutmaina, radiye, merdiye,* and *safiya* or *baqiya.*

3. Bayazid in J. Nurbakhsh, *The Psychology of Sufism* (New York: Khaniqahi Nimatullahi Publications, 1992), 14.

4. Qushairi in Nurbakhsh, ibid., 19.

5. Abu Bakr Temestani in Nurbakhsh, ibid., 12.

6. Mahmud Kashani in Nurbakhsh, ibid., 52.

7. Ibid., 16.

8. Ibid., 17.

9. Ibid., 17–18.

10. Ibid., 18.

11. Ibid.

12. Tosun Bayrak, *Inspirations: On the Path of Blame* (Putney, Vt.: Threshold Books, 1993), 51.

13. Rumi in Nurbakhsh, op. cit., 22–23.

14. J. Rumi, *We Are Three*, trans. C. Barks (Athens, Ga.: Maypop Books, 1987), 40.

237

15. This distinction was clarified for me by Sheikh Mehmet Selim.

16. The anonymous, unpublished eighteenth-century manuscript was translated several years ago from Ottoman Turkish into modern Turkish by Sheikh Safer Dal, and from Turkish into English by Sheikh Tosun Bayrak.

17. Nurbakhsh, op. cit., 45.

18. Ibid., 50.

19. Fadiman and Frager, op. cit., 21.

20. Cited in Nurbakhsh, op. cit. (original author not named), 55–56.

21. Ibid., 57.

22. Razi in op. cit., 58.

23. Nurbakhsh, op. cit., 67.

24. Ruzbehan in Nurbakhsh, op. cit., 59.

25. Kashani, in Nurbakhsh, op. cit., 59.

26. In Nurbakhsh, *Discourses*.

27. J. Rumi, *Open Secret,* trans. J. Moyne and C. Barks (Putney, Vt.: Threshold Books, 1984), 70.

28. 'Ayn al-Qudat in *Classical Persian Sufism: from Its Origins to Rumi,* ed. L. Lewisohn (New York: Khaniqahi Nimatullahi Publications, 1993) 289.

29. Ibid., 311.

30. Fadiman and Frager, op. cit., 23.

31. R. Carson, *Taming Your Gremlin* (New York: Harper & Row, 1983).

Chapter 4

1. J. Rumi, *Mathnawi*, trans. R. Frager (unpublished), IV 3901–5.

2. The discussions of brain function in this chapter are taken from E. de Beauport, *The Three Faces of Mind* (Wheaton, Ill.: Quest Books, 1996).

3. Najmaddin Razi in J. Nurbakhsh, *The Psychology of Sufism* (New York: Khaniqahi Nimatullahi Publications, 1992), 32–33.

4. Referred to as the *qalb*, or heart proper in chapter 2.

5. Sarraj Tusi in Nurbakhsh, op. cit., 123.

6. Abu Bakr Waseti in Nurbakhsh, op. cit., 126.

7. Abur-Razzaq Kashani in Nurbakhsh, op. cit., 125.

8. Abdul-Qadir al-Jilani, *The Secret of Secrets*, interpreted by Shaykh Tosun Bayrak (Cambridge, England: Islamic Text Society, 1992), 18–19, 22.

9. Hafiz, *I Hear God Laughing: Renderings of Hafiz*, trans. D. Ladinsky (Walnut Creek, Cal.: Sufism Reoriented, 1996), 95.

10. This exercise is adapted from the disidentification exercise of psychosynthesis.

Chapter 5

1. J. Fadiman and R. Frager, *Essential Sufism* (San Francisco: HarperSanFrancisco, 1997), 54–55.

2. Eckehart in Matthew Fox, *Original Blessing* (Santa Fe: Bear and Company, 1983), 280.

3. In J. Nurbakhsh, *The Psychology of Sufism* (New York: Khaniqahi Nimatullahi Publications, 1992), 77.

Chapter 6

1. J. Fadiman and R. Frager, *Essential Sufism* (San Francisco: HarperSanFrancisco, 1997), 37.

2. I here use here the term lower self as a translation for *nafs* because many Sufi authors use the word *nafs* to refer primarily to the lower levels of the self, especially the *nafs ammara*, or tyrannical self.

3. Hafiz, *I Hear God Laughing: Renderings of Hafiz*, trans. D. Ladinsky (Walnut Creek, Cal.: Sufism Reoriented, 1996), 129.

4. Rumi in W. Chittick, *The Sufi Path of Love* (Albany: State University of New York Press, 1983), 155.

5. This section is adapted from al-Ghazzali, *On the Duties of*

Brotherhood, trans. M. Holland (London: Latimer, 1975).

6. al-Ghazzali, op. cit., 33.

7. Abu Said in Fadiman and Frager, op. cit., 212.

8. al-Ghazzali in Fadiman and Frager, op. cit., 61.

9. al-Ghazzali, *Invocations and Supplications* (Cambridge, England: Islamic Text Society, 1990).

10. By heart, al-Ghazzali means the spiritual heart as a whole. He is referring mainly to the level of the heart proper, as opposed to the breast, inner heart or innermost heart.

11. By soul, al-Ghazzali means the secret soul.

12. The following section on *dhikr* and the section on the sheikh and dervish are taken from various discourses. Most of the material is from an unpublished talk by Sheikh Muzaffer Ozak, given at the Institute of Transpersonal Psychology in Menlo Park, California, on March 16, 1981.

13. M. Ozak, *Journey to the Lord of Power*, recording liner notes (New York: Inner Traditions).

14. Hafiz, *I Hear God Laughing: Renderings of Hafiz*, trans. D. Ladinsky (Walnut Creek, Cal.: Sufism Reoriented, 1996), 141.

15. From Sheikh Mehmet Selim.

16. Adapted from Bawa Muhaiyaddeen.

17. Ibid.

Chapter 7

1. J. Fadiman and R. Frager, *Essential Sufism* (San Francisco: HarperSanFrancisco, 1997), 141.

2. Ibid., 145.

3. From an unpublished talk by Sheikh Muzaffer Ozak, given at the Institute of Transpersonal Psychology in Menlo Park, California, on March 16, 1981.

4. Rumi in Shah, *The Way of the Sufi* (New York: Dutton, 1970). 37.

5. M. Shafii, *Freedom from the Self* (New York: Human Sciences, 1968), 11.

6. A. al-Shabrawi, *The Degrees of the Soul* (London: The Quilliam Press, 1997), xiii–xiv.

7. al-Ghazzali, *The Book of Knowledge* (Lahore, Pakistan: Muhammad Ashraf, 1997).

8. Shafii, op. cit.

9. J. Rumi, *We Are Three*, trans. C. Barks (Athens, Ga: Maypop Books, 1987), 12.

10. A. Nasafi in Shafii, op. cit., 77–78.

11. al-Shabrawi, op. cit., 50.

12. Hujwiri in Shafii, op. cit., 65.

13. Khan in Shafii, op. cit., 67.

Chapter 8

1. J. Fadiman and R. Frager, *Essential Sufism* (San Francisco: HarperSanFrancisco, 1997), 40.

2. Ibid., 247.

3. Ibid., 145.

4. Hafiz, *I Hear God Laughing: Renderings of Hafiz*, trans. D. Ladinsky (Walnut Creek, Cal.: Sufism Reoriented, 1996), 37.

5. Fadiman and Frager, op. cit., 37.

6. Hafiz, op. cit., 13.

7. Fadiman and Frager, op. cit., 39.

8. Adapted from Reshad Field.

INDEX

T

Tosun Bayrak, Sheikh, 63, 72,
    102, 192

U

understanding, 35–7

unity, 6, 8, 40, 82, 84, 161, 163

V

vampires, 116–17

veils, 2, 100, 207–33

W

woodcutter, 155

Y

Yunus Emre, 5, 9

Z

Zuleika, Potiphar's wife, 2, 3

ACKNOWLEDGMENTS

The author and publisher are grateful for permission to reprint passages from the following copyrighted material:

Emre, Y. *Yunus Emre and His Mystical Poetry*. T. Halman (transl.) Bloomington, Ind.: Indiana University Turkish Studies Publications, 1981.

Al-Jilani, A. *The Secret of Secrets*. T. Bayrak (transl.) Cambridge, England: Islamic Texts Society, 1991.

Hafiz, S. *I Heard God Laughing, Renderings of Hafiz*. D. Ladinsky (transl.) Walnut Creek, Cal.: Sufism Reoriented. 1996.

Nurbakhsh, J. *The Psychology of Sufism*. London: Khaniqahi-Nimatullahi Publications, 1992.

Rumi, J. *Open Secret*. J. Moyne & C. Barks (transl.) Putney, Vt.: Threshold Books, 1984.

Rumi, J. *We are Three*. C. Barks (transl.) Athens, Ga.: Maypop Books, 1987.

Al-Shabrawi, A. *The Degrees of the Soul*. M. Al-Badawi (transl.) London: The Quilliam Press Ltd., 1997.

Shafii, M. *Freedom from the Self*. New York: Human Sciences Press, 1985.

QUEST BOOKS
are published by
The Theosophical Society in America,
Wheaton, Illinois 60189-0270,
a branch of a world organization
dedicated to the promotion of the unity of
humanity and the encouragement of the study of
religion, philosophy, and science, to the end that
we may better understand ourselves and our place in
the universe. The Society stands for complete
freedom of individual search and belief.
For further information about its activities,
write, call 1-800-669-1571, or consult its Web page:
http://www.theosophical.org

*The Theosophical Publishing House
is aided by the generous support of
THE KERN FOUNDATION,
a trust established by Herbert A. Kern
and dedicated to Theosophical education.*

Medieval
July 15, 22, 29
aug 5, 12, 19   700PM

Franciscan
aug 9, 16, 23 + 30

LaVergne, TN USA
13 May 2010
182636LV00001B/140/P

9 780835 607780